P9-CKS-978

THE COLD WAR

Other Titles in the Greenwood Press Guides to Historic Events of the Twentieth Century
Randall M. Miller, Series Editor

The Persian Gulf Crisis
Steve A. Yetiv

World War I
Neil M. Heyman

The Civil Rights Movement
Peter B. Levy

The Holocaust
Jack R. Fischel

The Breakup of Yugoslavia and the War in Bosnia
Carole Rogel

Islamic Fundamentalism
Lawrence Davidson

Frontiers of Space Exploration
Roger D. Launius

The Collapse of Communism in the Soviet Union
William E. Watson

Origins and Development of the Arab-Israeli Conflict
Ann M. Lesch and Dan Tschirgi

The Rise of Fascism in Europe
George P. Blum

THE COLD WAR

Katherine A. S. Sibley

Greenwood Press Guides to
Historic Events of the Twentieth Century
Randall M. Miller, Series Editor

Greenwood Press
Westport, Connecticut • London

Library of Congress Cataloging-in-Publication Data

Sibley, Katherine A. S. (Katherine Amelia Siobhan), 1961–
The Cold War / Katherine A. S. Sibley.
p. cm.—(Greenwood Press guides to historic events of the twentieth century, ISSN 1092–177X)
Includes bibliographical references and index.
ISBN 0–313–29857–2 (alk. paper)
1. Cold War. 2. World politics—1945– I. Title. II. Series.
D843.S497 1998
909.82′5—dc21 98–4814

British Library Cataloguing in Publication Data is available.

Library of Congress Catalog Card Number: 98–4814
ISBN: 0–313–29857–2
ISSN: 1092–177X

First published in 1998

Greenwood Press, 88 Post Road West, Westport, CT 06881
An imprint of Greenwood Publishing Group, Inc.

Printed in the United States of America

The paper used in this book complies with the Permanent Paper Standard issued by the National Information Standards Organization (Z39.48–1984).

10 9 8 7 6 5 4 3 2 1

Front cover photo: Soviet missiles are carted into Red Square during the annual May Day parade. UPI/CORBIS-BETTMANN.

Back cover photo: Joseph Stalin and Winston Churchill at the Yalta Conference. National Archives.

Copyright Acknowledgments

The author and publisher gratefully acknowledge permission to use the following material:

Excerpts from *Masters of Deceit: The Story of Communism in America and How to Fight It* by J. Edgar Hoover, © 1958 by J. Edgar Hoover. Reprinted by permission of Henry Holt and Company, Inc.

Excerpts from "New Evidence on the Korean War" by Kathryn Weathersby in Cold War International History Project *Bulletin* 6–7 (Winter 1995–96): 37–51; "The Warsaw Pact and the Polish Crisis: Honecker's Call for Military Intervention" by Mark Kramer in Cold War International History Project *Bulletin* 5 (Spring 1995): 124. Reprinted by permission of the Cold War International History Project.

Excerpts from "Screen Guide for Americans" by Ayn Rand in Isaac Don Levine, ed., *Plain Talk: An Anthology of the Leading Anti-Communist Magazine of the 40s* (New Rochelle, N.Y.: Arlington House, 1976). Used by permission of the Estate of Ayn Rand. Copyright renewed in 1976 by Ayn Rand.

Every reasonable effort has been made to trace the owners of copyright materials in this book, but in some instances this has proven impossible. The author and publisher will be glad to receive information leading to more complete acknowledgments in subsequent printings of the book and in the meantime extend their apologies for any omissions.

Contents

Series Foreword

As the twenty-first century approaches, it is time to take stock of the political, social, economic, intellectual, and cultural forces and factors that have made the twentieth century the most dramatic period of change in history. To that end, the Greenwood Press Guides to Historic Events of the Twentieth Century presents interpretive histories of the most significant events of the century. Each book in the series combines narrative history and analysis with primary documents and biographical sketches, with an eye to providing both a reference guide to the principal persons, ideas, and experiences defining each historic event, and a reliable, readable overview of that event. Each book further provides analyses and discussions, grounded in both primary and secondary sources, of the causes and consequences, in thought and action, that give meaning to the historic event under review. By assuming a historical perspective, drawing on the latest and best writing on each subject, and offering fresh insights, each book promises to explain how and why a particular event defined the twentieth century. No consensus about the meaning of the twentieth century emerges from the series, but, collectively, the books identify the most salient concerns of the century. In so doing, the series reminds us of the many ways those historic events continue to affect our lives.

Each book follows a similar format designed to encourage readers to consult it both as a reference and a history in its own right. Each volume opens with a chronology of the historic event, followed by a narrative overview, which also serves to introduce and examine briefly the main themes and issues related to that event. The next set of chapters is composed of topical essays, each analyzing closely an issue or problem of interpretation introduced in the opening chapter. A concluding chapter suggesting the long-term implications and meanings of the historic event brings the strands of the preceding chapters together while placing the event in the larger historical context. Each book also includes a section of short biographies of the principal persons related to the event, followed by a section introducing and reprinting key historical documents illustrative of and pertinent to the event. A glossary of selected terms adds to the utility of each book. An annotated bibliography—of significant books, films, and CD-ROMs—and an index conclude each volume.

The editors made no attempt to impose any theoretical model or historical perspective on the individual authors. Rather, in developing the series, an advisory board of noted historians and informed high school history teachers and public and school librarians identified the topics needful of exploration and the scholars eminently qualified to examine those events with intelligence and sensitivity. The common commitment throughout the series is to provide accurate, informative, and readable books, free of jargon and up to date in evidence and analysis.

Each book stands as a complete historical analysis and reference guide to a particular historic event. Each book also has many uses, from understanding contemporary perspectives on critical historical issues, to providing biographical treatments of key figures related to each event, to offering excerpts and complete texts of essential documents about the event, to suggesting and describing books and media materials for further study and presentation of the event, and more. The combination of historical narrative and individual topical chapters addressing significant issues and problems encourages students and teachers to approach each historic event from multiple perspectives and with a critical eye. The arrangement and content of each book thus invite students and teachers, through classroom discussions and position papers, to debate the character and significance of great historic events and to discover for themselves how and why history matters.

The series emphasizes the main currents that have shaped the modern world. Much of that focus necessarily looks at the West, especially Europe and the United States. The political, commercial, and cultural expansion of the West wrought largely, though not wholly, the most fundamental changes of the century. Taken together, however, books in the series reveal the interactions between Western and non-Western peoples and society, and also the tensions between modern and traditional cultures. They also point to the ways in which non-Western peoples have adapted Western ideas and technology and, in turn, influenced Western life and thought. Several books examine such increasingly powerful global forces as the rise of Islamic fundamentalism, the emergence of modern Japan, the Communist revolution in China, and the collapse of communism in eastern Europe and the former Soviet Union. American interests and experiences receive special attention in the series, not only in deference to the primary readership of the books but also in recognition that the United States emerged as the dominant political, economic, social, and cultural force during the twentieth century. By looking at the century through the lens of American events and experiences, it is possible to see why the age has come to be known as "The American Century."

Assessing the history of the twentieth century is a formidable prospect. It has been a period of remarkable transformation. The world broadened and narrowed at the same time. Frontiers shifted from the interiors of Africa and Latin America to the moon and beyond; communication spread from mass circulation newspapers and magazines to radio, television, and now the Internet; skyscrapers reached upward and suburbs stretched outward; energy switched from steam, to electric, to atomic power. Many changes did not lead to a complete abandonment of established patterns and practices so much as a synthesis of old and new, as, for example, the increased use of (even reliance on) the telephone in the age of the computer. The automobile and the truck, the airplane, and telecommunications closed distances, and people in unprecedented numbers migrated from rural to urban, industrial, and ever more ethnically diverse areas. Tractors and chemical fertilizers made it possible for fewer people to grow more, but the environmental and demographic costs of an exploding global population threatened to outstrip natural resources and human innovation. Disparities in wealth increased, with developed nations prospering and underdeveloped nations starving. Amid the crumbling of former European colonial empires, Western technology, goods, and culture increasingly enveloped the globe, seeping into, and undermining, non-Western cultures—a process that contributed to a surge of religious fundamentalism and ethno-nationalism in the Middle East, Asia, and Africa. As people became more alike, they also became more aware of their differences. Ethnic and religious rivalries grew in intensity everywhere as the century closed.

The political changes during the twentieth century have been no less profound than the social, economic, and cultural ones. Many of the books in the series focus on political events, broadly defined, but no books are confined to politics alone. Political ideas and events have social effects, just as they spring from a complex interplay of non-political forces in culture, society, and economy. Thus, for example, the modern civil rights and woman's rights movements were at once social and political events in cause and consequence.

Likewise, the Cold War created the geopolitical framework for dealing with competing ideologies and nations abroad and served as the touchstone for political and cultural identities at home. The books treating political events do so within their social, cultural, and economic contexts.

Several books in the series examine particular wars in depth. Wars are defining moments for people and eras. During the twentieth century war became more widespread and terrible than ever before, encouraging new efforts to end war through strategies and organizations of international cooperation and disarmament while also fueling new ideologies and instruments of mass persuasion that fostered distrust and festered old national rivalries. Two world wars during the century redrew the political map, slaughtered or uprooted two generations of people, and introduced and hastened the development of new technologies and weapons of mass destruction. The First World War spelled the end of the old European order and spurred communist revolution in Russia and fascism in Italy, Germany, and elsewhere. The Second World War killed fascism and inspired the final push for freedom from European colonial rule in Asia and Africa. It also led to the Cold War that suffocated much of the world for almost half a century. Large wars begat small ones, and brutal totalitarian regimes cropped up across the globe. After (and in some ways because of) the fall of communism in eastern Europe and the former Soviet Union, wars of competing cultures, national interests, and political systems persisted in the struggle to make a new world order. Continuing, too, has been the belief that military technology can achieve political ends, whether in the superior American firepower that failed to "win" in Vietnam or in the American "smart bombs" and other military wizardry that "won" in the Persian Gulf.

Another theme evident in the series is that throughout the century nationalism has continued to drive events. Whether in the Balkans in 1914 triggering World War I or in the Balkans in the 1990s threatening the post–Cold War peace—or in many other places—nationalist ambitions and forces would not die. The persistence of nationalism is yet another reminder of the many ways that the past becomes prologue.

We thus offer the series as a modern guide to and interpretation of the historic events of the twentieth century and as an invitation to consider how and why those events have defined not only the past and present but also charted the political, social, intellectual, cultural, and economic routes into the next century.

Randall M. Miller
Saint Joseph's University, Philadelphia

Preface

This book is designed to provide a concise yet comprehensive overview of the Cold War's influence and implications both to the nations actively involved as well as to the larger world. Although it approaches the Cold War from the perspective of the United States, the surviving superpower, the book also closely examines the policies and goals of the Communist nations, as well as those of Western democracies that cooperated, and sometimes clashed, with America. The Cold War's major battlegrounds in the Third World are a key element in this story.

The book's narrative takes a topical approach to the Cold War. It starts by examining the Cold War's origins, and continues with a study of McCarthyism and internal security in the United States, followed by a survey of the principal Cold War sites of armed conflict in Asia, Latin America, Africa, and the Middle East. The book concludes with an analysis of the last two decades of the Cold War, including détente's heyday and bitter decline, the revived hopes for Soviet-American relations ushered in by Mikhail Gorbachev, and the Cold War's denouement in 1991.

The book is organized topically in order to emphasize better the key themes that characterized this era: the Cold War's origins amid the distrust that emerged in the aftermath of the World War II alliance; the historically pervasive and unifying force of American anticommunism; Washington's newly enhanced postwar global role, as exemplified by political, economic, and military initiatives in Europe and the underdeveloped world; the competing visions and strategies distinguishing the United States and the

U.S.S.R. in their respective pursuits of global influence; and the reasons why the Soviet Union did not survive the Cold War.

This book also includes seventeen primary documents that highlight the views of individuals such as George F. Kennan, Winston Churchill, Ayn Rand, Douglas MacArthur, Ronald Reagan, and Mikhail Gorbachev, as well as the policies of governments including the United States, the Soviet Union, the German Democratic Republic, and the Democratic People's Republic of Korea. These primary sources reveal the immediate concerns pressing on the various nations' leaders and opinion makers as they were caught up in the Cold War, and provide readers with concrete evidence of the hopes, fears, and opinions of those engaged in this polarized conflict. In addition, the book has fifteen capsule biographies of the Cold War's key actors, from Josef Stalin to Allen Dulles to Ronald Reagan. By illustrating the background and outlooks of such individuals, these biographies serve to flesh out the story told in this work, bringing to life the personalities of the leaders and officials most involved in making Cold War policies in their respective countries. The biographies should help readers understand the ways in which individuals have an impact upon their times, as well as how their personalities and priorities affect the manner in which they handle crises.

Just as Cold War initiatives were greatly enhanced by the collaboration of allies, so too did this book benefit immensely from the support of colleagues. I would like to thank the following people for their assistance: Jessica Gienow-Hecht, who provided a close reading and excellent suggestions on the manuscript; the staff of St. Joseph's University Library, who assisted so readily with book and information requests; Christian Ostermann of the Cold War International History Project, for permission to quote from his excellent *Bulletin*; the contributors to H-Diplo, whose lively debates have enriched this work; and Randall M. Miller, whose tireless assistance, helpful suggestions, and kindly mentoring with this project have made analysis of the Cold War such a pleasure. This book is dedicated to Nina Bakisian, in deep appreciation for her friendship and support through the oscillations of its writing.

Chronology of Events

1945

February 4–11	Yalta Conference: Roosevelt, Churchill, and Stalin discuss the nature of postwar governments in Europe.
April 12	Roosevelt dies and Harry S. Truman becomes U.S. president.
August 6 and 9	The United States drops atomic bombs on Hiroshima and Nagasaki.

1946

February 22	George F. Kennan's Long Telegram alerts Washington to Soviet threat.
March 5	Winston Churchill's Iron Curtain speech.
August	John Hersey's critical article, "Hiroshima," published in *New Yorker*.
September 20	Commerce Secretary Henry Wallace fired for unorthodox views on Soviet Union.
September 27	Soviet Ambassador to the United States Nikolai Novikov warns his government about newly hardened U.S. attitude toward U.S.S.R.

1947

March 12	Truman Doctrine announced.
June 5	Marshall Plan announced.

July	Kennan's "X" article published in *Foreign Affairs*; introduces containment theory.
October	House Un-American Activities Committee begins investigation of entertainment industry.
1948	
February	Communist coup in Czechoslovakia.
June	Soviets blockade Berlin, and the United States responds with airlift.
November	Harry S. Truman elected U.S. president.
1949	
April	NATO created.
August 29	First Soviet atomic blast.
August	Dean Acheson's "White Paper" on China absolves the United States of responsibility for Communist takeover there.
October 1	People's Republic of China established.
1950	
January	Alger Hiss convicted of perjury.
January 12	Acheson's speech to National Press Club leaves out Korea from U.S. "defensive perimeter."
February	Klaus Fuchs convicted of atomic espionage for Soviet Union.
February 3	Joseph McCarthy produces list of Communists in U.S. government.
April	National Security Council document #68 (NSC-68) issued; leads to great defense buildup in the United States.
June 25	Korean War begins.
1951	
April 11	Truman fires General Douglas MacArthur, commander in Korea, for insubordination.
1952	
May 10	Stalin writes peace note, calls for a neutral, unified Germany.
November	U.S. H-bomb developed; Dwight D. Eisenhower elected U.S. president.
1953	
March 5	Stalin dies; Mohammed Mossadegh overthrown in United States-sponsored coup in Iran.

July 27	Korean War ends.

1954

April	Army-McCarthy hearings begin.
May 7	Vietminh defeat French forces at Dien Bien Phu, Vietnam.
June	Guatemalan leader Jacobo Arbenz Guzman overthrown in United States-sponsored coup.
July	Geneva Conference settlement divides Vietnam at 17th parallel.
December	Senate censures McCarthy.

1955

January	"Taiwan Resolution," Congress to protect Taiwan and its offshore islands Quemoy and Matsu.
April	Bandung Conference of African and Asian countries, including many newly decolonized states.
May	Warsaw Pact established.
May	Geneva Conference: Soviet troops pull out of Austria; "spirit of Geneva" euphoria for better U.S.-Soviet relations.

1956

February	Nikita Khrushchev's secret speech attacking Stalinism.
July 4	First flights of U-2 spy plane.
October	Hungarian revolution crushed by Soviets.
October	Suez Crisis; Britain, France, and Israel attack Egypt.
November	Eisenhower reelected.

1957

Oct 4	Soviet Union launches Sputnik, first space satellite of human origin.

1958

March 9	Eisenhower Doctrine announced; United States to assist Middle Eastern countries fighting Communism.
November 10	Berlin Crisis begins with Khrushchev's ultimatum over status of city.

1959

January	Castro seizes power in Cuba.
September	Khrushchev comes to the United States.
July	Nixon visits Moscow for American Exhibition.

1960

May 1	U.S. U-2 pilot Francis Gary Powers shot down in Russia.
November	John F. Kennedy elected U.S. president.

1961

January 3	The United States and Cuba break off diplomatic relations.
April 17	Bay of Pigs invasion.
August 13	Berlin Wall erected.

1962

June	UN brokers Laotian political settlement.
October	Cuban Missile Crisis.

1963

July	The United States and the U.S.S.R. sign aboveground nuclear test ban treaty.
November 2	South Vietnamese leader Ngo Dinh Diem assassinated.
November 22	Kennedy assassinated; Lyndon B. Johnson becomes U.S. president.

1964

August	Gulf of Tonkin Resolution.
October 16	China blasts off first nuclear weapon.
October	Khrushchev ousted from power.

1965

March	U.S. Marines arrive at Da Nang, Vietnam.
April	U.S. intervention in Dominican Republic to prevent leftist-leaning reformer Juan Bosch from gaining power.

1967

October 16–21	Stop the Draft Week; fifty thousand march on Pentagon.
June	Soviet Premier Alexei Kosygin visits the United States.

1968

January	North Korea captures U.S. spy ship, *Pueblo*.
January 30	North Vietnamese Tet Offensive in Saigon.
August	Soviet crackdown on Czechoslovakia's "Prague Spring."
November	Richard M. Nixon elected U.S. president.

1969

July 25	Nixon Doctrine declares that the United States will no longer automatically fight Communists in Asia.

1970

April	U.S. invasion of Cambodia.

1971

June	Pentagon Papers released.

1972

February	Richard Nixon visits People's Republic of China.
May	SALT I ratified.
November	Nixon reelected.

1973

January	Peace treaty signed between the United States and Vietnam.
November	U.S. Congress approves War Powers Act, limiting the president's ability to dispatch troops without its authorization.

1974

August 9	President Nixon resigns; Gerald R. Ford becomes U.S. president.

1975

April	South Vietnam falls to Communists.
Summer	Conference on Security and Cooperation in Europe, Helsinki.

1976

November	Jimmy Carter elected U.S. president.

1979

December	Soviet invasion of Afghanistan.

1980

July	Solidarity union protests against rising meat prices in Poland.
November	Ronald Reagan elected U.S. president.

1981

December	Martial law imposed in Poland.

1983

March	Reagan calls the Soviet Union an "Evil Empire."

September 1	Soviet missile shoots down Korean Airlines Flight 007,
October 25	The United States invades Grenada.

1984

November	Reagan reelected.

1985

February	Reagan Doctrine calls for U.S. defense of "freedom fighters."
November	Reagan and Gorbachev first meet at Geneva Conference.

1986

October	Reykjavik summit; Gorbachev and Reagan suggest getting rid of all nuclear weapons.

1988

November	George Bush elected U.S. president.

1989

November 9	Berlin wall falls.

1990

March	Lithuania declares independence from Moscow.
June	Russia declares its sovereignty.
July	Ukraine and Belarus declare their sovereignty.

1991

August 19	Soviet hard-liners attempt to oust Gorbachev.
December 25	Mikhail Gorbachev resigns Soviet presidency; U.S.S.R. ceases to exist.

THE COLD WAR EXPLAINED

I

Historical Overview

From the end of World War II in 1945 until the dissolution of the Soviet Union in 1991, East-West relations were polarized between the liberal-democratic-capitalist "West"—the United States and its allies in western Europe, Latin America, Asia, and Africa—and the socialist-communist-authoritarian "East"—the Soviet Union and its camp in eastern Europe, the Caribbean, Asia, and Africa. This polarized state of international affairs was known as the Cold War, and in large part was a struggle between the United States and the U.S.S.R. for influence over other, less powerful nations. For almost half a century, the international Cold War between the United States and the Soviet Union defined foreign policy, military strategy, cultural initiatives, and domestic priorities in much of the world.

THE SUPERPOWERS AFTER WORLD WAR II

The Cold War emerged from a series of superpower initiatives and responses after World War II that created an environment of tension and distrust. The term "Cold War" itself was coined by journalist Walter Lippmann in a 1947 critique of U.S. policy toward Russia, especially the containment theory and the Truman Doctrine. These policies, he noted, were based on "a disbelief in the possibility of a settlement of the issues raised by this war"—a pessimistic outlook that Lippman did not share.[1] Both the United States and the Soviet Union bear a measure of responsibility for this outcome. Each nation's policymakers professed fervent belief in an ideology, whether liberal-capitalist or Marxist-Leninist, that they held as appropriate for their opponents as well as themselves. Each country built up extensive military-industrial complexes to protect both national security and the position of an expanding base of international clients. This competition sometimes convinced officials in Washington and Moscow that neighboring nations' pursuit of domestic reforms was tantamount to adopting the opposite superpower's political agenda, and thus intolerably dangerous. For this reason, the United States overthrew a left-wing reformer in Guatemala in 1954, and the Soviet Union crushed Hungary's anticommunist revolution in 1956.

Despite such parallels, there were important differences between the two powers after World War II. Both had spheres in Europe, for example. Yet the Soviet sphere, including Hungary, Czechoslovakia, Poland, and East Germany, was an involuntary one where Moscow manipulated and installed puppet socialist governments. The United States, meanwhile, created an " 'empire' by invitation," in which it introduced or preserved democratic governments, from Britain to Italy. Although its sphere was larger than the Soviet one, and just as self-serving, it generally relied on the consensus of the governments under its influence—a key difference.[2]

American public opinion had something to do with this. If U.S. policy could not be convincingly defended in the arena of democracy, it would be derailed, as the protests over Vietnam illustrate. On the other hand, covert initiatives, such as the overthrow of governments in the Third World, were subject to no such scrutiny until the U.S. Congress began looking more closely at them during the [Frank] Church Committee hearings in the mid-1970s.

Moreover, though both powers entered the Cold War with intensity, the methods to which the Soviet Union resorted in this early period were more aggressively provocative than those of the United States. Besides establishing a firm grip on eastern Europe, Moscow attempted a toehold in Iran, raided Manchuria, and blockaded Berlin. It refused to join such multilateral organizations as the International Monetary Fund or the World Bank, not to mention the Marshall Plan, which provided American aid to reconstruct war-torn Europe, citing the incompatibility of socialism and capitalism. General Secretary of the Communist Party of the Soviet Union Josef Vissarionovich Stalin (1928–1953) shoulders much responsibility for this. As historians Vladislav Zubok and Constantine Pleshakov note: "Stalin's imperialism was not a simple continuation of the Russian imperial tradition. It represented an externalization of his power-hungry ego." His actions drew the Western allies together and threatened fellow communist leaders like Josip Broz Tito of Yugoslavia, whose separate road to socialism proved troublesome to Stalin. Western nations became convinced that Stalin could only be faced sternly and warily.[3]

Although the Soviet Union bears a greater degree of culpability in the development of the Cold War, the United States was following no pristine path. In the Third World, the American Cold War record rivaled the Soviet Union's. There, covert U.S. operations attempted, and sometimes succeeded, in overthrowing popular leaders like Jacobo Arbenz Guzman in Guatemala, Patrice Lumumba in the Congo, Fidel Castro in Cuba, and Salvador Allende in Chile, not to mention a prolonged and agonizing attempt to create a noncommunist state of South Vietnam. These efforts were made in order to fight the spread of Communism or governments thought to be vulnerable to its influence. Yet the U.S. role in these countries, even abetted by the kingmaking proclivities of the Central Intelligence Agency (CIA) in its heyday, did not approximate the depth or duration of domination that the Soviets held for four decades in their satellites.

BACKGROUND EVENTS

Polarization between Washington and Moscow had started with the Bolshevik Revolution in 1917, when the United States refused to recognize the new Soviet republic and even contributed troops to the anticommunist coalition that under the rhetoric of democracy and the rubric of wartime exigency tried to reverse the Reds' takeover in 1919. But this initial ideological standoff, which evolved into a growing economic relationship even before President Franklin D. Roosevelt opened diplomatic ties with Russia in 1933, was not characterized by the intensity of the Cold War. There were certainly abundant propaganda and great distrust, but the two countries did not aim their military firepower at each other. It was only during World War II (1939–1945), when both the Soviet Union and the United States emerged for the first time as the dominant military powers of the world, that tensions began.

The Soviet Union, the United States, and Great Britain were allies during the war against the Axis powers of Germany and Japan, and this unity masked underlying ideological differences. All countries on the Allied side, for example, signed the Atlantic Charter, which promised self-determination of the peoples of the world in the choosing of their own governments, although the Soviet Union granted no such democratic rights to its people. It did, however, fight long and hard against Hitler's army, aided by U.S. lend-lease supplies, and made a critical contribution to the Allied victory, albeit at great cost. The United States and Britain did not open the long-awaited second front in western Europe to relieve the German onslaught in the East until June 1944. Most U.S. officials saw no reason to doubt that Washington could work out a friendly relationship with Moscow after the war, a view that prevailed until early 1946.

In addition to the distrust sowed by the long delayed second front, indications of the future difficult relationship between the United States and the U.S.S.R. also surfaced at the February 1945 Yalta conference. The conferees agreed upon a Provisional Government of National Unity in Poland that would include the leadership of both Communists and non-communists until democratic elections could be held. The Communists soon took over, however, and controlled the Polish government for the next four decades. Yalta's outcome infuriated American and British representatives as it appeared to facilitate the Sovietization of Poland—although the geographical position of the Red Army played a far greater role in this event than the conference did. President Franklin D. Roosevelt (1933–1945), unlike his British counterpart, Prime Minister Winston Churchill, remained willing to work with the Soviets, but the U.S. State Department and the Ambassador to Russia, Averell Harriman, felt increasingly betrayed by Soviet actions in Europe.

But just as the United States was alienated by events in eastern Europe, so too were the Soviets hedged out of Japan after the U.S. atomic attacks there in August 1945. The official explanation for the use of the bomb to end the war with Japan was based on projected American casualties (estimates varied from 250,000 to 1,000,000) in an invasion, a figure that was considered intolerably high. Many were convinced that an invasion would still be necessary even *with* the bomb. In hindsight, many historians believe that the precarious Japanese condition probably meant that the atomic attacks were unnecessary. But as historian Barton Bernstein points out, U.S. officials did not see it that way. Indeed, "they did not regard it as profoundly immoral, they were largely inured to the mass killing of the enemy, and they also looked forward to the A-bomb's international-political benefits—intimidating the Soviets."[4]

Other scholars, like Gar Alperovitz, have suggested that the chief purpose of the attacks was to get Japan to surrender before the Russians' promised invasion of Manchuria, and through this preemptive victory impress upon Moscow the extent of American power. Alperovitz disagrees with Bernstein's assessment of the politico-diplomatic effects on Russia as largely a "bonus" added to the military goal of defeating Japan, and declares, "What we now know even more strongly suggests—but does not definitively prove—that diplomatic factors were of far greater significance." He views the bomb as the opening salvo in the Cold War.[5] Soviet atomic scientist Yuli Khariton chimes in. "The Soviet government interpreted [Hiroshima] as atomic blackmail against the USSR, as a threat to unleash a new, even more terrible and devastating war." Russian leaders, moreover, believed that the attacks would cause the British and Americans "to renege on the Yalta agreement" because it appeared to make unnecessary a Soviet role in the East or in the postwar settlement of Japan.[6]

But the Soviet armies did play a major role in Manchuria, if not Japan itself, thus facilitating the end of hostilities on the Asian mainland, and the Yalta agreements were hardly abandoned—much to the disappointment of many Americans. Moreover, in 1946 the U.S. representative to the UN Atomic Energy Commission, Bernard Baruch, made what initially appeared to be a very liberal offer on behalf of his government to place nuclear weapons material under international control and eventually to destroy all existing weapons. Upon closer inspection, however, the Baruch plan proved unacceptable to Moscow, because it preserved the existing American monopoly in nuclear research and technology and would have required the Soviet Union, like other states, to host international inspectors to make sure that it was not producing atomic arms. Russian scientists were already working on their own bomb in any case, and the U.S. atomic monopoly lasted just four years.

These pivotal World War II events, Yalta and the A-bomb, did not cause the Cold War, though their legacies surely contributed to it. Americans and Soviet leaders remained in a cooperative relationship through 1945, agreeing on such matters as sharing access to the strategic Dardanelles Straits in Turkey. Instead, it was Britain, the once-great power that had led the world in the fight against Hitler, and the Soviet Union who were then at loggerheads, particularly in the old British colonial sphere of the Middle East (Document 1). Yet by early 1946, with the Soviet hold on eastern Europe tightening and its push into the Middle East widening—as Britain's position languished—a more distrustful attitude emerged in Washington. U.S. chargé George F. Kennan's "Long Telegram" from Moscow in February exemplified this new attitude (Document 2), and former British prime minister Winston Churchill's "Iron Curtain" speech (Document 3) in early March amplified it. Both addressed the pathologies of the Soviet Union and the dangers of Soviet expansionism. Kennan dissected Soviet motives, for which he would later prescribe "containment" in a pivotal article in *Foreign Affairs* in 1947; Churchill described an encroaching "iron curtain" and called for an Anglo-American alliance, hence predicting NATO.

THE COLD WAR HEATS UP

In September 1946 President Harry S. Truman fired the most prominent dove in his Administration, Commerce Secretary Henry Wallace, for publicly expressing views critical of the new hard-line approach to the Soviet Union. Less than a week later, presidential counsel Clark Clifford issued a report urging a strong military reponse to Russia, although Truman kept its incendiary contents a secret. In the first half of 1947 the United States publicly announced two major initiatives designed to further containment: the Truman Doctrine, which supported Greece and Turkey, and the Marshall Plan (European Recovery Plan), which aided Western Europe (Documents 4 and 5). The Truman Doctrine and its heated rhetoric made the Cold War an ideological contest rather than merely a balance-of-power struggle. The United States was intent to "help free peoples to maintain their free institutions," but the two governments being helped were hardly democracies.[7] And while Turkey was being threatened by Soviet demands for territory, the Communist insurrection in Greece was supported not by the Soviet superpower but by a much weaker neighbor, Yugoslav leader Josip Broz Tito. The Marshall Plan brought much more financial assistance to Europe in order to counter severe economic problems that made Communist solutions seem attractive to many Europeans. Together, these two programs brought a far greater American role to the world than any previously contemplated, both in resisting Communism and in shoring up the economies of countries that were in danger of falling under communist influence, especially France and Italy. At the same time, the House Un-American Activities Committee began hearings on Communist influence in American entertainment (Document 6), calling forth a series of witnesses and sending some artists to jail, and the newly created CIA, building on the legacy of the wartime Office of Strategic Services, widened its work from intelligence collection to covert operations, including attempts to destabilize Soviet regimes in eastern Europe.

By the late 1940s, Soviet satellites had been established in Poland, Romania, Hungary, East Germany, and Czechoslovakia. One month after the brutal Soviet-sponsored overthrow of the democratically elected Czech government in February 1948, Britain, France, Belgium, Luxembourg, and the Netherlands formed a security agreement, the Brussels Pact. This became the core of the North Atlantic Treaty Organization (NATO) in 1949, an alliance in all but name which brought in both the United States and Canada to protect western Europe. That year, too, Germany was formally divided, although the Western powers maintained their hold on West Berlin, located 110 miles inside East Germany. In 1948 the Soviets had blockaded that city, but a continuous U.S. airlift brought food and supplies until Stalin lifted the blockade a year later.

DEVELOPMENTS IN ASIA

In Asia, Japan was securely glued to the American sphere after the war with U.S. occupying forces and a new constitution. In the countries Japan had formerly occupied, such as China, Korea, and Vietnam, rival factions struggled for power, including returning imperialists like the French in Vietnam and nationalists such as the Kuomintang in China. By 1949 Chinese Communists under Mao Zedong (Mao Tse-tung) had decisively defeated the Nationalists under Jiang Jieshi (Chiang Kai-shek). The Nationalists were chased to the island of Taiwan, upsetting many Americans who blamed Washington officials for the "fall" of China (Document 7).

In divided Korea, where the United States had been conspicuous by its limited postwar role, Communist North Korea invaded South Korea in June 1950, drawing in the United States and other nations to defend the South in a "police action." Truman saw Korea as "the Greece of the Far East," and the invasion as an example of Communist domino-toppling. According to the "domino theory," popular among U.S. policymakers in the early Cold War, countries were like dominoes; once one "fell" to Communism, its neighbors would also fall. "There's no telling what they'll do, if we don't put up a fight now," said Truman.[8] The UN response to Korea would also serve as a test of the merits and strength of collective security.

While the Soviets provided military equipment and other encouragement to North Korea (Document 9), the Chinese Communists sent troops after General Douglas MacArthur had escalated the war far into North Korea in his hope to unify the country in late 1950. This Chinese response confined the U.S. role to containment rather than a rollback of Communism in Korea, greatly disappointing MacArthur and his supporters (Document 10). Korea thus set a pattern for limited war that was followed in Vietnam. The Korean War, which ended in an armistice in 1953, created many Cold War precedents for American foreign policy. It provided a justification for the vast expansion in U.S. military capabilities that had been proposed in the secret National Security Council Paper No. 68 (Document 8). The veiled threat of nuclear response that the United States used to convince the Chinese to accept an armistice at the end of the Korean War also set a precedent that was followed later in the Eisenhower administration, both in Vietnam (discussed later) and in the Taiwan Strait (see Chapter 4). As Secretary of

State John Foster Dulles declared in 1954, Korea had ended because China was made aware that the United States was willing to take the war "beyond the limits and methods which . . . [the enemy] had selected."[9] This "brinksmanship" and its corollary threat of "massive retaliation" were typical of Eisenhower's presidency, which resorted more frequently to making nuclear threats in response to crises than did any succeeding administration.

DOMESTIC DEVELOPMENTS

Korea also greatly heightened domestic insecurity in the United States as both the notorious revelations of the Rosenberg spy case and the shaky statistics of Wisconsin Senator Joseph McCarthy first made their stamp on the national consciousness, and raised doubts that containment was going far enough to fight international Communism. Fear of Communist influence in and espionage against the U.S. government and other American institutions was widespread, as reflected in laws, employment regulations, and the media. By 1950 the Cold War was underway in earnest inside the United States. Congress brought hundreds of professors, teachers, actors, and filmmakers in front of hearings about supposed communist subversion in American culture during what is known as the McCarthy Era (1950–1954). Many lost their jobs, introducing a spirit of conformity and fear in American society in the 1950s, which ironically paralleled the straitjacket of Soviet society. Neverthless, anticommunism itself was not merely "an irrational and indefensible persecution of a group of American reformers," write historians John Earl Haynes and Harvey Klehr. There *were* Communists in the United States, and socialist Irving Howe offered perhaps the most telling criticism of them, charging that they "helped destroy whatever possibilities there might have been for a resurgence of serious radicalism in America."[10]

ESCALATION AROUND THE GLOBE

Although McCarthy was disgraced by 1954, the domestic anticommunist consensus (Document 11) and its foreign counterpart, the domino theory, survived. In Latin America, this theory brought such relatively benign programs as President Dwight D. Eisenhower's Inter-American Development Bank and President John F. Kennedy's Alliance for Progress, aid programs with anticommunist overtones to keep revolutionary movements in the region under control. These programs reflected, too, the American conviction in the beneficence of U.S. nation-building efforts abroad, such as those conducted in Japan and Germany after the war, and were rooted in a New Deal belief in the salutary effects of technology to mitigate economic distress. Thus the Tennessee Valley Authority projects of the 1930s would reappear in Vietnam's Mekong Delta of the 1960s as another symbol of American ingenuity and responsibility for progressive nation building. But it was precisely nine thousand miles away in Vietnam that the domino theory was applied most disastrously.

In the spring of 1954 colonial French troops, in the midst of a seven-year struggle to hold onto their position in Indochina, were trapped by the Communist Vietminh forces at Dien Bien Phu in North Vietnam. Dulles dangled the hope of U.S. military assistance to the desperate French, yet this assistance would only come, he declared, if the United States acted in "united action" with a coalition of Southeast Asian nations, Britain, and the Philippines—a somewhat improbable prospect. But in such an eventuality, Dulles was prepared to send nuclear weapons. His rhetoric clearly took the United States to the "brink" of war, part of Dulles's policy of "brinksmanship," an all-or-nothing approach to the Communist threat. Yet Congressional approval was needed too, and despite the fears of many in Congress that the Chinese Communists would intervene in Indochina as they had done in the Korean War, that conflict was too recent for most Americans to feel comfortable with an all-out commitment to the French. Even Dulles, who had lectured the Chinese against contemplating a "second aggression" in the region, conceded, "We don't want to be committed to a series of Koreas around the globe."[11]

It was too late for Washington's help, in any case. Dien Bien Phu fortress fell to the Vietminh on May 7. The only option now was negotiation, and world attention turned to the Geneva Conference, where conferees had begun deliberating a number of Asian issues, including the political future of Vietnam and its neighbors, Cambodia and Laos, and the intransigent issue of Korean unification. The conference included Chinese, Russian, British, and North and South Korean representatives, as well as American. Dulles, who found the very idea of compromises and negotiations with Communists unpalatable, acted at Geneva "with the pinched distaste of a puritan in a house of ill repute," refusing to shake hands with Chinese foreign minister Zhou En-lai.[12]

Yet it was in part owing to Dulles's efforts at Geneva that the border between North and South Vietnam ended up at the 17th parallel and not farther south at the conclusion of the conference in July. After the Vietminh replaced the French in North Vietnam, Washington became increasingly active in the South. The Eisenhower administration's use of "domino theory" rhetoric at Geneva reflected the official view that leftist regimes from Iran to Indonesia represented outreaches of the "Communist monolith" (though it was already cracking as the Soviets and Chinese moved apart) and led the United States covertly to assist in the overthrow of a series of foreign governments in the 1950s and early 1960s as well as to support the new Republic of South Vietnam beyond the limits that the Geneva Conference had granted outside powers. This was not empire by invitation but imperialism, and led to blunders like the Bay of Pigs invasion of Cuba in 1961.

Meanwhile, the death of Stalin and the emergence of a more conciliatory leader, Nikita S. Khrushchev (1953–1964), in the Kremlin led to a softening of the Soviet stance in Europe. Eastern European satellite nations were told to de-Stalinize, make economic concessions to workers, and separate the Communist party from the national governments. But after East German leader Walter Ulbricht had reluctantly lifted the lid, only to slam it down again, a riot erupted and Soviet tanks rolled in. De-Stalinization was clearly a limited concept.

When the Federal Republic of Germany joined NATO in 1955, the Soviet Union and its satellites formed the Warsaw Pact military organization. This new balance between the superpowers' camps offered an opportunity for cooling tensions. In May the United States, Soviet Union, Britain, and France signed the Austrian State Treaty, and for the first time Soviet tanks rolled out of a European country. In July, President Eisenhower (1953–1961) and Khrushchev met for the first time, drawing hopes of a new and conciliatory "spirit of Geneva," in honor of the city where the summit took place. But both sides made far-reaching demands: The Soviets wanted to terminate NATO, have American soldiers leave the continent, and ban nuclear arms, while the United States called for unification of Germany with elections and an "open skies" weapons monitoring program. In the end, the conference's contributions were limited. The Soviet Union recognized West Germany, and the two countries began cultural exchanges.

After Moscow refused to share maps of its military installations, the United States launched secret espionage flights over Russia on July 4, 1956, using U-2 aircraft with special cameras that filmed a 750–mile swath from 12 miles up. Although extremely provocative and a source of heightened superpower tensions, U-2 flights allowed Washington to know about Russia's intercontinental ballistic missile (ICBM) capabilities, its space program, and its nuclear testing and missile deployment. Over two hundred missions were flown before pilot Francis Gary Powers crashed into a field on the Soviet holiday of May Day in 1960 and created a superpower crisis that led to the cancellation of the Paris summit that year. After issuing denials of responsibility, which gave the impression that low-level officials could send risky missions into Russia, Eisenhower finally acknowledged that he had authorized the policy of U-2 flights. At the same time, he also made sure there was " 'no specific tie' of the May Day flight to him." This "lying" to Khrushchev—and the American people—about his approval of this mission, and initially of the policy itself, contributed to a growing trend of Americans' distrust of their leadership.[13]

Khrushchev, meanwhile, had continued de-Stalinization with an unprecedented attack on Stalin's crimes, his cult of personality, and his paranoia in a secret speech to the Twentieth Congress of the Communist Party of the Soviet Union in February 1956. The CIA procured a copy of this speech and leaked it to the *New York Times* in June. But just as in East Germany three years earlier, a slackening in repression destabilized the satellites, this time leading to riots and a split in the Polish Communist party. Wladyslaw Gomulka, a nationalist who had been rehabilitated after Stalin's death, became First Secretary despite Moscow's initial concerns. He soon proved a devoted client.

Hungary's reaction to de-Stalinization was much more dangerous. Imre Nagy, another post-1953 Communist reformer, led a revolution against the existing government in October 1956. As the previous leaders fled to Moscow, rebelling Hungarians trashed secret police headquarters and Nagy announced plans to leave the Warsaw pact, asking for help from the West. Washington, which sent anti-Soviet messages through Radio Free Europe and the Voice of America, was deeply gratified at this effort at freedom. Yet, though the CIA trained East European émigrés for intervention, there was little the United States was prepared to provide in the form of direct assistance to the revolutionaries.

Soviet tanks appeared on November 4 and brutally suppressed the revolution. Thirty thousand Hungarians died in the failed effort, and Nagy was executed and buried without a headstone in a cemetery for zoo animals. (In 1989, when the Soviet grip loosened on Hungary, his coffin was exhumed and reburied). Two hundred fifty thousand Hungarians emigrated, many to the United States.

Although American officials shied away from meddling where the Soviets had established a firm hold, Washington was more assertive in areas where Soviet influence was a threat rather than a fact. In the Middle East, the United States attempted to entice Egyptian leader Gamal Abdul Nasser to join an anticommunist defense league, promising to assist him with building a dam on the Nile River. But when he resisted joining the defense pact, the United States cancelled aid for the dam. This tit-for-tat response was typical of Dulles's brinksmanship. As a result, Nasser nationalized the Suez Canal, taking control of the Suez Canal company from its foreign-dominated board (with its twenty-five British and French directors but only five Egyptian). According to Egypt's 1949 agreement with the Suez Canal Company, it received only 7 percent of Canal profits, and Nasser saw the nationalization as a way to raise money for his dam after Dulles's pullout. The resulting French-British-Israeli military attack on Egypt drew a furious U.S. response, because Washington feared that such neocolonialism would drive Nasser even closer to the Soviets. After the Suez crisis, Moscow capitalized on the Western countries' differences and became Egypt's patron, though Nasser was no pro-Communist.

Meanwhile, Khrushchev began a policy in the Third World of aiding left-wing nationalist struggles or "wars of national liberation," such as Ho Chi Minh's in Vietnam or Patrice Lumumba's in the Congo, as the undeveloped world increasingly became the chief battleground in the Cold War. Along with this new adventurism was an apparent Soviet technological edge, represented by the 1957 launching of Sputnik. This space satellite, which closely followed the Soviet development of an ICBM, alarmed Americans and drew loud denunciations from early Democratic contenders for the presidency, like John F. Kennedy and Lyndon B. Johnson, as evidence of Republican complacency about a "missile gap." However, American intelligence reports indicated that no such gap existed, and that the Soviets still lacked the airplanes and missile capability to deliver nuclear warheads to American targets. Moreover, Sputnik was only "a prototype," as Eisenhower, who had been quietly watching development of Sputnik through the U-2, knew.[14] He also saw a silver lining: If Sputnik convinced the Soviets that freedom of international space was legitimate, then his "open skies" goal could become a reality. Indeed, after the Soviets acquired satellite technology in the 1960s, both nations quietly spied on each other, which cooled tensions by limiting imaginary fears.

THE ARMS BUILDUP

Such fears were thick in the United States after Sputnik, as the Ford Foundation's secret and alarmist Gaither report revealed, demanding a huge arms program in response to putative Soviet economic and military successes. Consequently, the United States conducted a rapid buildup between 1958 and 1960, tripling the number of nuclear arms to eighteen thousand weapons, including Polaris nuclear submarines, and sending intermediate-range ballistic missiles to NATO. Washington launched its own satellite in January 1958, the Explorer I, and established the National Air and Space Administration in July. This Cold War agency would be responsible for the U.S. space program, which sent the manned Apollo missions to the moon in the 1960s and continues to launch research missions into outer space to this day. In September 1958 Congress passed the $1 billion National Defense Education Act, with an emphasis on improving Americans' abilities in mathematics, science, and foreign languages, which soon helped the United States lead the world in doctorate production (at ten thousand in 1960 alone). A rueful Eisenhower left office warning about the dangers of a "military-industrial complex" more threatening than the perceived missile gap.[15]

Meanwhile, flush with his Sputnik triumph, Khrushchev decided to press his advantage on the ground, in the sore spot of Berlin. By 1958 three million refugees had fled from Communist East Germany into the attractive, rich city of West Berlin. More than just a drain on population, the city was also a spy and propaganda center. Khrushchev was also angry about the arming of West Germany in NATO, which he saw as a clear violation of wartime agreements, and in November 1958 declared that the Western allies (Britain, France, and the United States) must leave West Berlin. If the ultimatum were not met, the Soviets would sign a separate peace with East Germany, terminating the occupation. The Western powers would then have to negotiate passage rights with the East German government, which thus far had not gained their recognition.

Eisenhower heeded the pleas of West German Chancellor Konrad Adenauer against taking this step and decided that there should be no weakness in the U.S. "forward position." If East Germany tried to stop American passage to West Berlin, he would send a convoy to the city and prepare for further measures. Khrushchev subsequently made several more ultimatums but did not act on them.

At the same time, a slight warming trend in Soviet-American relations developed following the death of Secretary Dulles in May 1959. The hard-line and dominating Dulles was replaced by the more subdued former Governor of Massachusetts Christian Herter, and this transition allowed Eisenhower, often underestimated as a key player in U.S. foreign policy, to take a noticeably active role. Without Dulles, "the conscience and strait-jacket of the free world," the president moved toward an opening with the Soviet Union, with Vice President Richard Nixon traveling to Moscow and Khrushchev to Camp David that year.[16] This trend was not to last, however. After Francis Gary Powers was shot down in his U-2 in 1960, relations deteriorated, and the blusterous Khrushchev declared at the UN that September, "We will bury you."

Then, early in the Kennedy administration (1961–1963), the Soviet leader again made the West sweat over Berlin. The disastrous American-sponsored Bay of Pigs invasion of Cuba had encouraged yet another ultimatum from the pugnacious Soviet leader, this time at the Vienna Summit in 1961. Furious, John F. Kennedy muttered, "That son of a bitch won't pay any attention to words. He has to see you move."[17] The president activated the reserves and called for an expanded civil defense in case of nuclear attack. He also sent Jupiter missiles to Turkey, a U.S. ally on the Russian border.

INTERNATIONAL CRISIS

A concrete solution to the intractable problem of the evaporating East German population finally arose on August 13, as workers constructed twenty-eight miles of wall, barbed wire, and armed guards between East and West Berlin. General Lucius Clay, the U.S. representative in Berlin, responded—without Kennedy's authorization—by fitting American tanks with bulldozer attachments to stop the construction. After the Soviets readied their own tanks to defend the barrier, Kennedy and Khrushchev hastily defused the situation. As the president said, "A wall is a hell of a lot better than a war."[18] In sympathy with the West Germans, Kennedy would later travel to Berlin to utter his immortal words, "Ich bin ein Berliner [I am a Berliner]," signaling America's continued commitment to a free Berlin.[19] Yet the wall did not address the diplomatic status of East Germany. Even as the Kennedy administration was preparing to talk to the Soviets about that issue, Khrushchev ratcheted up the pressure by installing missiles in Cuba.

Believing that the missiles would make his position even more powerful in Europe and prevent further American invasions of the Caribbean island after the Bay of Pigs, the Soviet leader reached too far. Khrushchev wanted to deploy forty 1100–mile medium-range ballistic missiles (MRBMs) with warheads, and Cuba's leader Fidel Castro did not object. But U.S. U-2s identified the missile sites before they were fully operational, and Khrushchev was forced to retreat in October 1962 after a harrowing showdown. Khrushchev's weakness in Cuba prevented further demands over Berlin. The wall remained, a blight on the landscape, a deadly barrier, and a symbol of what a Communist government had to do to keep people from leaving the workers' paradise, for the next three decades. In 1971, under President

Nixon's policy of détente, or lessened tensions, the United States finally recognized East Germany in return for unalterable transit rights.

As part of the resolution of the missile crisis, the United States had to remove its missiles in Turkey and promise never to invade Cuba again. The crisis did allow for better relations between Washington and Moscow. A telex was installed connecting the White House and the Kremlin to prevent further surprises. In 1963 the two superpowers signed an aboveground test-ban treaty that was an important step on the road towards arms control.

But in the Third World, tensions were building. JFK was in the process of increasing U.S. involvement in Vietnam, more than quadrupling the number of American military advisers there since he came to office. After what many American officials saw as an unsatisfactory solution next door in Laos—the creation of a neutralist coalition government, including Communists, in 1962—the Kennedy administration determined that the United States was not going to let Vietnam also slip away. In the speech he was scheduled to give at Dallas on November 22, 1963, the day he was shot, the president had written, "Our assistance to . . . nations can be painful, risky and costly, as is true in Southeast Asia today. But we dare not weary of the task." Yet his Defense Secretary, Robert McNamara, has since contended that had the president continued in office, he "would have sensed that the conditions he had laid down—i.e., it was a South Vietnamese war, that it could only be won by them, and to win it they needed a sound political base—could not be met."[20] Other former members of JFK's cabinet who continued to shape policy in the Johnson administration are not so sure what course JFK might have taken.

Unfortunately, American diplomats encouraged the assassination of Ngo Dinh Diem, president of South Vietnam, thus drawing Washington in more deeply in November 1963. As Kennedy told Ambassador to South Vietnam Henry Cabot Lodge upon the accession to power of the new president, General Duong van Minh: "We . . . have a responsibility to help this new government to be effective in every way that we can."[21] JFK himself was assassinated two weeks later. His successor, Lyndon B. Johnson (1963–1969), would place much greater emphasis on victory in South Vietnam. He believed strongly in fighting Communism and in building a nation in South Vietnam, just as Kennedy had tried to do. Because of his great interest in effecting his Great Society social programs at home, however, Johnson did not make the war his top priority. By not placing a strong emphasis on rallying support for the war, Johnson saw a limited level of patience from the American people when the U.S. effort in Vietnam began to flag in 1968, despite the presence of 543,000 American soldiers there. U.S. military involvement created an agonizing dilemma: stay in for "credibility," despite what was evidently "an unwinnable war"—because to protect South Vietnam adequately from the North, the United States risked the entry of China—or leave, and suffer a serious loss of prestige and world position. American officials decided to stay in a limited, frustrating effort that only exacerbated Vietnam's problems and created maximum dissent at home. So great was the need to project consensus in the administration, however, that McNamara, despite harboring doubts beginning in 1966, kept them to himself. It was not until 1968, during the Tet Offensive (actually a military disaster for the communist attackers) that many Americans began to realize that things were not going well in Vietnam. The war greatly damaged U.S. foreign policy, as some government officials had predicted it would as early as the first year of the Kennedy administration (Document 12). The failure of this overambitious effort was a blow to American prestige and was followed by a period of vigorous Communist expansion in the Third World.

The Soviet Union faced challenges too in 1968, when Czechoslovaks attempted to replace their regime with "socialism with a human face" during the Prague Spring. They were crushed by Soviet tanks and the troops of neighboring Warsaw Pact countries. This event likely helped Republican Richard Nixon win a close presidential election in the United States, as did his promise to end the war in Vietnam "with honor." Nixon's administration (1969–1974) was the first to reduce the number of troops in Vietnam through a policy of "Vietnamization," whereby the United States withdrew its forces in tandem with an attempted buildup of South Vietnam's military capabilities. In this way, Nixon and his chief foreign policy adviser, Henry Kissinger, planned to end direct American involvement without the appearance of defeat. Through his détente policy of lowering tensions with the Communist bloc, Nixon was determined to end the U.S. role as global policeman, and thereby also to cut the increasingly heavy financial costs of the Cold War. The Nixon Doctrine declared that the United States would in the future let Asian nations take care of their own problems (Document 13).

EFFORTS AT DÉTENTE

Nixon and Kissinger planned a policy of "triangulation" to maintain strategic balance. They played to the existing Sino-Soviet split, which had broken out in skirmishes at the Chinese-Russian border in 1969, and provided an opportunity for Nixon in his attempt to extricate America from Vietnam. In 1972 he opened relations with China with the goal of pressuring the Soviet Union to take a more conciliatory position towards the United

States, and thus to facilitate movement at the Vietnam peace negotiations in Paris (Russia was Hanoi's major patron). The triangular relationship—such a drastic departure from the old American view of monolithic Communism—did have some effect. It increased tensions between the two Communist giants, which benefited the United States, as Nixon and Soviet leader Leonid Brezhnev (1964–1982) agreed to a significant arms limitation agreement (SALT I) the same year that the United States and China opened talks. Unfortunately, the Paris talks did not live up to their promise. The 1973 peace treaty, designed to preserve Saigon's role in a future government while removing "foreign" forces from South Vietnam, extricated Washington from its longest war but only postponed the Communist takeover of the South. By early 1975, after American aid was cut off, North Vietnam invaded the South and reunited the country, as millions of Vietnamese struggled to escape.

Yet there were victories on other fronts. As South Vietnam fell, the United States and the Soviet Union reached an agreement on the postwar settlement of Europe in the Helsinki Accords of 1975. Though skeptics blasted these accords as providing window dressing for the Soviet grip on Europe, the agreements actually helped to undermine Soviet legitimacy by requiring the monitoring of human rights in eastern Europe. This empowered dissidents and contributed to the end of the Cold War.

This emphasis on human rights expanded during the Jimmy Carter administration (1977–1981). Carter had come into office hopeful to create better relations with the Kremlin, though Brezhnev was put out by his human rights agenda. Carter's hopes were dashed by the Soviet invasion of Afghanistan in 1979, and in protest his administration pursued a much harder line toward the Soviet Union thereafter. Carter announced an embargo on grain sales to Russia, an effective form of leverage against the agriculturally backward Russians, but one that had the unfortunate effect of harming American farmers as well. The president also called for a boycott of the 1980 Moscow Olympics. Young men had to register for the draft, too. Less publicly, Carter issued Presidential Directive 59, a hard-line nuclear policy that envisioned atomic weapons as more than a deterrent force. It provided, noted Defense Secretary Harold Brown, "the option for more selective, lesser retaliatory attacks that would exact a prohibitively high price from the things the Soviet leadership prizes most—political and military control, nuclear and conventional military force, and the economic base needed to sustain a war."[22] The administration thus moved toward "realpolitik" and away from idealistic notions like human rights, which few Americans held as a high priority anyway.[23]

SETBACKS TO DÉTENTE

The Soviet invasion of Afghanistan, which capped a series of events favorable to Soviet interests in the Third World in the late 1970s, from the placement of Cuban proxy soldiers in Angola to the promotion of Communist control of Yemen to the establishment of a Marxist regime in Nicaragua, seemed to call for a stronger American posture. In the wake of Vietnam, the United States appeared to be losing the Cold War and détente to be facilitating the trend, as the Soviet Union and China and their clients made new probes around the globe. Though Nicaraguan and Cambodian Marxists were very different in their policies (Daniel Ortega's Sandinistas in Nicaragua did not conduct the kind of murderous policies that Pol Pot's Khmer Rouge did in Cambodia, for instance), the leftist trend appeared to indicate that the capitalist West was no longer in the vanguard of history.

The demise of the Shah of Iran, long an American client, his replacement by a fundamentalist Muslim government in 1979, and finally Iranian militants' taking hostage of the U.S. embassy for 444 days amounted to the worst crisis of Carter's presidency and the disappearance of a key Cold War ally. Yet it was also in the Middle East that Carter experienced his greatest achievement. After years of bloodshed, in 1978 he was able to bring Egyptian President Anwar Sadat and Israeli Prime Minister Menachim Begin together to sign the Camp David accords, a peace treaty between Egypt and Israel, which was a solid step toward peace in that troubled region.

During Carter's last year in office, Poland became the site of the first sustained challenge to a satellite regime in the history of the Cold War. The Polish workers' protest movement, Solidarity, began as a protest over meat prices. Centered in a shipyard in Gdansk, led by the charismatic electrician Lech Walesa, and supported by the Catholic Church in Poland, it drew Soviet concern as well as panic from neighboring satellites like East Germany (Document 14). Eventually, the Polish Communists installed martial law to keep order, but Solidarity continued underground, aided by U.S. and Papal assistance, and eventually emerged, triumphant, in 1989.

THE COLLAPSE OF THE SOVIET UNION AND THE END OF THE COLD WAR

President Ronald Reagan (1981–1989) continued Carter's tough position toward the Soviets and greatly increased defense spending. As a result, he helped exacerbate the economic crisis in the Soviet Union, already in trouble from flattening oil prices and years of economic and political stagnation. The Soviet Union lacked the financial or technological capacity to keep up with the U.S. buildup. Reagan condemned the Soviet Union in harsh terms, referring to it as the "focus of evil in the modern world" (Document 15) in 1983. But in his second term, when Mikhail S. Gorbachev became leader of the Soviet Union, superpower relations improved considerably. Gorbachev pushed strongly for an end to the arms race (Document 16). But his domestic reforms, *glasnost* (openness) and *perestroika* (restructuring), though long needed, unleashed forces beyond the Kremlin's control, as the Soviet people demanded an end to their repressive government. Satellites like Poland and Hungary freed themselves from the Warsaw Pact during 1989 and 1990, and Soviet occupying troops left soon after. The two Germanies unified and became part of NATO in October 1990. The peoples who lived directly under Soviet domination, in the Baltic States, Ukraine, Moldova, Belarus, and even Russia liberated themselves, and in 1991 the Soviet Union disintegrated. The collapse of the U.S.S.R., the most important nuclear-armed enemy of the United States and its allies, effectively ended the Cold War.

Economic problems and other sources of instability in the post-communist states have led to crises in many of these nations, and in some of them, like Hungary, Communists have returned to power in socialist garb. Russia itself has struggled with severe economic, political, and nationalist challenges, including a vicious war in Chechnya that was settled in 1997. Moreover, although President George Bush crowed about the death of Communism in 1992 (Document 17), it lives on in China, Cuba, North Korea, and Vietnam, among other countries. Within the United States, the Cold War's legacy continues to shape economic policy, the military, diplomacy, and domestic culture to this day, as this book's concluding chapter illustrates.

Nevertheless, the Cold War was certainly over when Bush spoke in 1992. This nearly fifty-year struggle, which ended in 1991 with the demise of the Soviet Union and the survival of the United States as the world's greatest economic and military superpower, has been painted by some as a vindication of American "can-do" spirit, or even as the product of Ronald Reagan's hard-line policies in vanquishing the "evil empire." But in reality, Mikhail S. Gorbachev and his agenda served as the midwife for the birth of post-Soviet Russia and the concomitant end of the Cold War—whether Gorbachev wanted this end or not—and Americans, who badly wanted to be delivered from two generations of tensions, but could hardly believe it was happening, merely coached the process along and claimed its reward in prestige and power.

NOTES

1. Walter Lippmann, *The Cold War: A Study in U.S. Foreign Policy* (New York: Harper and Brothers, 1947).

2. Geir Lundestad, *The American "Empire" and Other Studies of U.S. Foreign Policy in a Comparative Perspective* (New York and Oslo: Oxford University Press and Norwegian University Press, 1990), 54–55.

3. Vladislav Zubok and Constantine Pleshakov, "The Soviet Union," in David Reynolds, ed., *The Origins of the Cold War in Europe* (New Haven: Yale University Press, 1994), 63.

4. Barton Bernstein, "Understanding the Atomic Bomb and the Japanese Surrender: Missed Opportunities, Little-Known Near Disasters, and Modern Memory," *Diplomatic History* 19 (Spring 1995), 236.

5. Gar Alperovitz, *The Decision to Use the Atomic Bomb and the Architecture of an American Myth* (New York: Knopf, 1995), 665.

6. Khariton quoted in Vladislav Zubok and Constantine Pleshakov, *Inside the Kremlin's Cold War: From Stalin to Khrushchev* (Cambridge, Mass.: Harvard University Press, 1996), 42; David Holloway, *Stalin and the Bomb: The Soviet Union and Atomic Energy, 1939–1956* (New Haven: Yale University Press, 1994), 125.

7. See Document 4 in the Primary Documents chapter.

8. Quoted in Alonzo L. Hamby, *Man of the People: A Life of Harry S. Truman* (New York: Oxford University Press, 1995), 537.

9. Quoted in Frederick W. Marks III, *Power and Peace: The Diplomacy of John Foster Dulles* (Westport, Conn.: Praeger, 1993), 106.

10. Harvey Klehr, John Earl Haynes, and Fridrikh Firsov, *The Secret World of American Communism* (New Haven: Yale University Press, 1995), 16; Howe as cited in Stephen J. Whitfield, *Culture of the Cold War*, 2nd ed. (Baltimore: Johns Hopkins University Press, 1996), 114.

11. Quoted in Marks, *Power and Peace*, 107.

12. Townsend Hoopes, *The Devil and John Foster Dulles* (Boston: Little Brown, 1973), 222.

13. See Michael Beschloss, *May Day: Eisenhower, Khrushchev, and the U-2 Affair* (New York: Harper and Row, 1986), 252–53.

14. Henry A. Kissinger, *Diplomacy* (New York: Simon and Schuster, 1994), 570.

15. Eisenhower Farewell Address, January 17, 1961, quoted in Stephen E. Ambrose, *Eisenhower: The President* (New York: Simon & Schuster, 1984), II: 612.

16. Hoopes, *Devil and John Foster Dulles*, 492.

17. Kennedy quoted in Arthur M. Schlesinger, Jr., *A Thousand Days: John F. Kennedy in the White House* (Boston: Houghton Mifflin Company, 1965), 391.

18. Quoted in Paterson et al., *American Foreign Relations: A History since 1895*, 4th ed. (Lexington, Mass.: D.C. Heath, 1995), II: 390.

19. Quoted in Richard Reeves, *President Kennedy: Profile of Power* (New York: Simon and Schuster, 1993), 536.

20. Kennedy quoted in Lawrence J. Bassett and Stephen E. Pelz, "The Failed Search for Victory: Vietnam and the Politics of War," in Thomas G. Paterson, ed., *Kennedy's Quest for Victory: American Foreign Policy, 1961–1963* (New York: Oxford University Press, 1989), 249; Robert S. McNamara, *In Retrospect: The Tragedy and Lessons of Vietnam* (New York: Random House, 1995), 96.

21. Quoted in Richard Reeves, *President Kennedy*, 652.

22. Quoted in John Dumbrell, *The Carter Presidency: A Re-evaluation*, 2nd ed. (Manchester and New York: Manchester University Press, 1995), 201.

23. Only 1 percent of Americans polled saw human rights as among the top three priorities of U.S. foreign policy in a 1978 poll. See Dumbrell, *Carter Presidency*, 185.

2

Origins of the Cold War, 1945–1950

At the end of World War II, the victorious United States and Soviet Union stood as the most powerful economic and military powers on the globe. Though not inevitable, the rivalry that developed between these two countries and their respective spheres of influence was in part the product of the war's outcome. After its stunning defeat of Nazi forces at Stalingrad in February 1943, the Soviet Union began its push into Europe, setting the stage for the map revisions that followed the war. The U.S. State Department realized that once Nazi Germany had fallen, "the Soviet Army will be the most powerful on the European continent" and Soviet leaders would have "governments acting in substantial compliance with their desires in Poland, Romania, Bulgaria, Czechoslovakia, and Hungary" (see Document 1). Revealing the then limited U.S. ambitions for postwar involvement, the Department predicted: "The degree of American influence in the situation will tend to diminish. . . . The United States has not yet become the protagonist of any set of ideas or policies which would give rise to great influence in Europe on doctrinaire grounds."[1] Cold War rivalry could hardly be foreseen. Nevertheless, it became reality by early 1946, and it is the problem of the origins of the Cold War and its early intense and accelerated phase that form the subject of the current chapter.

YALTA SETS THE STAGE FOR THE COLD WAR

In early February 1945 the three leaders of the anti-Nazi alliance, U.S. President Franklin D. Roosevelt, British Prime Minister Winston Churchill, and Soviet leader Josef Stalin—met at Yalta in the U.S.S.R. The conference agenda included Russia's entry into the war against Japan; the composition of the postwar government of Germany; voting arrangements in the new United Nations (UN) organization; and the future of the liberated governments of eastern Europe. All were important issues, but the Yalta Declaration on Liberated Europe, which called for free elections and constitutional liberties in Eastern Europe, became the most controversial. In Soviet-occupied Poland, for instance, the allies agreed on a provisional government including the Communist Lublin Committee and noncommunist Polish exiles. The noncommunists were soon squeezed out, however, and the Soviets consequently used the Declaration to provide legitimacy for their occupation of Hungary, Czechoslovakia, East Germany, Poland, and Romania—and later transformed these countries into satellites.

Journalist Walter Lippmann suggested that Roosevelt and Churchill had unrealistic expectations. "Had [the United States and Britain] seen clearly the significance of the military situation, they would not have committed the United States to anything in Eastern Europe while the Soviet Government had the power to oppose it, while the United States had no power to enforce it." But to idealistic Americans, swallowing "the realities of the balance of power" was unpalatable. Instead, Washington later attacked Soviet ideology and sought to contain it and transform it, even as two spheres would be effectively carved out in Europe—one by force, the other by consensus.[2]

FDR died on April 12, 1945, and the war in Europe ended on May 8. The last war conference, at Potsdam in July, coincided with the first successful testing of the U.S. atomic bomb, the best kept secret of the war despite its $2 billion cost. But after the nuclear attacks on Hiroshima and Nagasaki on August 6 and 9, which killed 150,000 people, and the Russian invasion of China, Japan surrendered. After World War II, the United States restructured Japan with a new democratic constitution, greater access to education, and a less regimented economy.

The attacks drew great controversy at the time, and still do, as evidenced by the 1995 flap over the Smithsonian National Air and Space Museum's planned interpretive exhibit of the bomb-carrying plane, the *Enola Gay*. In 1946 the Federal Council of Churches declared, "[T]he suprise bombings of Hiroshima and Nagasaki are morally indefensible." That August, John Hersey's critical essay, "Hiroshima," was published in *The New Yorker* and caused a sensation. The bad press demanded a response, as officials worried that "the lurking, inchoate, anomic terror of living in the strange new atomic age might coalesce into an unstoppable demand for the elimination of

America's nuclear arsenal—or almost as damaging, vitiate its diplomatic usefulness."[3] To prevent this outcome, Former Secretary of War Henry L. Stimson explained the use of the bomb in a February 1947 article: "I believe that no man, in our position and subject to our responsibilities, holding in his hands a weapon of such possibilities for accomplishing this purpose and saving those lives, could have failed to use it and afterwards looked his countrymen in the face."[4] In this way, Stimson prepared Americans for the eventuality of using the bomb again.

In the immediate aftermath of the war, the Soviet Union and the United States were more detached than focused on each other, however. Indeed, they were friendly: Eisenhower visited Russia, and Truman invited Soviet Marshal Georgi Zhukov to the United States. The United States was pulling back to the Western Hemisphere, and for Moscow this was an opportune time to pursue its imperial goals, not only in eastern Europe but in Greece, Turkey, and Iran—traditionally a British area of interest. During the war, Washington had been prepared to accept such "a Soviet 'sphere of influence' . . . operated in somewhat the same fashion as we have operated the good neighbor policy in Mexico and the Caribbean area."[5] But the U.S. chargé in Moscow, George F. Kennan, was increasingly concerned about Soviet expansion, which became ever more blatant in 1946. Owing to its commitment in the war to the principle of self-determination, Washington officials were disturbed by Moscow's ambitions and aggressive behavior in eastern Europe, the Middle East, and Asia, where the Soviets looted $2 billion in infrastructure as they departed Manchuria. Particularly vexing to the West was the Red Army's overstaying its wartime occupation of Iran in order to establish a sphere of influence in that country, a situation that led Teheran to complain to the UN Security Council in January 1946.

A fed-up Truman asserted that he would no longer acquiesce in Soviet aggression. "Unless Russia is faced with an iron fist and strong language another war is in the making. Only one language do they understand—'how many divisions have you?' I do not think we should play compromise any longer. . . . I'm tired [of] babying the Soviets."[6] George F. Kennan's Long Telegram (Document 2) and Winston Churchill's "Iron Curtain" speech (Document 3) were each emblematic of this shift in outlook. Kennan sent his influential 5,540–word message on February 22, noting that "world communism is like [a] malignant parasite which feeds only on diseased tissue." He urged that the United States "formulate and put forward for other nations a much more positive and constructive picture of [the] sort of world we would like to see than we have put forward in the past."[7] No longer should the United States passively allow other powers to set the agenda. His missive, which described not only the geopolitical ambitions but the ideological basis of the Soviets, became the received gospel for American officials seeking to understand Soviet behavior.

"AN IRON CURTAIN HAS DESCENDED"

On March 5 Winston Churchill spoke at Westminster College in Fulton, Missouri—Truman's home state. He vilified the Soviet Union for pulling down an "iron curtain" across Europe, "[f]rom Stettin in the Baltic to Trieste in the Adriatic." Churchill's emphasis on Anglo-American cooperation against Soviet Communism was compelling. U.S. ambassador to Russia Walter Bedell Smith reported that the speech rattled Stalin, who saw it as "an unwarranted attack upon the USSR."[8] Although Washington was not yet ready for an alliance with Britain, U.S. officials did urge the Soviets to leave Iran on the same day as the Iron Curtain speech, and Soviet troops departed in May. That summer, the president shifted course to support Turkey's refusal to share control of the Dardenelles Straits with Russia.

Although a growing number of Truman administration advisers—such as Navy Secretary James V. Forrestal, Secretary of State James Byrnes, former Ambassador to Russia Averell Harriman, and president of the World Bank and American proconsul in Germany John J. McCloy—were becoming convinced that the Soviet Union was not to be trusted, there were still dissenting voices. Secretary of Commerce Henry Wallace strongly disagreed with the Iron Curtain speech, which he thought tied the United States too closely to British imperialism. Wallace, indeed, believed that the United States was responsible for the emerging Cold War: "After we got the atomic bomb and acted the way we did, the Russians felt it necessary to enter upon an armaments race with us. . . . [S]ince we proposed to have bases clearly aimed at Russia, a large number of atomic bombs, and a large Navy, the Russians could feel that we were aiming the whole thing directly at them." Wallace's views were increasingly unacceptable to the administration, and his downfall came with his speech on September 12 to the left-leaning National Citizens Political Action Committee and the Independent Citizens Committee of the Arts and Sciences—a speech that Truman had read and approved. The Secretary argued that "whether we like it or not, the Russians will try to socialize their sphere of influence just as we try to democratize our sphere of influence."[9] An argument for catering to Soviet "insecurity" and a sphere in eastern Europe was not acceptable to many members of the administration. Truman backtracked, and asked Wallace to resign on September 20. He fulminated in his diary, "He is a pacifist 100 percent. He wants us to disband our armed forces, give Russia our atomic secrets and trust a bunch of adventurers in the Kremlin Politbureau [*sic*]." Truman added, "The Reds, phonies and the 'parlor pinks' seem to be banded together and are becoming a national danger."[10]

Soviet Ambassador to the United States Nikolai Novikov, detecting a new chill in the air, cabled home: "Wallace's resignation means the victory of the reactionary course that Byrnes is conducting in cooperation with [Senators] Vandenberg and Taft." The cooperative war Democrats were gone, and the U.S. government was now dominated by "President Truman, a politically unstable person but with certain conservative tendencies." Novikov concluded: "The foreign policy of the U.S., which reflects the imperialist tendencies of American monopolistic capital, is characterized in the postwar period by a striving for world supremacy." Stalin himself saw the Western leaders as "bear[ing] a striking resemblance to Hitler and his friends."[11]

Four days after Wallace's address, Clark Clifford, Special Counsel to Truman, handed the president a secret report that was the antithesis of Wallace's views. It declared that "The Soviet Union will never be easy to 'get along with.' " The Kremlin was expanding its influence and "unless the United States is willing to sacrifice its future security for the sake of 'accord' with the U.S.S.R. now, this government must . . . seek to prevent additional Soviet aggression." The United States could no longer assume a shared interest with the Soviets; and "must be prepared to wage atomic and biological warfare."[12] Desiring not to inflame an already agitated situation, Truman locked the report away.

Although the U.S. nuclear monopoly may have appeared to offer just the sort of edge Clifford was talking about, it was not in fact very useful. In 1945 Secretary of War Stimson had suggested that the U.S. monopoly would "almost certainly stimulate feverish activity on the part of the Soviet toward the development of this bomb." He recommended consulting with the British and offering to the Soviet Union a plan "to control and limit the use of the atomic bomb as an instrument of war and . . . encourage the development of atomic power for peaceful and humanitarian purposes."[13] Nuclear physicists and other scientists also sought to enlighten the public to the dangers of atomic energy and to shape legislation that governed its use. Their work led to the Atomic Energy Act of 1946, which granted civilian control of atomic energy but maintained many secrecy provisions in accordance with Army wishes.

Scientists also worked on a plan for international control of atomic technology in the UN, known as the Baruch plan after its chief negotiator, Bernard Baruch. However, because it gave the United States the right to continue producing and testing weapons if it was not satisfied with the plan's inspection system or had security concerns, and because the Soviets saw these loopholes as perpetuating American superiority, delegate Andrei Gromyko rejected it. In a postmortem to the failed movement for international control, physicist Edward Teller wrote: "The United States, immediately after World War II, had a unique opportunity to ensure peace. . . . But we let the opportunity slip by." Concludes historian Paul Boyer: "[T]he scientists' movement did not occur in a political void. . . . [U]ltimately the American people succumbed to an intense and all-pervasive anticommunist ideology."[14] That consensus made technological superiority over the Soviet Union through the bomb a priority, as the United States began a rapid expansion in the number of nuclear weapons, from thirteen in 1947 to three hundred three years later.

CONTAINMENT

But in 1947 Washington still relied on London's power to counter Moscow's. Great Britain, however, was broke, and its leaders announced in February 1947 that they would cut off aid to Greece and Turkey. They asked the United States to take on the burden. This request, building on Washington's hardening attitude toward Russia, launched a new U.S. security policy based on "containment," as articulated by George Kennan, now Director of the State Department Policy Planning Staff. In a famous article published in July 1947, "The Sources of Soviet Conduct," he urged the United States to pursue a policy of "long-term, patient but firm and vigilant containment of Russian expansive tendencies."[15] Kennan believed that if the West was vigilant and well-armed, it could "win" the Cold War, although not necessarily by military means—measures like the Truman Doctrine or Marshall Plan would be more effective. The success of the Soviet Union's staying power, he had noted in his Long Telegram, "is not yet finally proven." In any case, normal diplomatic relations would not be effective with the Soviets, working as they were amid the Kremlin's "atmosphere of oriental secretiveness and conspiracy," perpetuating a "neurotic view of world affairs . . . which [pictures] outside world as evil, hostile, and menacing."[16]

Journalist Walter Lippmann critiqued this policy in a contemporary book auspiciously titled *The Cold War* (he was the first to use the term). Instead of containment, Lippmann argued, it was only through negotiation with the Soviets leading to the evacuation of Russian forces from Europe, and the similar removal of American troops, that "a balance of power [may] be established which can then be maintained." Lippmann asked how the United

States could have "the money and the military power always available in sufficient amounts to apply 'counterforce' at constantly shifting points all over the world." But Kennan later protested that containment "was not something that I thought we could, necessarily, do everywhere successfully, or even needed to."[17] Yet by too often taking this kind of wholesale response, the United States would become exhausted and frustrated in places like Korea and Vietnam.

But American officials were not yet able to distinguish the drawbacks of containment. Although they did not envision a Soviet attack in Europe in 1947, they remained concerned that the continent's postwar weakness would render its people vulnerable to the influence of Communist parties and Soviet bullying. On February 27 Secretary of State George Marshall declared, "It is not alarmist to say that we are faced with the first crisis of a series which might extend Soviet domination to Europe, the Middle East and Asia."[18] On March 11, without mentioning the Soviets by name, Truman asked Congress for $400 million for economic and military aid for Greece and Turkey, pointing out that it was a tiny sliver of the war investment of $341 billion. Truman's appropriation request was enshrined in its accompanying "Truman Doctrine": "I believe that it must be the policy of the U.S. to support free peoples who are resisting attempted subjugation by armed minorities or by outside pressures . . . [and] that we must assist free peoples to work out their own destinies in their own way."[19]

This proposal put the United States in the position of supporting an oligarchic Greek regime, a fact somewhat mitigated by that regime's fighting a Communist insurrection sponsored by Bulgaria, Albania, and Yugoslavia. Turkey, the other recipient, had a similarly repressive government, but was facing Soviet imperial demands for land and other concessions that the United States considered threatening. Democratic Senator Claude Pepper of Florida, however, argued that Russia's demand to share in administering the Dardenelles Straits was no more unreasonable than the U.S. role in the Panama Canal, and proposed that Turkey be denied any aid. Others, like isolationist Sentator Robert Taft of Ohio, disliked the concept of guaranteed foreign aid, especially to help Britain, but eventually voted for it. The measure was approved in May.

Meanwhile, an economic crisis was brewing in the western zones of Germany, where both food and coal were in short supply, adversely affecting the recovery of Western Europe. Secretary Marshall and Soviet Foreign Minister Vyacheslav Molotov differed over the best way to handle Germany at the Council of Foreign Ministers meeting in Moscow in April 1947. The Soviet Union badly wanted reparations from Western Germany to alleviate its own economic difficulties, and asked for a role in the industrial Ruhr valley. In return, the Soviets promised to permit greater output from Germany as well as economic unification of the four allied zones—American, British, French, and Soviet. But Marshall did not want to see Western Germany's economy so closely linked with Russia's recovery. If Western Germany provided reparations from current industrial production, moreover, its own reconstruction might be adversely affected. There was no desire on the part of the United States, either, to have the Soviets in the Ruhr, where they could "meddle in West European economic affairs." Even the idea of a unified German government was unpalatable, because it could enhance the position of the Communists. The meeting ended at an impasse, with the Soviets still holding out for reparations, while the United States placed the needs of Western Germany and Western Europe first. The State Department declared that summer that it would work to combine the three Western zones to build up industry and draw Germany closer to the West through a new recovery plan. Four-power unity in Germany was no longer possible.[20]

THE MARSHALL PLAN

This new European recovery plan had been announced on June 5 by Secretary of State George C. Marshall (Document 5), and it sought to cure the "diseased tissue" that Kennan had so graphically described as the breeding ground for Communism. Despite billions in aid from the United Nations Relief and Rehabilitation Administration, largely in American money, and a $4.4 billion loan to Britain, Europe faced shortages, despair, and a large Communist following in Italy and France, where the party drew 20 percent of the voting public. As the origins of World War II had shown, Western Europe's economic health was a vital matter for U.S. national security.

In order to forestall charges of dividing Europe, the Soviet Union and its satellites were also invited to participate in the aid program that became known as the Marshall Plan. The program's requirements for divulging domestic economic information and providing resources deterred the Soviets, as did its emphasis on Germany as the keystone to Europe's recovery. Molotov assailed the plan as a "new venture in American imperialism."[21] Molotov walked out of a planning meeting in July 1947, and representatives of Yugoslavia, Albania, Bulgaria, Poland, Romania, Czechoslovakia, Hungary, and Finland followed him. With British Foreign Secretary Ernest Bevin and French Premier Georges Bidault in the lead, sixteen countries eagerly accepted the money, for a total of $22 billion in assistance. The Soviet bloc in turn created the Council of Mutual Economic Assistance, which required each nation to specialize in the production or cultivation of certain items for the Soviet empire.

Many U.S. Congressmen had made visits to Europe in 1947, and the devastation there had convinced them to vote for the unprecedented aid package, as did the Communist coup in Czechoslovakia in February 1948. Soon after the Marshall Plan's passage in Congress, the United States, Britain, and France installed a new currency, the deutsche mark, in Western Germany. In response, the Soviet Union introduced the *ostmark* for use in Berlin, claiming that the city was under its control. U.S. General Lucius Clay, military governor of Western Germany, immediately circulated the deutsche mark in West Berlin. Refusing to accept this, the Soviet Union blockaded traffic to Berlin on June 24, and Stalin made it clear that he wanted either a unified Germany or the Western powers to leave Berlin. U.S. planes then began flying in food, and the airlift continued until a four-power agreement was reached on May 5, 1949. It is likely that Stalin's eventual shift had something to do with the United States having delivered sixty B-29 bombers with atomic bomb-carrying capacity to Britain.

The blockade strengthened Western unity. In April 1949 the West Europeans and their transatlantic allies created the North Atlantic Treaty Organization, or NATO. As Bevin declared in 1948, Europe's own defense treaties "cannot be fully effective nor relied upon when a crisis arises unless there is assurance of American support for the defense of Western Europe."[22] The consolidation of the Western sphere became complete when the western Federal Republic of Germany was formed on September 21, 1949. The eastern German Democratic Republic followed on October 7. For the United States, NATO represented the formal abandonment of a long-held principle of no entangling alliances in peacetime, and the enshrinement of the principle of collective security. Although NATO was not technically an "alliance" but a "treaty organization," the United States was now obliged to protect Europe, contributing sizeable percentages of its naval, air, and ground troops, amounting to $6 billion in military assistance alone in 1953.

U.S. initiatives like the Truman Doctrine, the Marshall Plan, and the integration of Western Germany and Japan into the Western economy, along with overseas bases and atomic bombs, made the Cold War more frigid. Historians Vladislav Zubok and Constantine Pleshakov confirm that Truman's economic and military plans contributed to the division of Europe, but point out that "Stalin helped the polarization a great deal."[23]

Truman's measures were "prudently conceived," notes Melvyn P. Leffler.[24] U.S. policymakers believed that totalitarianism must be confronted before it required a response that curtailed the American way of life, with increased centralization of the U.S. economy, suppression of freedom, and vast expansion in defense expenditures. Truman's Cold War policies were designed to keep the Communists and their then-appealing ideology from spreading further. Risky, expensive, and lengthy as the process was, it was also successful.

U.S. POSITIONS IN THE EARLY YEARS OF THE COLD WAR

American policies and programs during the first years of the Cold War were especially effective in Europe, where U.S. interests were long-standing—especially among American diplomats—and U.S. objectives of spreading democracy and developing consensus for liberal values were most clear. These policies established a stable military balance between East and West in Europe that lasted the duration of the Cold War, and the American people consistently provided wide support for these initiatives, along with the troop commitments they required. Except in Japan and South Korea, Americans did not favor such an involvement outside of Europe. In the Third World, where U.S. objectives were decidedly more murky than they were in the West, American popular backing for military, financial, or political engagement was often lacking or at best, short-lived. Thus, much to the disappointment of "Asia-first" advocates like General Douglas MacArthur, there was no Marshall Plan for Asia, although the U.S. fought its two major conflicts of the Cold War in this unstable region, as Chapter 4 shows.

In the late summer and early fall of 1949, two major events deepened Cold War fears in the United States. The Soviets detonated their first atomic bomb on August 29, and Communists assumed power in China in early October. These developments helped spawn the creation of the secret National Security Council Paper No. 68 of April 1950, which recommended a dramatic increase in defense spending (Document 8). The proposal created a debate in the State Department between George F. Kennan and Paul Nitze, who replaced Kennan as head of the Policy Planning Staff, over the likelihood of the Soviets using their military against the United States. Nitze's view of an increasingly bellicose and ambitious Russia dominated the debate.

NSC-68 was an ambitiously ideological document. As Nitze noted: "If we had objectives only for the purpose of repelling invasion and not to create a better world, the will to fight would be lessened."[25] In contrast to the position articulated in 1944, in 1950 the United States had a set of ideas to impart to the globe and a mission to defend the "free world," those nations that had not yet fallen under the Communist yoke. The Cold War had begun and was rapidly intensifying, and the United States and the Soviet Union saw each other as intractable foes. When the Korean War came, NSC-68 became enshrined as the permanent security state that Americans still live with. Today, the document appears to be an exaggerated, Machiavellian portrayal of the Soviet threat in order to create a consensus on national security priorities. But a half-century ago, Americans lived in fear. Although their government played a significant role in generating that fear, it was not the sole cause of it.

NOTES

1. See Document 1.

2. Walter Lippmann, *The Cold War: A Study in U.S. Foreign Policy*, 38.

3. See James G. Hershberg, *James B. Conant: Harvard to Hiroshima and the Making of the Nuclear Age* (New York: Knopf, 1993), 304.

4. Henry L. Stimson, "The Decision to Use the Atomic Bomb," *Harpers* 194 (February 1947), 106, cited in Gar Alperovitz, *The Decision to Use the Atomic Bomb and the Architecture of an American Myth* (New York: Random House, 1995), 461.

5. See Document 1.

6. Truman to James F. Byrnes, January 5, 1946, as quoted in Alonzo L. Hamby, *Man of the People: A Life of Harry S. Truman* (New York: Oxford University Press, 1995), 339.

7. See Document 2.

8. Document 3; Smith as quoted in Fraser Harbutt, *The Iron Curtain: Churchill, America, and the Origins of the Cold War* (New York: Oxford University Press, 1986), 211.

9. Wallace quoted in John Morton Blum, ed., *The Price of Vision: The Diary of Henry A. Wallace, 1942–1946* (Boston: Houghton Mifflin, 1973), February 12, 1946, 548; September 12, 1946, 665.

10. Truman quoted in Hamby, *Man of the People*, 359.

11. "Novikov telegram," September 27, 1946, trans. Kenneth M. Jensen and John Glad, in *Diplomatic History* 15 (Fall 1991), 527–37, underlined by Vyacheslav Molotov; Vladislav Zubok and Constantine Pleshakov, *Inside the Kremlin's Cold War: From Stalin to Krushchev* (Cambridge, Mass.: Harvard University Press), 76.

12. Clark Clifford, cited in William Dudley, ed., *The Cold War: Opposing Viewpoints* (San Diego: Greenhaven Press, 1992), 33, 35.

13. Stimson to Truman, September 11, 1945, cited in Hamby, *Man of the People*, 340.

14. Teller quoted in Paul Boyer, *By the Bomb's Early Light: American Thought and Culture at the Dawn of the Atomic Age*, rev. ed. (Chapel Hill: University of North Carolina, 1994), 101; Boyer, *idem.*, 101.

15. George F. Kennan, "The Sources of Soviet Conduct," *Foreign Affairs* (July 1947), 575–76 (originally pseudonymously-published by "X").

16. Kennan to the Secretary of State, February 22, 1946 ("Long Telegram"), *FRUS* 1946 6: 707, 701, 699–700. (See Document 2 in the Documents section.)

17. Lippmann, *Cold War*, 15, 38–39; George F. Kennan, *Memoirs, 1925–1950* (Boston: Little Brown, 1967), 359. Kennan had indeed called for "the adroit and vigilant application of counterforce at a series of constantly shifting geographical and political points" in his article, and in his Memoirs he conceded that this statement "lent itself to misinterpretation." See Kennan, *Memoirs*, 359.

18. Quoted in Hamby, *Man of the People*, 391.

19. See Document 4.

20. Melvyn P. Leffler, *A Preponderance of Power: National Security, the Truman Administration, and the Cold War* (Stanford: Stanford University Press, 1992), 153; on the conference, see 151–157 *passim.*

21. Molotov quoted in David Holloway, *Stalin and the Bomb: The Soviet Union and Atomic Energy, 1939–1956* (New Haven: Yale University Press, 1994), 255.

22. Bevin as quoted in Geir Lundestad, *The American "Empire" and Other Studies of U.S. Foreign Policy in a Comparative Perspective* (New York and Oslo: Oxford University Press and Norwegian University Press, 1990), 57.

23. Vladislav Zubok and Constantine Pleshakov, "The Soviet Union," in David Reynolds, ed., *The Origins of the Cold War in Europe* (New Haven: Yale University Press, 1994), 65.

24. Leffler, *Preponderance of Power*, 516.

25. Quoted in Hershberg, *Conant*, 483.

3

Domestic Security and Insecurity during the Cold War

During the early 1950s, domestic anticommunism reached its height in the United States, appealing to all sides of the political spectrum. Anticommunism provided "a firm foundation of morality" to the doctrine of containment.[1] This chapter examines how concern about Communist subversion manifested itself within the United States, by looking at the cases, investigations, hearings, and personalities that dominated the domestic Cold War during its height, 1945–1960. The 1960s saw the waning of this extreme anticommunist effort, and in the 1970s its credibility sank further with revelations of the excesses and violations of civil liberties carried out by zealous antisubversives. Nevertheless, Americans remained anticommunist in their outlook throughout the Cold War, and their attitudes helped sustain an unprecedented defense apparatus.

During World War II, membership in the Communist Party of the United States of America [CPUSA] had risen to eighty thousand, a trend that greatly alarmed FBI Director J. Edgar Hoover, who saw it as indicating the resurgence of a Red Menace like the one he remembered following World War I. In 1945, after he first heard the revelations of Soviet espionage in the United States from former spy Elizabeth Bentley, and his agency had discovered classified State Department reports in the offices of the journal *Amerasia*, a magazine of Asian affairs, he was doubly convinced of this renewed threat. Although Bentley lacked documents to prove her case, the FBI had wiretapped a conversation of *Amerasia* editor Philip Jaffe, where he had agreed to provide Soviet agent Joseph Bernstein his "dope . . . on Chungking [the Chinese Nationalist base] out of the Far Eastern Division of the State Department." But the FBI only belatedly figured out Bernstein's connections, and the agency was meanwhile impugned by both Congress and the Justice Department for searching *Amerasia* without a warrant and turning up "gossip." Jaffe faced only a fine, and Hoover seethed that his bureau was "the victim of a liberal-engineered cover-up."[2]

THE HOUSE UN-AMERICAN ACTIVITIES COMMITTEE

President Truman's permanent Loyalty-Security Program, a Cold War initiative launched in March 1947 that screened federal employees to prevent members of "totalitarian, communist, fascist, or subversive" groups entering or remaining on the government's payroll, was no consolation to the FBI chief.[3] Hoover testified to the House Un-American Activities Committee (HUAC)—which was investigating potential subversives in government, the media, and other areas of American life—that stronger action than that contemplated by Truman was needed, and that both HUAC and the FBI should lead it. Hoover, in fact, helped HUAC with confidential information. The loyalty program, meanwhile, screened twenty thousand employees by 1952. More than 10 percent resigned, and four hundred were fired. These procedures have been vilified by scholars, some of whom argue that those investigated were simply misguided idealists who should have been left alone. Historian Ellen Schrecker writes: "[N]either devils nor saints, American Communists were people who had committed themselves to a political movement that they hoped would make a better world." Many influential studies have identified the postwar anticommunist surge as flatly irrational. Yet despite the contention that "after all, there was nothing intrinsically illegal about what Communists did," Soviet archives now confirm what the Bentley and Jaffe cases showed in 1945, that many American Communists did break the law by assisting the Kremlin through espionage.[4]

However, most of those accused—Communists, former Communists, or simply fellow travelers—had not done anything illegal, but were targeted simply because they worked in cultural or educational pursuits where they could influence others. Film's propagandistic power, for instance, made Hollywood a special target, and in October 1947 HUAC investigated the Hollywood Ten, present or previous members of the CPUSA, including screenwriters Dalton Trumbo, Ring Lardner, Jr., and Alvah Bessie. The Hollywood Ten pled the First Amendment, attesting to their right of freedom of association, but were found guilty of contempt of Congress for refusing to reveal their political affiliations, and eight were sentenced to a year in jail with a $1,000 fine, their sentences upheld by the Supreme Court. The only recourse now remaining for those who feared self-incrimination was to take the Fifth Amendment, which allows defendants the right to remain silent rather than be witnesses against themselves.

The hearings were a great public relations coup for HUAC. In response to the verdicts, studio producers banned the Ten from working at their studios, and this blacklist expanded to other suspected Communists. There were certainly Party members in Hollywood as elsewhere, and they had supported, often with mind-numbing regularity, the policy shifts of the Soviet Union. Yet the humiliation, prosecution, and loss of employment they suffered far outweighed their crime. Moviemakers also began producing more stridently anticommunist fare such as *I Married a Communist* (1949) or *My Son John* (1952), as well as the television series *I Led Three Lives* (1953–1956) about Herbert Philbrick, an undercover FBI agent in the Communist party, who had published a book of the same name in 1952. Anticommunist scenarists like the novelist Ayn Rand came to Washington to point out to HUAC some of the anticapitalist messages in past Hollywood fare (Document 6). In 1951 HUAC brought in a parade of Hollywood artists to "name names." Refusal to comply could result in being put on a blacklist. While many used the Fifth Amendment against self-incrimination, one-third of the witnesses cooperated. One of them was Elia Kazan, a former Communist and brilliant director then at the zenith of his career, who felt compelled to alert his fellow citizens to the danger of Communism. Hollywood has not forgiven him, and in 1996 he was denied the lifetime achievement award of the San Francisco Film Festival.[5]

Such identification methods were piecemeal, however, and in 1948 a HUAC subcommittee chaired by Richard Nixon (R-Calif.) considered "legislation to curb or control the Communist Party of the United States." The Mundt-Nixon Bill, coauthored with Senator Karl E. Mundt (D-S.D.), mandated registration of the CPUSA and its fronts and would present to any Communist who registered the prospect of jail time. Although it failed to pass the Senate in 1948, another version of it was enacted in 1950. HUAC also heard from Elizabeth Bentley in 1948, who named more than forty government employees who had supplied her with information during the war. She had no evidence with her, however, and only two of the accused were ever convicted, whereas others took the Fifth Amendment or left the country. Bentley's allegations have been maligned by critics as the "imaginings of a neurotic spinster."[6] Yet several of her names have turned up in the papers of the NKVD's (People's Commissariat of Internal Affairs) foreign intelligence directorate, and in Soviet wartime cable traffic, lending some credence to her story.[7]

A federal grand jury in New York used Bentley's information in 1948 to find the leaders of the CPUSA guilty of violating the Smith Act, which prohibited the teaching and advocacy of overthrowing the government by force. The FBI supplied massive quantities of documents, seeking to show that the CPUSA had changed its domestic and foreign policies in accordance with the Kremlin. The defendants were found guilty, and seven were sent to prison, as were five of their lawyers, who failed to keep them in order. The Supreme Court upheld the decision in *Dennis et al. v. United States* (1951). Hoover devoted much energy to bringing the rest of the Party leadership to trial; his efforts resulted in 126 indictments, 93 convictions, and 10 acquittals. By the end of the 1950s, there were only three thousand CPUSA members.

THE CASE OF ALGER HISS

After Bentley's revelations, HUAC became preoccupied with a new spy case, that of Alger Hiss. Former Soviet agent Whittaker Chambers had told government officials in 1939 that Hiss, then at the Far Eastern division of the State Department, had supplied him with confidential files from 1936–1938. But his story went unheeded until the appearance of Bentley's revelations and those of cipher clerk Igor Gouzenko, who defected from the Soviet Embassy in Ottawa in 1945 exposing a spy ring that included atomic targets in both Canada and the United States. Chambers, unlike Bentley, had plenty of evidence, including the "pumpkin papers," microfilms of Hiss's notes that Chambers had hidden on his Maryland farm.

Supported originally by high-powered friends like Secretary of State Dean Acheson, Hiss refuted the charges, denied to a grand jury he had ever been a Communist or had known Communists, or that he knew Chambers. For these denials, Hiss was tried for perjury. He would not be tried for espionage, because the statute of limitations prevented it—Chambers' last acknowledged contact with Hiss to collect information for the Soviets was in 1938. Truman attacked the hearings as a "red herring," which the "do-nothing" Congress was using to hide its "reactionary" history, but HUAC, led by Nixon, doggedly pursued the case, with Hoover's ready help.[8] Hiss was found guilty in January 1950 on two counts of perjury: He had lied when he said he didn't know Chambers and when he had denied giving him documents. Hiss went to his grave in 1996 denying his culpability, but the consensus of scholarly opinion is that he was guilty.[9] Truman was chagrined, but Nixon's career took off.

As the Hiss case demonstrates, the Cold War presented profound challenges to liberal Americans. Harvard University president James B. Conant, for example, boldly opposed the methods of HUAC: "Only the enemies of American democracy could desire a witch hunt as a consequence of our attempt to protect our security from a military point of view." Yet in 1949, Conant joined the National Education Association's Educational Policies Commission in agreeing that Communists should not teach in America's schools, a policy that if enforced would require the vigilance he had previously denounced. Meanwhile, Brown University president Henry Wriston and his Yale counterpart, A. Whitney Griswold, declared that those who took the Fifth Amendment had to be aware that it "places upon a professor a heavy burden of proof of his fitness to hold a teaching position and lays upon his university an obligation to re-examine his qualifications for membership in its society."[10]

In 1952–1953 the Senate Internal Security Subcommittee heard more than one hundred school teachers take the Fifth Amendment on questions about their political involvement, all of whom lost their jobs. Nationwide, six hundred educators (out of a million) were fired. Many of them had earlier belonged to left-leaning or communist-sympathizing groups. This pursuit of teachers had a chilling effect in classrooms, where innocuous conformity became the order of the day.

THE RISE OF JOSEPH McCARTHY

The man who has been most notoriously associated with domestic anticommunism during the Cold War is Senator Joseph McCarthy (R-Wis.), who professed that a witness's use of the Fifth Amendment "is the most positive proof obtainable that he is a Communist."[11] McCarthy came to prominence on February 9, 1950, when he spoke to the Ohio County Women's Republican Club of Wheeling, West Virginia, and declared, "I have here in my hand a list of 205 that were known to the Secretary of State as being members of the Communist party and who, nevertheless, are still working and shaping the policy of the State Department."[12] McCarthy's numbers, which changed in subsequent reports, had little meaning. They were merely suspects who had been charged by others, and there was no proof that they were fellow travelers or even Communists. McCarthy's was a crude conspiracy theory, but for a time he had powerful friends like Hoover willing to supply him with information. In the process, he nearly destroyed the cause of anticommunism.

A skeptical Senator Millard Tydings (D-Md.) soon brought McCarthy in to testify to his committee, which was investigating the Wisconsin senator's charges. McCarthy charged that Owen Lattimore, a Far Eastern specialist at Johns Hopkins University, was the "top Russian espionage agent in this country."[13] Lattimore had served as a consultant to the Chinese Nationalists as well as to the State Department's Far Eastern Division. But he was hardly "the architect of our far eastern policy," nor was he responsible for "losing China," as McCarthy claimed, echoing charges leveled against Lattimore by a group of American defenders of Nationalist China known as the China Lobby. Not even Hoover believed that Lattimore was a Communist or an espionage agent.[14] The Tydings Committee called McCarthy's work "a fraud and a hoax" on July 17.[15] The committee report was accepted by the Senate, yet McCarthy's moment continued, aided by the arrest of Julius and Ethel Rosenberg on a charge of treason and by the outbreak of the Korean war.

THE ROSENBERG CASE

The Rosenberg case broke after the British charged Klaus Fuchs, a scientist who had done atomic research at Los Alamos National Laboratory during the war, as being a spy. Historian David Holloway notes that "Fuchs's information undoubtedly enabled the Soviet Union to build the atomic bomb more quickly than it could otherwise have been done."[16] Fuchs identified Harry Gold as his courier, and Gold identified machinist David Greenglass as another of his sources. Greenglass then named his brother-in-law, engineer Julius Rosenberg, and his sister Ethel as his recruiters. The Rosenbergs declared that they were innocent, but the government alleged that their assistance to Russia, along with that of the other accused spies in their ring, including Morton Sobell, had encouraged the Communists to launch the Korean War. The trial began in New York City in March 1951, led by Prosecutor Irving Saypol, successful veteran of several previous trials of suspected Communists, including the aforementioned Smith Act convictions and the Hiss perjury trial. A jury found the Rosenbergs guilty of treason and Judge Irving R. Kaufman, charging them of "a crime worse than murder," sentenced them to die in May 1951. Sobell received a lengthy prison term.[17]

Their case became a cause célèbre, stirring an international outcry for their release. Eisenhower, who became president during the appeals process, refused to pardon the couple. Acknowledging his discomfort with putting a woman to death, he declared erroneously that "in this instance it is the woman who is the strong and recalcitrant character. . . . [S]he has obviously been the leader in everything they did in the spy ring." If he commuted her sentence, Communists would recruit women from then on, he believed.[18] The Rosenbergs were executed on June 19, 1953. Their fate has remained controversial, in part because the decrypted Soviet cables that the government relied upon in making its charges were released only in 1995. The appearance of Julius Rosenberg's aliases in these cables, along with other newly available Soviet sources, is persuasive evidence of his espionage activity, as even some of his longest defenders have had to admit.[19] Yet Alexander Feklisov, the Soviet intelligence officer who handled Rosenberg between 1943 and 1946, points out that the spy's role was largely confined to supplying technical information, not atomic intelligence. Other spies whose work was far more dangerous to U.S. security escaped abroad. Scholars agree, moreover, that Ethel Rosenberg was only peripherally involved.[20] The stiff sentencing of the Rosenbergs—spies whose contribution to Soviet technological development was modest at best—demonstrates clearly the tenor of fear that typified the United States during the Korean War and the period of McCarthyist hysteria.

Just as the Rosenberg case appeared, Senator Pat McCarran (D-Nev.) introduced the "Internal Security Act," which passed over Truman's veto in the summer of 1950. This bill, a remake of the Mundt-Nixon bill, made it a crime to conspire to introduce totalitarian dictatorship in the United States, and it required Communist groups or fronts to register with a Subversive Activities Control Board (SACB). Registrants faced job restrictions and the prospect of internment. Nine states mimicked the law, some of them banning the CPUSA outright. The Communist Party refused to register (indeed, no groups registered), and its case eventually reached the Supreme Court, which decided in 1961 that registration was constitutional, as it did not violate the First Amendment, and found the Party guilty for failure to register. However, the Court of Appeals of the District of Columbia, addressing the Fifth Amendment implications of the registration requirement, reversed this conviction in 1963 and noted that "the government had not proved there was anyone alive willing to run the risk of incriminating himself by registering as an officer or member of a party that had been labeled 'a criminal conspiracy.' " After Congress ruled to allow SACB to hold hearings to determine if groups were Communist in 1968, the D.C. Court of Appeals threw that out, too, finding the act in contradiction of the first amendment.[21] SACB finally died during the Nixon administration, never having registered a single Communist.

McCARTHY'S ACCUSATIONS

The Korean War added to the atmosphere of fear in the early Cold War and allowed demagogues like McCarthy to keep the pressure on. In June 1951 he railed for an amazing three hours in the Senate, accusing Secretary of Defense and war hero George Marshall of the most traitorous acts. Marshall's aid to Russia—he was " 'side by side' with Stalin," the senator remarked—was central to "a conspiracy on a scale so immense as to dwarf any previous such venture in the history of man."[22] McCarthy's flagrant distortions of the truth in order to defame others and build up his own agenda and career would ultimately backfire on him, as well as gravely damage the anticommunist cause. Meanwhile, the 1952 presidential election, which pitted the popular Commander of NATO, Republican candidate Dwight D. Eisenhower, against Democratic Governor of Illinois Adlai Stevenson, was infused with the issue of Communism. Nixon cracked that Stevenson had a Ph.D. from "Dean Acheson's Cowardly College of Communist Containment," and Joseph McCarthy kept referring to "Alger—I mean Adlai."[23] McCarthy, reelected that year himself, became chairman of the Permanent Subcommittee on Investigations. But this prominent role would be his undoing, beginning with the preposterous junket of McCarthy's staff counsel Roy Cohn and his assistant, G. David Schine. They went to investigate the contents of United States Information Agency libraries in Europe, and proceeded to toss out as subversive books written by eminent historians Arthur Schlesinger, Jr., and Foster Rhea Dulles, cousin of the Secretary of State.

McCarthy made a further mistake by hiring as executive director of his committee a scurrilous red hunter, J. B. Matthews, who had recently written that "[t]he largest single group supporting the Communist apparatus in the United States today is composed of Protestant clergymen."[24] Matthews soon had to resign, and not long after, McCarthy also lost the cooperation of Hoover, who was fed up with the excesses and incompetence of the senator's staff.

With the execution of the Rosenbergs and the ending of the Korean War in 1953, the country was growing less interested in Communism. But McCarthy was not finished. That summer, he began hearings into allegations of "communist infiltration" at the Army's Ft. Monmouth (N.J.) Signal Corps installation.[25] The committee charged that the Army was harboring and promoting a Communist dentist, Irving Peress. But the Army had charges of its own against the senator, who with Cohn had pressured the agency to give Schine a soft commission to free him from basic training.

THE ARMY-McCARTHY HEARINGS

The Senate Army-McCarthy hearings began in April 1954, and the senator's popularity dropped to 30 percent by the end of that year, as the eloquent Boston lawyer Joseph Welch exposed McCarthy's brutish methods. Edward R. Murrow, the CBS television journalist, vilified McCarthy on his show, *See It Now*. In Murrow's clips, McCarthy was "belching, picking his nose, contradicting himself, giggling at his own vulgar humor . . . and harshly berating witnesses."[26] The senator's final mistake was to make another accusation of Communist sympathies, this time against one of the lawyers in Welch's office, Fred Fisher. By doing so, he violated an agreement made between himself and Welch that McCarthy was not to mention the lawyer (who belonged to a Communist front known as the National Lawyers' Guild), while Welch was not to mention rumors of a homosexual relationship between Cohn and Schine. But because Welch had earlier referred to a photo of Schine with Army Secretary Robert T. Stevens as being cropped by a "pixie," McCarthy believed Welch had broken the agreement. Welch accused McCarthy of an attempt to "assassinate" Fisher, and when the senator continued his hectoring, Welch said the immortal words: "You have done enough. Have you left no sense of decency, sir, at long last? Have you left no sense of decency?"[27] Senators introduced a resolution in June demanding that McCarthy be stripped of his chairmanships, and later changed it to a censure "for conduct unbecoming a senator."[28]

Refusing to give up, McCarthy used a public hearing of his committee "to apologize for having supported Eisenhower in the 1952 campaign." He wrote a resolution attacking Eisenhower's planned visit with Soviet leader Khrushchev at Geneva, and asked supporters to consider his own chances for capturing the nomination for president from Eisenhower.[29] This incredible prospect did not materialize. Instead, McCarthy died in 1957 of hepatitis, brought on by excessive drinking.

THE COURTS AND THE FBI

Extreme anticommunism was on the wane by the mid-1950s, with the death of Stalin and the new "spirit of Geneva." This was paralleled by a series of decisions by the Supreme Court. In 1956 *Pennsylvania v. Nelson* canceled antisubversion laws in forty-two states. In 1957 two more important cases limited antisubversive investigations. *Jencks v. United States* declared that accused persons had the right to see evidence presented against them, undercutting some of HUAC's practices. In *Yates v. United States,* the Court overthrew the Smith Act convictions of eleven Communist party officials, basing its decision on the notion that one's advocacy had to be more than academic—it had to be, as the Court noted in a later free speech decision, "directed to inciting or producing *imminent* lawless action and [be] likely to incite or produce such action."[30] The Court made it impossible for the government to refuse to hire or to fire accused Communists from certain jobs solely because of their beliefs.

Despite, or perhaps because of, such laws, J. Edgar Hoover began a new initiative against the Communist party, a counterintelligence program called COINTELPRO-CPUSA that lasted until 1971 and was designed with the goal of "keeping the pot boiling" for domestic Communists.[31] This program aggressively employed harassment, disinformation, "dirty tricks," and other unsavory techniques. Additional COINTELPROs were inaugurated in 1961 against the Socialist Workers Party, in 1964 against the Ku Klux Klan, in 1965 against black nationalists, and in 1968 against antiwar militants. Sometimes these efforts came at presidential initiative, such as when the Johnson Administration, in response to demonstrations and bombings on college campuses during the Vietnam War, urged the FBI to act, and the agency created COINTELPRO-New Left.

Yet, growing criticism of the Vietnam War itself helped discredit the FBI's methods of seeking out subversives. In 1971 a group called the Citizens Commission to Investigate the FBI broke into the resident agency in Media, Pennsylvania, and seized thousands of FBI documents, which showed that the agency had illegally harrassed activists at colleges like Swarthmore and Bryn Mawr. Attacks grew on the FBI and its director, Hoover, who died of a heart attack six months later, even as the Nixon administration "plumbers" hatched plans to steal papers inside the Democratic party headquarters in the Watergate complex. Such tactics had been used by Hoover in the search for domestic Communists, and their exposure during Watergate served to discredit what he, and others, had done for so long in the name of domestic security. This new scrutiny of secret government operations was reflected as well in congressional investigations of the CIA that began in the late 1960s. Senator Stuart Symington (D-Mo.) questioned the CIA's "waging war" in Laos during the height of the Vietnam War in 1969. Senator Frank Church (D-Ida.) went further in his Foreign Relations Committee investigation of the mid-1970s, which gathered over one hundred thousand pages of documents and led him to ask if the CIA had become a "rogue elephant."[32] Thus, just as Washington realized that it could no longer be the world's military policeman as made evident in policies like the Nixon Doctrine, so too were domestic and international

U.S. covert security forces reined in and made to scale back from their overreaching efforts.

NOTES

1. Richard Gid Powers, *Not without Honor: The History of American Anti-communism* (New York: Free Press, 1995), 191.

2. Harvey Klehr and Ronald Radosh. *The Amerasia Spy Case: Prelude to McCarthyism* (Chapel Hill: University of North Carolina Press, 1996), 65, 144; Athan G. Theoharis and John Stuart Cox, *The Boss: J. Edgar Hoover and the Great American Inquisition* (Philadelphia: Temple University Press, 1988), 284, 241. Klehr and Radosh suggest that the case was likely fixed to prevent leaking of information embarrassing to prominent members and friends of the Truman Administration. See *Amerasia*, Chapter 5.

3. Executive order 9835, March 21, 1947, cited in Ellen Schrecker, *The Age of McCarthyism: A Brief History with Documents* (Boston and New York: Bedford Books of St. Martin's Press, 1994), 150–54.

4. Schrecker, *McCarthyism*, 3, 42.

5. "Why Won't Hollywood Forgive Elia Kazan?" *Los Angeles Times Magazine*, January 14, 1996, 14.

6. Earl Latham, *Communist Conspiracy in Washington: From the New Deal to McCarthy* (Cambridge: Harvard University Press, 1966), 160.

7. Harvey Klehr, John Earl Haynes, and Fridrikh Firsov, *The Secret World of American Communism* (New Haven: Yale University Press, 1995), 317; John Earl Haynes and Harvey Klehr, "Two Gentlemen of Venona," *Weekly Standard*, November 13, 1995.

8. Quoted in Richard Gid Powers, *Secrecy and Power: The Life of J. Edgar Hoover* (New York: Free Press, 1987), 298–99.

9. See especially, Allen Weinstein, *Perjury: The Hiss-Chambers Case* (New York: Knopf, 1978). In 1992 Russian historian Dmitri A. Volkogonov created a sensation claiming that Hiss had not spied for the Soviet Union, a statement he had to retract later because it was based on an incomplete investigation. See *New York Times*, October 29, 1992, B14; *Los Angeles Times*, December 17, 1992, A16. Volkogonov conceded on the later date that he had looked only at KGB files and not at those of the GRU, or Soviet Military Intelligence, many of which have been destroyed. The lack of attention to the retraction is evident in Ellen Schrecker's book on McCarthyism, which cites only the first letter of Volkogonov to Hiss's intermediary, John Lowenthal. (See Schrecker, *McCarthyism*, 135.) Recently released intercepted VENONA cables of Soviet messages to Moscow have also identified Hiss, code-named "Ales." Comintern documents, too, have revealed Chambers' involvement in Soviet secret work during the 1930s, when "a thriving Communist underground was in place" in the United States. (See Klehr, Haynes,

and Firsov, *Secret World*, 96, 87–94.) These documents do not prove Hiss's culpability, but they certainly strengthen Chambers' credibility.

10. Quoted in James G. Hershberg, *James B. Conant: Harvard to Hiroshima and the Making of the Nuclear Age* (New York: Knopf, 1993), 405, 635.

11. McCarthy quoted in Ellen W. Schrecker, *No Ivory Tower: McCarthyism and the Universities* (New York, 1986), 176.

12. Wheeling *Intelligencer*, as quoted in Roy Cohn, *McCarthy* (New York: New American Library, 1968), 2; see also "Speech at Wheeling, West Virginia," February 9, 1950, published in the *Congressional Record*, 81st Cong., 2nd Sess., February 20, 1950, 1954–1957 (there were only fifty-seven names in this printed version); quoted in Schrecker, *Age of McCarthyism*, 214. The information came from a four-year-old letter of former Secretary of State James F. Byrnes and was based on "simple arithmetic": Byrnes had stated that only 79 of 285 of these "individuals unfit for Government service because of Communist activities and other reasons" had been fired. McCarthy's sources used faulty subtraction to get 205. See Cohn, *McCarthy*, 1–2.

13. Quoted in Hershberg, *Conant*, 619.

14. McCarthy as quoted in Schrecker, *Age of McCarthyism*, 68.

15. Quoted in Peter H. Buckingham, *America Sees Red: Anticommunism in America, 1870s to 1980s* (Claremont, Calif.: Regina Books, 1988), 72.

16. David Holloway, *Stalin and the Bomb: The Soviet Union and Atomic Energy, 1939–1956* (New Haven: Yale University Press, 1994), 222.

17. Ronald Radosh and Joyce Milton, *The Rosenberg File: A Search for the Truth* (New York: Holt, Rinehart and Winston, 1983), 4.

18. Eisenhower to John Eisenhower, June 16, 1953, quoted in Stephen E. Ambrose, *Ike's Spies: Eisenhower and the Espionage Establishment* (Garden City, N.Y.: Doubleday, 1981), 277.

19. See Walter Schneir and Miriam Schneir, "Cryptic Answers," *The Nation* 261 (August 14–21, 1995), 153.

20. See Michael Dobbs, "Julius Rosenberg, Spy," *Washington Post National Weekly Edition*, March 24, 1997, 6–7; on Ethel Rosenberg, see Radosh and Milton, *Rosenberg File*, 450–51. Theodore Hall, who provided atomic information to the Soviet Union from Los Alamos, escaped to England and is still alive. See Joseph Albright and Marcia Kunstel, *Bombshell: The Secret Story of America's Unknown Atomic Spy Conspiracy* (New York: Random House, 1997).

21. Walter Goodman, *The Committee: The Extraordinary Career of the House Committee on Un-American Activities* (New York: Farrar, Straus, and Giroux, 1968), 293.

22. Quoted in Powers, *Not without Honor*, 244.

23. See Buckingham, *America Sees Red*, 84–85.

24. Quoted in Powers, *Not without Honor*, 265–66.

25. See Cohn, McCarthy, 95.

26. Michael D. Murray, "Persuasive Dimensions of *See It Now*'s 'Report on Senator Joseph R. McCarthy,' " *Today's Speech* 23 (Fall 1975), 18, quoted in Robert L. Ivie, "Cold War Demagoguery: Murrow versus McCarthy on 'See It Now,' " in Martin J. Medhurst, Robert L. Ivie, Philip Wonder, and Robert L. Scott, *Cold War Rhetoric: Strategy, Metaphor, and Ideology* (Westport, Conn.: Greenwood Press, 1990), 83.

27. Quoted in Powers, *Not without Honor*, 269–70.

28. Buckingham, *America Sees Red*, 97.

29. Ivie, "Cold War Demagoguery," 81.

30. *Brandenberg v Ohio* 395 U.S. 444 (1969), quoted in Henry J. Abraham and Barbara A. Perry, *Freedom & the Court: Civil Rights & Liberties in the United States*, 6th ed. (New York: Oxford University Press, 1994), 162.

31. Powers, *Secrecy and Power*, 339.

32. John Prados, *Presidents' Secret Wars: CIA and Pentagon Covert Operations from World War II through the Persian Gulf*, Rev. ed. (Chicago: Ivan R. Dee, Inc., 1996), 284–85, 336.

4

The Cold War in Asia

A balance between East and West had been established in Europe by 1949, but in Asia stability was elusive. Japan's wartime occupation and control of China, Vietnam, Indonesia, Malaya, Burma, Thailand, and the Philippines had fueled nationalism in the region, and the United States worried that many of these nationalists, though quoting Thomas Jefferson, were following Marxist dictates. Indeed, the Communists would see important gains in Asia despite vigorous Western resistance. There, the Cold War often broke into military engagement, and these wars left legacies that continue to this day. This chapter takes a close look at Asia during the Cold War and highlights concepts such as decolonization, the defensive perimeter, the domino theory, and détente in shaping Cold War history.

SOUTHEAST ASIA FOLLOWING WORLD WAR II

Asia provides a clear illustration of the tension between American ideals and Cold War imperatives. Although the United States had called for an end to colonialism in World War II, President Harry S Truman's need to hold western Europe together against Soviet expansion meant that he encouraged the return of Western imperialism in Asia to preempt Soviet-style governments there. The United States thus supported the French return to power in Vietnam despite the efforts of the Vietminh independence movement and its leader, Ho Chi Minh. The State Department wanted to strengthen France's position, and many officials doubted the Vietnamese people's ability for self-government.

In contrast to the situation in Vietnam, in Indonesia American "idealism and self-interest merged" in the struggles against both colonialism and communism.[1] In the Dutch East Indies, Dutch controllers and the Republic of Indonesia had signed an agreement in 1946 that pledged an independent Indonesia by January 1, 1949. Yet, persistent Dutch military intervention was undermining the nascent republican government of Mohammed Hatta, which had won plaudits for crushing a Communist insurrection in September 1948. Initially reluctant to use the Marshall Plan as a bargaining chip (the Dutch were receiving $500 million), the United States was pushed to do so when Senate critics proposed cutting off aid to the Netherlands if their adventurism in Asia continued. The Netherlands finally surrendered control, even as the French received European Recovery Program aid plus American military assistance in order to maintain their hold in Vietnam under the "domino theory."

REVOLUTION IN CHINA

Indonesia and Indochina were small dominoes, however, compared to China. During World War II, the leading opposition forces fighting Japan's occupation of that country were Jiang Jieshi's (Chiang Kai-shek) Nationalists and Mao Zedong's (Mao Tse-tung) Communists. Jiang was recognized by both the Soviets and the United States and gained a spot on the UN Security Council. The Chinese Communists remained implacable foes of Jiang, however, and when Truman sent Secretary of State George C. Marshall to bring Communists and Nationalists together after the war, he was unable to do so. When Marshall returned in January 1947, the Communists, who were better organized, held the upper hand in China. General Albert Wedemeyer traveled to China next, and despite his sympathies for Jiang, found conditions just as bad: Not only were the Nationalist troops unwilling to fight, their leaders were "spiritually insolvent" and lacked the support of the people.[2]

As George F. Kennan of the State Department's Policy Planning Staff pointed out, the fall of the Nationalists "probably would not be a catastrophe for American interests in China." But he nevertheless recommended that it not happen overnight and "that the U.S. should extend the minimum aid necessary to satisfy American public opinion."[3] Marshall agreed. The United States sent $2 billion there between 1945 and 1949. These expenditures were necessary to obtain congressional support of Europe's recovery.

Nevertheless, by the end of January 1949 all of China north of the Yangtze River was in Mao's hands. Dean Acheson, who became Secretary of State in January, realized that there was no point in spending any more money on Nationalist China. Acheson prepared a White Paper that blamed the Nationalists for the imminent "fall" of China in August: "Nothing that this country did or could have done within the reasonable limits of its capabilities could have changed that result. . . . It was the product of internal Chinese forces which this country tried to influence but could not."[4] Some Americans, including a vociferous group known as the China Lobby, were not prepared for this accommodationist stance to events in China (Document 7). The paper did, however, attack the Soviets for inspiring the Communist takeover and accused the Chinese of "publicly announc[ing] their subservience to a foreign power, Russia."[5]

The People's Republic of China (PRC) was born on October 1, 1949. The Soviet Union immediately recognized it, but the United States offered support for the Nationalists, who retreated to the island of Formosa. (Formosa, the Japanese name for the island, was soon renamed Taiwan, its Chinese name). Despite Mao's announcing that his country was "leaning to the side" of the U.S.S.R., relations were not as close as the United States assumed. To Stalin, Mao was only a "Margarine Marxist." Some American China experts believed that the United States should keep channels open to Mao's government, as had happened with Josip Broz Tito in Yugoslavia, whose "different road to socialism," independent of Stalin's, was welcomed by Washington in 1948. But acceptance of Communist China proved difficult because of the long-held myth of a "special relationship" between the United States and China, in which the American role was to rescue China and introduce its people to liberal democracy.[6] California Senator William Knowland thundered on January 5, "[F]ifty years of friendly interest on the part of our people . . . in a free and independent China" were gone, "frittered away by a small group of willful men in the Far Eastern Division of the State Department who had the backing of their superiors."[7] This was the same conspiracy theory that had driven McCarthy to attack Owen Lattimore (see Chapter 3).

In February, Stalin formed a thirty-year mutual defense pact with Mao. He also offered a $300 million low-interest loan, yet maintained privileges to exploit resources in Manchuria. In his move toward China, suggests William Stueck, Stalin was promoting a "forward policy" in Asia, to "serve the same twofold purpose of perpetuating China's isolation from the West and turning U.S. efforts away from Europe," where the West had recently experienced a series of successes.[8] North Korean leader Kim Il Sung's invasion of the South in 1950, encouraged by Stalin, certainly presented an opportunity to get the United States focused on Asia, although the possibility of American involvement was dismissed at the time by Mao (see Document 9).

THE KOREAN WAR

Korea had been temporarily divided after World War II by the United States and the U.S.S.R. In the South, under American auspices, Dr. Syngman Rhee had formed the Republic of Korea (ROK). In the North a youthful Kim Il Sung began a nearly fifty-year reign as head of the Communist Democratic People's Republic of Korea. By the spring of 1949 both the Soviets and the Americans had departed, but the Soviets left behind a well-armed North Korean military whereas the United States had done little to build up South Korea's defenses. Kim began lobbying Stalin for assistance in reunification with the South, and the Soviet leader provided matériel and planes (see Document 9).

After a small force was repulsed by the ROK in 1949, Kim convinced Stalin to give the nod to a full-scale attack on the South. Mao seconded the idea. In January 1950 Acheson left the country out of his "defensive perimeter" speech to the National Press Club, when he declared: "The Asian peoples are on their own."[9] The same month, the House defeated Korean aid.

On June 25, 1950, 110,000 North Korean soldiers tore across the border. The North Koreans took South Korea's capital, Seoul, within three days, and soon trapped the Southern forces inside the Pusan perimeter in the southeast. Once the war started, Stalin pulled his advisers out, and Khrushchev recalled his reasoning: "We don't want there to be evidence for accusing us of taking part in this business. It's Kim Il Sung's affair."[10] To the United States, the invasion appeared as an inevitable outgrowth of the Communist monolith—another "Munich" if it were allowed to stand. Washington felt that it must show the Communist bloc the strength and credibility of the "free world," and immediately committed American men, money, and military hardware to a "police action" under General Douglas MacArthur. One day after the invasion, Truman promised aid to Nationalist China, Indochina, and the newly independent Philippines, and two days later, the president sent the Seventh Fleet into the Taiwan Strait.

The United States and eight other nations voted to send in troops under UN auspices. The Soviets could not protest as they were then boycotting the Security Council over the denial of a seat to Communist China. By September, sixteen nations had joined the UN effort. Rather than remove Washington from European concerns, the Korean outbreak tightened the North Atlantic alliance. Korea gave great impetus to the U.S. military's plan to rearm Germany in order to enhance NATO's strength. Some NATO members, most especially France, were disturbed about the plan to add ten German divisions to NATO's fourteen, and in order to placate such worries, Washington promised money, four U.S. divisions, and an American general (Dwight D. Eisenhower) as leader of the organization. The U.S. Senate passed NATO's expansion in January 1951. The expenditures of European governments on defense grew to $8.2 billion by 1951, from $5.3 billion a year earlier.[11]

On September 15, 1950, MacArthur engineered the spectacular amphibious landing behind enemy lines at Inchon. Shortly thereafter, UN forces recaptured Seoul and escaped from Pusan, and the Communists started fleeing north. In a fateful decision, MacArthur ordered UN forces to follow the Communists into North Korea. In the eyes of U.S. officials, writes one historian, a victory over the North "would provide an important psychological boost to U.S. prospects in the cold war."[12] But how much was it worth?

On October 3 China warned the United States that it would take action as UN forces approached the Yalu River border with China. Then, when three hundred thousand Chinese were unleashed south in late November, smashing through UN lines, UN forces turned south in a hurry. It would be containment of Communism, not rollback, in Korea. By the following March the opposing armies were locked in a stalemate, even as MacArthur still hoped for a large assault against China and called for atomic weapons on an "on call basis." Truman wanted to negotiate a cease-fire, but the general disagreed and publicly criticized Truman's policy. Only if the Korean war were "won," declared MacArthur, would Europe "most probably avoid war and yet preserve freedom."[13] In a highly unpopular move, Truman fired the insubordinate general on April 11. An outraged *Chicago Tribune* declared Truman "unfit to be president." The state legislature of Michigan thundered, "*Whereas*, at 1 a.m., of this day, World Communism achieved its greatest victory of the decade in the dismissal of General MacArthur."[14] Upon his return, the popular general gave a stirring speech to a joint session of Congress (Document 10). In time, public opinion retreated in its support for MacArthur's call for an all-out war with the Chinese. Led by General Omar Bradley, the head of the Joint Chiefs of Staff, who said a war with China would be "the wrong war, at the wrong place, at the wrong time and with the wrong enemy," military men joined Truman in pointing out that the real danger lay with Russia, not China.[15] Although the psychological frustration of "containment" took its toll, the reality of the Cold War led to a settlement in Korea.

That summer, China agreed to peace talks while the fighting continued. The Chinese wanted the United States and UN out of Korea and for Americans to stop helping Formosa and to admit the Chinese Communists into the UN Security Council, but the United States rejected these demands. Repatriation of 170,000 UN prisoners of war was the stickiest issue—half of them did not wish to return to North Korea. During this interval, the United States signed a treaty with Japan, ending occupation in September 1951. The Americans and Japanese joined in a security pact, and Washington obtained a base on Okinawa. Japan's role as a staging area in the Korean war jump-started its expanding economy. Japan's position augmented existing U.S. arrangements in Asia. Also, by implanting democratic institutions and encouraging economic growth in Japan, the United States secured an Asian showcase for Western values in the Cold War, as well as a strong ally in the Pacific. As in Europe, American officals sought to stabilize relationships by way of mutual defense pacts in Asia. Washington had already signed a security agreement with the Philippines, and the ANZUS pact with Australia and New Zealand in August 1951.

In May 1953 a newly elected Eisenhower resolved on the use of nuclear weapons against China, plus a new ground offensive in Korea to break the stalemate in the talks. The United States quietly delivered the message that it was prepared to use the weapons if no settlement was reached within a year. The Communists finally agreed to the UN's turning over North Korean POWs to a neutral nation. A balkish Rhee only accepted the deal in return for a U.S. security pact.

The war cost the United States 54,246 soldiers' lives; North Korea lost 2,000,000 civilians and 500,000 troops; South Korea lost 1,000,000 civilians and 100,000 troops; and China lost 1,000,000 soldiers' lives. Korea's settlement was only an armistice, and the two Koreas remain officially at war, their border the site of the greatest concentration of troops in the world. Preliminary peace talks, however, began in early 1997. The war also brought new forces to NATO, new bases, and new defense spending under NSC-68 (see Document 8). Korea set a precedent for American involvement against Communism in far-flung regions. Historian William Stueck suggests that it also played "a stabilizing role" in the Cold War, as did Stalin's death that year.[16]

QUEMOY AND MATSU

Conditions were not so calm among the United States and the two Chinas in 1954 when a crisis broke out in Jinmen and Mazu (Quemoy and Matsu). For the next four years, there were periodic clashes between Jiang, who held the two islands just off the coast of China and used them as a base from which to attack PRC shipping, and the Communists, who shelled back. The U.S. Congress boldly declared that it would protect the offshore islands as well as Taiwan in the "Formosa Resolution" of January 1955. This view was in accordance with that of Dulles and Eisenhower, who saw the islands' security as essential for Taiwan's "morale," despite the fact that the People's Republic of China lacked the military might to use them as an effective base to take over Taiwan. Dulles believed that their defense required "atomic weapons," and Eisenhower agreed. In March the president threatened the PRC with the use of precision-targeted nuclear arms over the issue. Despite the administration's (inaccurate) contention that such atomic weapons were "conventional," this brinksmanship upset many American allies.[17] Canadian and British officials declared they would not participate in any U.S.-led intervention. Eisenhower, too, soon distanced himself from the precipice, deciding in April, despite Dulles's opposite inclinations, that the islands were no longer inherently connected with Taiwan's defense. He made attempts to persuade Jiang that the United States could no longer be committed to their wholesale protection. He also issued an appeal to the conferees at the Bandung Conference of Asian and African nations that spring, directing their attention to the PRC's buildup as a threat to peace in the area. The Communists responded positively, with Chinese Prime Minister Zhou En-lai declaring that "The Chinese people do not want to have a war with the United States of America," and the crisis was averted.[18] Finally, after a repeat standoff over the islands in the summer of 1958, Jiang, at Dulles's behest, renounced the use of force against the mainland and removed a number of his troops from the offshore bases. Mao himself was soon preoccupied with the Great Leap Forward, a disastrous program of wiping out China's social classes that killed tens of millions of Chinese between 1958 and 1962.

U.S. INVOLVEMENT IN VIETNAM

Despite his willingness to use the nuclear threat, Eisenhower refused to consider deploying atomic weapons to rescue the French in Vietnam, whose forces were trapped at Dien Bien Phu in 1954. Instead, a UN peace conference at Geneva addressed Vietnam that year, and the country was divided in half, with Communist Ho Chi Minh in Hanoi and the pro-Western Emperor Bao Dai in Saigon. By 1956 the U.S.-backed South Vietnamese leader, anticommunist Catholic Prime Minister Ngo Dinh Diem, was installed in Saigon, where U.S. advisers and aid soon propped up Diem's regime. The United States was in for its longest military involvement of the Cold War. For President John F. Kennedy, who ran on a platform of closing the "missile gap" with the U.S.S.R., Vietnam became a key symbol of U.S. credibility in 1961, particularly after the Bay of Pigs fiasco, Khrushchev's declaration of support of wars of "national liberation" at the Vienna summit of the two superpowers, and the building of the Berlin Wall.

Diem, however, was a repressive leader. Secretary of Defense Robert McNamara found him "an enigma . . . autocratic, suspicious, secretive, and insulated from his people."[19] Culturally, he was more Confucian than Catholic, in his outlook "hierarchical and elitist, emphasizing loyalty to family, institutions, and authority." Diem's brothers held half of the cabinet posts.[20] Yet compared to the French or Ho, he was no worse, and certainly better from the American perspective. The United States also misundertood Ho. "We saw him first as a Communist," rather than as a nationalist, writes McNamara.[21] Chiefly, U.S. officials accepted the domino theory without question, as they did the notion that the fate of Vietnam was vital to American national security. The debate turned instead over how the United States would help the South. Kennedy declared that he would make no "unconditional commitment." Washington would lend weapons and logistical support, but the South Vietnamese must fight their own war.[22] The United States tripled Vietnam military advisers to three thousand in 1961 and then to nine thousand at end of 1962 as the Pentagon pressed for more.

By 1963 Diem was having difficulties with Buddhist protesters, whose religion drew 80 percent of the South's population. Protests erupted in May in response to a law forbidding the flying of Buddhist flags, and nine protesters were killed in Hue, where Diem's brother was bishop. In June some Buddhists immolated themselves with gasoline as a public protest. After the Diem government's particularly repellent anti-Buddhist campaign in August, *Newsweek* asked: "Is the anti-Communist struggle, with the Ngo clique in charge, hopeless?"[23] Later that month, members of the administration first raised the possibility of Diem's removal. JFK remained indecisive, but on November 2, Diem and his brother Ngo Dinh Nhu were killed for $42,000 in CIA money.[24] JFK was severely shaken and in a bizarre coincidence was himself assassinated three weeks later. A series of unstable military governments ran South Vietnam until Premier Nguyen Cao Ky and General Nguyen van Thieu came to power in 1965.

President Lyndon B. Johnson (1963–1969) would take America's Vietnam involvement much further than his predecessors, convinced that "South Vietnam is both a test of U.S. firmness and specifically a test of U.S. capacity to deal with 'wars of national liberation.' "[25] In the summer of 1964, two

American destroyers were attacked by North Vietnamese gunboats in the Gulf of Tonkin, an event that drastically changed America's conduct of the war. Congress unanimously approved a resolution that authorized the president to "take all necessary measures to repel any armed attacks against the forces of the U.S. and to prevent further aggression."[26] The war in Vietnam played an important role in the 1964 presidential election. Johnson pledged he would not send "our boys" to fight in foreign wars, and portrayed his Republican opponent in the 1964 presidential election, Senator Barry Goldwater, as a dangerous warmonger. Goldwater did nothing to help his cause with such pronouncements as "extremism in the defense of liberty is no vice, and . . . moderation in the pursuit of justice is no virtue."[27] Johnson was elected by a landslide, yet he too was unable to avoid a deepening commitment to the conflict in Southeast Asia.

In February 1965, bombing of Communist targets in Vietnam began (given the righteous appellation "Rolling Thunder"), and the first U.S. Marines arrived at Da Nang on March 8. Bombing was very costly, as well as largely ineffective. By 1967 the North was infiltrating 8,400 men into the South per month, which when added to the National Liberation Front's (or Vietcong's) monthly recruitment of 3,500 men, provided a total of 142,800 troops for the Communists—more than enough to make up for battle losses. By 1968 this figure had more than doubled. The Chinese and Russians both helped with equipment and advisers, and the legacy of the Korean War, where hundreds of thousands of Chinese soldiers had stormed into North Korea after the United States had expanded its efforts in 1950, hindered any U.S. response to the larger powers' role. After Mao became preoccupied with the upheaval of the Cultural Revolution in 1966, his reckless and disastrous attempt to reform Chinese society, the Soviets became the major foreign suppliers of Hanoi.

There were 184,000 American troops in South Vietnam by the end of 1965, and 400,000 a year later. Along with the combat role, U.S. officials also attempted nation building in Vietnam, emphasizing private landholding and "western liberal capitalist viewpoints."[28] These efforts were not sufficient to win the support of the South Vietnamese. The war's greatest effect was destroying consensus in America. On January 30, 1968, public opposition to the Vietnam war crystallized after the North Vietnamese launched a massive strike during the national holiday of Tet. On the heels of the latest U.S. military pronouncement that the Communists were "on the run," the Vietcong swept into every South Vietnamese city and, for a moment, sent the American and South Vietnamese forces reeling. The Communists even exploded a hole in the U.S. embassy wall in Saigon, killing two military police, and thereby suggesting that no place was safe from their attack. This image was played again and again on U.S. television news reports, and the media's role was pivotal in creating the deep disillusionment among many Americans as a result of Tet, in response to what seemed a blatant "credibility gap" between what officials had been telling the country about the war's progress, and what seemed evident from their TV sets. Walter Cronkite, the popular CBS news anchor, assessed the war as a stalemate. Public opinion polls showed that 20 percent of American war-supporting voters, or "hawks," became antiwar "doves" the month after Tet.[29]

DOMESTIC REPERCUSSIONS OVER VIETNAM

U.S. and South Vietnam forces eventually threw back the Communists, killing forty thousand of the enemy, but the psychological shock of the offensive overwhelmed these losses. Amid a firestorm of antiwar protests and criticism in the United States, LBJ left the 1968 presidential race himself at the end of March. He had suffered badly in the New Hampshire primary, where many war advocates had voted against him for not doing enough in Vietnam, even as antiwar adherents despised him for keeping the war going. Both sides claimed the moral high ground, contributing to great bitterness at the 1968 Democratic primary, where candidate and nominee Hubert Humphrey committed to stay in the war. By doing so, he gained the support of the Democratic hawks, largely blue-collar men and women and Southerners, but outraged the Democratic doves, who were predominantly college students, senior citizens, African-Americans, and well-heeled liberals.

These divisions in the Democratic party over Vietnam assisted Republican Richard Nixon to win the 1968 presidential election, aided also by the Soviet crackdown in Czechoslovakia. During the campaign, he had promised a "secret plan" to end the Vietnam War, but just like Johnson, his downfall would originate in Vietnam-related developments. First, though, he began drastic U.S. troop reductions under the rubric of "Vietnamization," as well as peace negotiations in line with the new policy of détente, which called for relaxing tensions with the Communist bloc. But in order to gain more leverage, Nixon also widened the war by secretly bombing Cambodia, the Vietcong's supply route. When Americans learned about it in May 1970, many reacted with outrage and violence, part of a wave of destruction that school year in which 250 structures were bombed, including ROTC offices, draft board headquarters, corporations, and campus buildings. Innocent people died—including a math student at the University of Wisconsin who was working in a building that protesters blew up; four students at Kent

State University in Ohio, who were killed by the National Guard after the bombing of a ROTC office; and two students at Jackson State College in Mississippi, who were shot by police in the wake of protests.

In 1971, after former Defense Department analyst Daniel Ellsberg leaked the Pentagon Papers, a classified history of decision making in the Vietnam War, to the *New York Times*, it was Nixon's turn to be outraged, even though the documents mainly embarrassed Democratic administrations. The Nixon administration tried to discredit Ellsberg as mentally unfit, and the White House "Plumbers Unit"—so named because it was aimed to stop leaks—organized a raid of the office of Ellsberg's psychiatrist in order to make their case. This was only the most extreme example of Nixonian dirty tricks against antiwar activists, the prelude to the Watergate break-in of the Democratic party headquarters the following year that would lead to the president's resignation.

ENDING THE WAR IN VIETNAM

On January 27, 1973, Nixon's negotiator, Henry Kissinger, and his North Vietnamese counterpart, Le Duc Tho, reached a peace agreement, which earned them the Nobel Peace Prize. Among its provisions: Hanoi would return POWs, Thieu would stay in office provided that the United States left after a cease-fire and Thieu had to share power with the Vietcong. Privately Nixon promised the South Vietnamese leader assistance if the North violated the cease-fire; but Congress cut off all funds for bombing that summer. In November, Congress passed the War Powers Act, which required that the president gain congressional approval if American forces were sent abroad for more than sixty days.

The peace agreement did not last. In January 1975 the North invaded the South in a final crushing blow. The last, fitting vista for Americans was that of angry ARVN troops shooting at departing U.S. helicopters on April 30, as 150,000 South Vietnamese fled on boats or by foot. Not until 1996 did Washington exchange ambassadors with a Vietnamese government. Shortly after the fall of Saigon, Communist Pol Pot's murderous Khmer Rouge took over in Cambodia, and Laos too became Communist. The Communists were soon fighting among themselves—so much for the domino theory—and in 1978 Vietnam invaded Cambodia (renamed Kampuchea), and China responded by invading Vietnam briefly in 1979. The United States and China, meanwhile, both supported the ousted Pol Pot as legitimate ruler of Cambodia. Vietnam became a Russian client. Although Vietnam and its settlement were disastrous for the United States, Nixon also enjoyed his greatest success in Asia, where he opened relations with Communist China in 1972 in the spirit of détente (see Chapter 5).

The Cold War and its related polarities created much instability and change in Asia, from Japan to Indonesia, from the two Chinas to the two Koreas, which remain to this day. This region was the Cold War's chief battleground, and as a result, that long-running conflict left its stamp all over the area, politically, militarily, and economically. It was in Asia—specifically, in Vietnam—that long-held Cold War assumptions met their greatest challenge, and did not survive. For most Americans, the Cold Warriors' mantra of the domino theory and monolithic Communism no longer made sense in light of post-Vietnam War realities. Certainly, such ideas no longer could stir Americans to send young men and women nine thousand miles away to fight. Vietnam dealt a death blow to the Cold War consensus, and never again would such an ambitious struggle be waged in the name of fighting Communism.

NOTES

1. Robert J. McMahon, *Colonialism and Cold War: The United States and the Struggle for Indonesian Independence, 1945–49* (Ithaca and London: Cornell University Press, 1981), 12.

2. Quoted in William Stueck, *The Wedemeyer Mission: American Politics and Foreign Policy during the Cold War* (Athens: University of Georgia Press, 1984), 35.

3. Kennan to Marshall, as quoted in Wilson D. Miscamble, C.S.C., *George F. Kennan and the Making of American Foreign Policy, 1947–1950* (Princeton: Princeton University Press, 1992), 220–21.

4. U.S. Department of State, *United States Relations with China with Special Reference to the Period 1944–1949* (Washington, D.C., 1949), xvi, (China White Paper), as cited in Stueck, 107.

5. Letter of transmittal, Acheson to Truman, July 30, 1949, China White Paper, xvi, cited in Miscamble, *Kennan and American Foreign Policy*, 232.

6. See Ross Terrill, *Mao: A Biography* (New York: Harper and Row, 1980), 201; David McLean, "American Nationalism, the China Myth, and the Truman Doctrine: The Question of Accommodation with Peking, 1949–1950," *Diplomatic History* 10 (Winter, 1986): 25–42.

7. Knowland quoted in Thomas G. Paterson and Dennis Merrill, eds., *Major Problems in American Foreign Relations*, 4th ed., Vol. 2 (Lexington, Mass.: D. C. Heath, 1995), 334.

8. William Stueck, *The Korean War: An International History* (Princeton: Princeton University Press, 1995), 34.

9. See Acheson's speech to the National Press Club, January 12, 1950, U.S. Department of State, *Bulletin*, January 23, 1950, 111–19.

10. Quoted in Nikita S. Khrushchev, *Khrushchev Remembers: The Last Testament*, ed. and trans. Strobe Talbott (Boston: Little Brown, 1974), 370.

11. Melvyn P. Leffler, *A Preponderance of Power: National Security, the Truman Administration, and the Cold War* (Stanford: Stanford University Press, 1992), 412.

12. Stueck, *Korean War*, 357.

13. MacArthur quoted in Michael Schaller, *Douglas MacArthur: The Far Eastern General* (New York: Oxford University Press, 1989), 231; Burton Kaufman, *The Korean War: Challenges in Crisis, Credibility, and Command* (New York: McGraw-Hill, 1986), 161.

14. Schaller, *Douglas MacArthur*, 241; Stephen J. Whitfield, *Culture of the Cold War*, 2nd ed. (Baltimore: Johns Hopkins University Press, 1996), 59.

15. Bradley quoted in Schaller, *MacArthur*, 249.

16. Stueck, *Korean War*, 350–51.

17. Townsend Hoopes, *The Devil and John Foster Dulles* (Boston: Little Brown, 1973), 274–78.

18. Ibid., 283.

19. Robert S. McNamara, *In Retrospect: The Tragedy and Lessons of Vietnam* (New York: Random House, 1995), 41.

20. Henry A. Kissinger, *Diplomacy* (New York: Simon and Schuster, 1994), 638.

21. McNamara, *In Retrospect*, 33.

22. Ibid., 38–39.

23. *Newsweek*, September 2, 1963, 37.

24. See McNamara, *In Retrospect*, 61.

25. Quoted in Ibid., 107.

26. Quoted in Ibid., 147.

27. Quoted in Richard Gid Powers, *Not without Honor: The History of American Anticommunism* (New York: Free Press, 1995), 317.

28. Michael Tolle, " 'In the Realm of Theory': The Study of Nation Building in Viet Nam," unpublished conference paper, Society for Historians of American Foreign Relations, June 1996.

29. Guenter Lewy, *America in Vietnam* (New York: Oxford University Press, 1978), 434.

5

The Cold War in Latin America, the Middle East, and Africa

Although the Cold War was largely a standoff between two superpowers with forward positions in Europe, the United States and the Soviet Union, the Third World became the arena for all of the Cold War's military conflicts. Chief among these were the two major Asian engagements, Korea and Vietnam, addressed in Chapter 4. But there were numerous smaller wars, interventions (political and economic), and covert operations in Latin America, the Middle East, and Africa, often fought by local clients or proxy armies, but also with Soviet and American troops. The United States intervened frequently in Latin America (in Guatemala, Cuba, the Dominican Republic, Nicaragua, Grenada) as well as the Middle East (Egypt, Iran, Israel) and, to a lesser extent, Africa (Ethiopia, Somalia, Angola). The Soviet Union was more active in Africa, often through Cuban proxies (Ethiopia and Somalia), and set up client states in Yemen and Angola. It was involved in the Middle East (Egypt, Afghanistan), but less so in Latin America (chiefly Cuba). This chapter surveys the non-Asian battlegrounds of the Cold War, from the public heights of nuclear showdown to the secret depths of covert intervention, as well as addresses the more widespread practice of cultivating Cold War client states.

THE COLD WAR IN LATIN AMERICA

In Latin America, the United States continued the hands-off "Good Neighbor" policy of Franklin D. Roosevelt after World War II but with a Cold War spin. In many ways this Cold War relationship harked back to the nation's nineteenth-century Monroe Doctrine, where the United States had assumed a prerogative to police Latin America from foreign intervention, first by relying on British power, and then through direct military intervention or "gunboat diplomacy" to collect debts and "keep order." On numerous occasions this policy had involved the dispatch of American troops, to such countries as the Dominican Republic, Nicaragua, and Haiti, both before and after World War I. After World War II, worries about international Communism making inroads in Latin America provided American officials with another pretext to stop "foreign intervention" in the region, and the Cold War saw many instances of U.S. intervention to stop or derail its putative expansion.

On September 2, 1947, Washington signed the Rio Pact with other American states, which "permitted collective action when a member state was subject to armed attack or when it declared its independence and sovereignty threatened by subversive intervention." The following year, the Act of Bogotá more explicitly asserted that "the political activity of international communism . . . is incompatible with the concept of American freedom."[1] Soon enough, the Cold War tested the meaning of that declaration.

In 1950 leftist reformer Jacobo Arbenz Guzmán was elected president of Guatemala, but it was only in 1952, when the American-owned United Fruit Company suffered a land expropriation, that U.S. opposition to Arbenz "solidified." The firm's banana business dominated Guatemala's economy and paid almost no taxes, and its fate under Arbenz is often cited as the catalyst for U.S. intervention in 1954. Yet as historian Richard Immerman points out, the "cold war ethos" was probably more important. At the Inter-American Conference at Caracas in March 1954, Secretary of State John Foster Dulles pressured the conferees to ratify the "Declaration of Solidarity for the Preservation of the Political Integrity of the American States against International Communism."[2] Guatemala was not mentioned, but it was the only country to oppose the declaration. U.S. Ambassador John E. Peurifoy thought that Arbenz was a Communist, noting, "he talked like a Communist, he thought like a Communist, and he acted like a Communist, and if he is not one, he will do until one comes along."[3] Arbenz was not unsympathetic to Communism, and there was an active Communist labor party in his country. Historian Lester Langley writes that Arbenz's representatives "brazenly followed a pro-Soviet line" in the UN.[4] But as Immerman suggests, at a time when "monolithic communism" loomed large in American thinking, officials erroneously conflated "Guatemalan Communism" with Soviet Communism.[5]

In May 1954 the Guatemalan government received a shipment of arms from Czechoslovakia. Although publicly the United States announced plans to use the Organization of American States (OAS), an association of the nations of North and South America, to stop the buildup, Eisenhower gave the green light to PBSUCCESS, a secret CIA plan to overthrow Arbenz. CIA chief Allen Dulles strongly endorsed covert operations to effect desired policies, particularly after his success in Iran (discussed later). Arbenz's chosen replacement was Carlos Castillo Armas, an American-trained Guatemalan soldier. Armas and his mercenaries trained in Honduras and Nicaragua, and assisted by U.S. planes and radio propaganda, entered Guatemala with a band of less than five thousand troops. Arbenz was overthrown by a combination of invading forces and his own military on June 30. As the intervention showed, Eisenhower's Latin American policy was that the threat of international Communism took precedence over local problems like land reform. Not surprisingly, when Vice President Richard M. Nixon traveled to Caracas on a goodwill tour in 1958, he was pelted with rocks by angry crowds protesting U.S. support for right-wing dictatorships, including that of the recently overthrown Venezuelan dictator Marcos Pérez Jiménez, then living in exile in the United States. "*Muera Nixon* [Death to Nixon]!" the crowds cried. Nixon's wife Pat, despite having her new suit splotched by spat tobacco juice, kept her cool during the fracas while her husband, whose car was being rocked by angry protesters, managed to stop his driver from shooting at them.[6]

This violent attack on an American vice president was only a foretaste of the insults that Cuban leader Fidel Castro would throw America's way. In the mid-1950s, Cubans struggled to find an alternative to their oppressive dictator, Fulgencio Batista, who was receiving arms and support from the United States. One of his leading opponents was law-graduate Fidel Castro, who offered a program of industrialization and land reform, as well as elections and a constitution. Batista fled into exile, and Castro seized power on New Year's Day 1959.

Washington recognized the new government, and the American media applauded Castro. *Reader's Digest* cited his "daring and determination," and *Life* hailed him as a "soldier-scholar." But by mid-1960, as Castro moved toward the socialism espoused by his brother Raoul and his principal adviser, the revolutionary Ernesto "Che" Guevara, U.S. opinion changed. *Time* now asserted that Castro was "the Reds' best tool in Latin America since Jacob Arbenz fled Guatemala."[7] Castro cut rents, nationalized businesses, and enacted agrarian reform. More ominously, he also signed trade agreements with the Soviet bloc and showed no signs of holding an election.

In the minds of U.S. officials, the Cuban revolution "had been perverted" by Castro. In 1955 CIA Director Allen Dulles had instructed Batista to set up a Bureau for the Repression of Communist Activities—and now a Communist was running Cuba. In March 1960 Eisenhower authorized $13 million for a secret CIA project to train 1,400 Cuban exiles in Guatemala and Nicaragua for the invasion of Cuba and overthrow of Castro. Eisenhower also stopped the import of Cuban sugar and told American firms on the island to refuse to refine Soviet oil, thus losing the refineries. This economic pressure significantly chilled relations and likely hurried Castro's move toward Marxism-Leninism. Every American firm was nationalized, amounting to almost $1 billion in losses, more than occurred in the Bolshevik or Chinese revolutions. On January 3, 1961, the United States and Cuba broke diplomatic relations, and they remain ruptured to this day. Contemporary polls showed that Americans agreed with the hard-line policy against Castro. As no one would voluntarily become a Communist, the thinking went, the Soviets must be behind the Cuban leader, who was in any case "off his rocker" and "psycho."[8]

The Kennedy administration, while acting militarily to remove Cold War threats, also advanced the notion that it could win over the Third World through social and economic progress. The *Alianza para Progreso* (Alliance for Progress), announced in March 1961 as Kennedy's program in Latin America, left Castro out. Instead, Kennedy continued the invasion plan, Operation "Zapata," which fit well his defense posture of "flexible response." The exiles' invasion was set for April 17, 1961, at the swampy Bay of Pigs. Planners counted on the anti-Castro underground to join in, followed by an uprising, leading to a new provisional government. But Castro learned about the mission, and his army was ready when the invaders splashed ashore.

With Kennedy's doubts already growing, a second air strike to assist the mission was cancelled. Now the project really was "not feasible," as chief of naval operations Arleigh Burke admitted.[9] Three hundred of the invading forces fell to Castro's army and another 1,200 surrendered, to be stuck for two years in Cuban jails. A successful operation would probably have been worse, however, because it would have tied the United States down in defending a new leader who would be an "American stooge."[10] The entire imbroglio firmly established the Cold War in the Caribbean for the next three decades, as the Soviet Union became Cuba's patron. The United States did not immediately give up the idea of overthrowing Castro. "Operation Mongoose" continued with sabotage, espionage, assassination attempts, and other plots carried out by Cubans and U.S. agents, including plans for placement of the hallucinogen drug LSD in Castro's broadcasting studio to disrupt his speech-making ability and a scheme to dust his shoes with thallium salts so that his virile beard would fall out. In 1974–1975 Senator Frank Church's (D-Idaho) Select Committee to Study Governmental Operations determined that neither Eisenhower nor Kennedy knew about these methods. Indeed, Kennedy made efforts to recover American prestige and allay fears of U.S. intentions in the region after the Bay of Pigs through such efforts as the Peace Corps, a voluntary organization for Americans who wished to lend their skills abroad in impoverished countries, the aforementioned Alliance for Progress, and a personal trip to Caracas in December 1961, where his reception was as glowing as Nixon's had been gruesome three years earlier.

After the Bay of Pigs fiasco, the Soviets believed that the United States might try another, more successful invasion. Khrushchev above all wanted "to preserve the impression of Communism on the march," note Russian historians Zubok and Pleshakov.[11] Having already sent arms, advisers, and KGB consultants for Castro's security service, Moscow had a sizable investment in the island, which offered a strategic location second to none. Khrushchev wanted to deploy forty 1,100–mile medium range ballistic missiles (MRBMs) with warheads there, and Castro did not object. Khrushchev rashly shipped over the missiles figuring that once they were installed, only a war could get them out. There were other motivations besides Soviet "image" for this initiative: The missiles would counter the U.S. 17:1 advantage in nuclear warheads, and offer further leverage in West Berlin. An embarrassment in the middle of East Germany, the city was a destination for millions of citizens escaping Communist tyranny. Beginning in 1958, in what became the "Berlin Crisis," Khrushchev periodically threatened to turn the administration of the city's border over to the East Germans, which would have required the Western powers to recognize the state. Khrushchev had built a concrete wall to divide Berlin in August 1961, but in 1962 neither side yet realized how long-lasting that solution would be.

In early October 1962, U.S. reconnaissance photos picked up the Cuban MRBM sites, with indications that more missiles were coming with double the capacity (it was not known that the nuclear warheads had already arrived). With forty-two thousand Soviet servicemen already on the island, the United States was gravely concerned. Soviet representatives insisted that the missiles were defensive, but a dubious Kennedy established an Executive Committee of the National Security Council to look into the matter. Its consensus was that the missiles posed a threat to the United States and should not stay. For Secretary of State Dean Rusk and Secretary of Defense Robert McNamara, the Munich analogy was compelling—the United States must not allow Soviet aggression as Europeans had appeased

Hitler in 1938. The committee decided to blockade Cuba with over 180 ships. Kennedy addressed the nation on television on October 22, informing one hundred million viewers of the crisis and the decision, as the world held its breath. The American military, including an invasion force of ninety thousand men, twelve nuclear-armed Polaris submarines, and sixty nuclear-loaded B-52s, waited on high alert, and the blockade, or "quarantine" as it was delicately called, began at 10:00 A.M. on October 24.

On October 26 the Soviets signaled that they would remove the missiles under UN auspices, provided that the United States dropped the quarantine and promised no invasion of Cuba. The next day a different proposal arrived, demanding that the United States remove its Jupiter missiles from Turkey. Kennedy responded publicly to the first letter. He announced that the United States would leave Cuba alone if the Soviets would take out their weapons. But privately, Attorney General Robert Kennedy told Soviet Ambassador Anatoly Dobrynin that once the crisis passed, Washington would remove the Jupiter missiles. On October 28 Khrushchev agreed. Cuba was safe from U.S. invasion, and the Western Hemisphere was secure from Soviet missiles. Khrushchev, blamed by the Politburo for the humiliating showdown and other failures, was ousted in 1964.

The presence of Communist Cuba was never accepted by the United States, and after nearly four decades of Castro's rule, Washington still does not recognize his government. Indeed, Castro's regime served as a justification for continued American anticommunist interventions in the region well into the 1980s, in order to limit any "export of revolution" from Cuba. In 1973, for example, the CIA covertly assisted in the overthrow of Marxist Chilean President Salvador Allende and his leftist Popular Unity government. Allende's nationalization policies were threatening the profits of the utility, International Telephone and Telegraph (ITT), and several copper mining firms, including Kennecott and Anaconda, and the United States feared that the Soviet Union and Cuba might capitalize on Allende's victory to extend their influence in the region. The CIA spent millions of dollars on its effort, chiefly in support of political parties and media outlets opposed to Allende, and worked with American firms to limit Chile's access to credit and supplies.[12] The end of the Cold War and the resulting demise of the threat of international Communism has not diminished U.S. official hostility to the last Communist in Latin America. Washington's continued isolation of Castro is sustained in part by the efforts of an influential voting bloc, the community of Cuban-American exiles who live in Florida and who have sought to maintain a hard-line position against Castro.

Twenty years after Castro's takeover, in 1979, another opportunity to replace an oppressive Central American dictator with a moderate and liberal alternative presented itself. The Carter administration and many Americans looked forward to the departure of Nicaraguan *caudillo* or dictator Anastasio Somoza, just as they had to Batista. But Somoza's main rivals were the well-organized, -armed, and -funded left-wing Sandinista National Liberation Front (FSLN), which threw out Somoza in 1979. Carter's National Security Adviser, Zbigniew Brzezinski, expressed concern about the Marxist nature of the new government. However, it was not until the Reagan administration that opposition crystallized, when the United States assisted the anti-Sandinista *Contra* forces under the auspices of the Reagan Doctrine and its support of "freedom fighters." This policy, which included mining the harbors of Nicaragua, became very unpopular among the U.S. Congress and the American public, who feared another Vietnam-style foreign engagement, and unraveled completely after the Iran-Contra affair of 1986, where American officials secretly used profits from arms sales to Iran in order to finance weapons for the Contras. Four years later, in the anti-Marxist wave sweeping the globe, a democratic election limited the power of the Sandinistas.

THE COLD WAR IN THE MIDDLE EAST

Though the Cold War in Latin America was closely tied to traditional American interests going back to the Monroe Doctrine, the Middle East represented a new departure for American diplomacy, and was closely related to the decline of British imperialism (Document 1). U.S. interests in this area included restricting Soviet influence, promoting stability, and assuring access to oil and other commercial opportunities. Truman Doctrine aid to Turkey and Greece stabilized these nations against Communist or Soviet influence, and the postwar U.S. construction and operation of the Dhahran Airfield in Saudi Arabia was an opening wedge for U.S. economic interests. The United States also rushed to recognize the state of Israel on May 15, 1948, the day it was created, with the Soviet Union right behind. The Holocaust, in which six million European Jews had died, as well as the unraveling of the British empire, made a solution to the question of a Jewish homeland a pressing matter. But Palestinian Arabs, who lost their homes, were embittered, and an Arab-Israeli conflict that continues to this day began immediately.

In 1953, developments in Iran led to the CIA's first covert overthrow of a government. At first, Washington had urged calm when Premier Mohammed Mossadegh nationalized the Anglo-Iranian Oil Company in 1951, infuriating the British. Two years later, however, when Mossadegh attempted to take over the Army from the Western-leaning Shah of Iran, Mohammed Reza Pahlavi, closed down Parliament when it resisted to move, and obtained financial support from the Soviet Union, the United States cut off aid, convinced that Mossadegh's actions were evidence of Communist leanings. The CIA's Kermit Roosevelt led Operation Ajax, and Mossadegh was overthrown in a bloodless coup. The Shah returned with American assistance, weapons, and propaganda in August 1953. He declared to Roosevelt, "I owe my throne to God, my people, my army—and to you."[13] But this connection would eventually serve to undermine the Shah. Communism was vanquished, and oil companies enjoyed new access, but within three decades another form of extremism removed Western influence from Iran.

The United States also attempted to enlist Arab states like Egypt, Syria, and Jordan in a pro-Western defense league. Egypt was the most important target, both because of location and its large population, but its leader, Colonel Gamal Abdul Nasser, did not choose to join the Western-oriented Baghdad Pact in 1955. He wanted to retain his options, and at the Bandung Conference that year heard from Indian Prime Minister Jawaharlal Nehru about the virtues of "positive neutralism" to avoid falling under the superpowers' sway. Having recently suffered an Israeli attack in Gaza, Nasser needed weapons, and in September he obtained them from Czechoslovakia after the United States had turned him down. In a last-ditch attempt to woo Nasser, the United States offered to build the Aswan Dam in December, which would increase Egypt's arable land by one-third as well as provide power, with most of the $1.3 billion project paid for by the U.S.-subsidized World Bank. But this did not make Nasser more malleable to Western influence. He continued trading with the Soviets, criticized the Baghdad Pact, and in April 1956 joined Saudi Arabia, Yemen, and Syria in an alliance aimed at Israel. The United States began a policy, pointedly code-named Omega (meaning "the end"), that was "designed to limit Nasser's influence, undermine his prestige, and perhaps depose him from power by covert methods."[14]

When Nasser insisted that the World Bank commit to financing the entire dam project, the Western negotiators grew testy. Distrust deepened when Nasser recognized Communist China, bought more Soviet-bloc arms, and partied with the Russians at the long-awaited departure of the British from the Canal Zone. Southern Congressmen were increasingly cool to supporting production of foreign cotton. Secretary of State Dulles withdrew support for Aswan the day that the Egyptian foreign minister was coming to Washington to discuss the project, July 19, 1956.

Nasser responded by nationalizing the Suez Canal Company. He would use canal tolls, with their annual profit of $25 million, to pay for his dam and compensate the shareholders of the canal. The British and French, the largest shareholders, were outraged, but Eisenhower, whose country had little economic stake in the canal, recognized that nationalization was legal and that Nasser was able to run the waterway. British plans for military action commenced, however, and on October 29, Israeli planes swooped down on Egypt, taking arms and six thousand soldiers. Pretending to be surprised, the French and British called for a cease-fire ten miles from the canal, which gave Israel a large chunk of Egypt. Nasser retaliated by sinking shipping in the canal. British and French troops started bombing Egyptian airstrips and occupied Port Said, and a furious Eisenhower rebuked them.

Dulles fumed that the canal fracas had come "at this very time, when we are on the point of winning an immense and long-hoped-for victory over Soviet colonialism in Eastern Europe."[15] The United States had in fact done almost nothing to help the Hungarian revolution that month, which was being crushed by Soviet tanks. The Kremlin, meanwhile, sent threatening letters to Israel, France, and Britain over the Suez crisis, and the U.S. Strategic Air Command went on alert. Britain and France finally yielded to the superpower pressure from both the United States and the Soviet Union acting in rare concert, and a UN Emergency Force went to Gaza. Israel returned to its original boundaries the following year.

As Khrushchev noted correctly, "Dulles's policies backfired and helped bring us and Egypt closer together." He added modestly, "We wanted only to help these peoples to cast off the yoke of their servile dependence on their colonialist masters. Ours has been a noble mission in the Near East."[16] Moscow financially supported the Aswan Dam, although it proved a drain for them. The Suez crisis also heightened Nasser's prestige in the Arab world. Nasser drove the British out of the Canal Zone, expropriated their property, and cut off diplomatic relations, as the U.S. became the unchallenged Western power in the region. Reacting to Nasser's new coziness with Moscow, in 1957 Congress endorsed the Eisenhower Doctrine, which stated that the president could use military force to assist any government of the Middle East that wanted help in resisting "armed attack from any country controlled by international communism."[17]

During the Vietnam War era, Congress repealed the Eisenhower Doctrine, though the U.S. role in the Middle East increased. The Yom Kippur War brought the world nearly as close to nuclear war as had the Cuban Missile Crisis. On October 6, 1973, Yom Kippur, the holiest day on the Jewish calendar, Eygpt and Syria, backed by Russia, attacked Israel. The

United States assisted Israel, which soon encircled Egypt. Egyptian president Anwar Sadat wanted Russia and the United States to rescue him, but the United States refused while Moscow pressured Washington for joint action. Nixon then ordered the Sixth Fleet on high alert, Defense Condition 3, and the Soviets backed down.

Americans were hit hard by the resulting five-month Arab oil embargo, when the Organization of Oil-Exporting Countries, or OPEC, cut off supplies to the United States. The entire world paid a stiff price as OPEC quadrupled oil and gasoline prices between 1973 and 1975. Henry Kissinger soon began "shuttle diplomacy" between Tel Aviv and Cairo to prevent further clashes and to remove Israel from the Sinai Desert, which it had occupied since the 1967 Six-Day War with Egypt. In 1979, leavened by American money, Sadat and Israeli prime minister Menachim Begin signed a historic peace agreement under President Jimmy Carter's auspices, and Israel left the Sinai in 1982. Egypt, like Israel, became a U.S. client, supported by billions in aid. It had long since thrown out its Soviet advisers.

THE COLD WAR IN AFRICA

Egypt is a dramatic example of the shifting alliances typical of many Third World states in the Cold War. In the Horn of Africa a quieter but just as persistent struggle ensued. The Arab and African states beneath the strategic "Northern Tier" in the Middle East had not seemed vulnerable to Soviet meddling in the early Cold War. Thus, the United States had ignored Ethiopia's requests for a military agreement, even as Americans operated Kagnew Station, a former Italian communications center in Eritrea. In 1953 priorities changed. The U.S. State Department gave several reasons for a closer bond—including Ethiopian Emperor Haile Selassie's sending of one thousand troops to Korea ("colored troops . . . [were] of great value to us in the propaganda war," noted the State Department in a letter to the Defense Department); Kagnew's security; the emperor's pro-American position; and a way to demonstrate American assistance to the Horn.[18] The United States proffered military aid in exchange for the use of Kagnew, evidence of how Third World countries benefited economically from the bipolar system. Kagnew became very important in monitoring Soviet ICBMs, and Washington shipped fighter planes to Addis Ababa in 1960 in a secret agreement that doubled assistance, provided training of forty thousand Ethiopian soldiers, and secured access to Ethiopian installations. The Johnson administration continued the aid, but Selassie now wore neutralist garb, as the nonaligned Organization of African Unity was headquartered in Addis Ababa.

The end of colonization introduced instability that also increased the value of a client like Selassie. In the Congo, a bloody crisis developed after Belgium granted independence in 1960. The army revolted and attacked white settlers, and in mineral-rich Katanga province, leader Moise Tshombe and Belgian businessmen called for secession. After the UN failed to restore order, Congolese Premier Patrice Lumumba, who was considered "a Castro or worse" by Allen Dulles, asked the Soviet Union for help. But Lumumba was assassinated by his enemies in 1961, to Washington's delight; the CIA itself had plotted to have Lumumba killed, sending a "biological poison that would leave no traces upon a corpse." The Congo's troubles were far from over, however.[19] The secession was eventually crushed, and in 1965 the United States helped bring in notorious dictator Mobutu Sese Seko, who changed the country's name to Zaire and systematically looted its wealth and oppressed its people. He was finally forced out by domestic opponents in 1997, and the country's name changed back to the Republic of the Congo.

While American clients were firmly entrenched in Ethiopia and the Congo, another superpower entered the Horn of Africa. In 1969 Marxist-Leninist Major General Mohammed Siad Barre seized power in Somalia, and the Soviet Union quickly signed a military treaty with him. In addition to the port at Berbera, Moscow built a base in neighboring South Yemen. The situation became more complex when U.S. client Selassie was overthrown in 1974. Ethiopia became a Marxist-Leninist state under brutal dictator Mengistu Haile-Mariam. With the arrival of Cuban proxy troops in Somalia to assist in attacks on the disputed Ogaden territory that divided Ethopia and Somalia, along with 2,500 Soviet advisers, the United States felt compelled to increase aid to Mengistu, despite his ideology and his abysmal human rights record. Mengistu's success was a clear example of how the Cold War created an environment where the emerging nations effectively played one superpower off against another.

In 1977 Jimmy Carter came to office on a platform of reducing arms sales and increasing human rights, and he cut ties with Mengistu. By then, advances in satellite technology had made Kagnew Station obsolete. Mengistu already had a willing patron. The Soviets switched sides to pour in weapons and seventeen thousand Cuban troops to help the Ethopians, whom they saw as more reliable and more strategically important, to fight Somalia. Somalia survived the breakup by courting Washington. After the Shah fell in Iran and the Soviet Union invaded Afghanistan in 1979, both Somalia and North Yemen became beneficiaries of U.S. largesse as part of the Carter Doctrine to prevent any outside power from gaining access to the Persian Gulf (see Chapter 6). The United States paid $40 million for a ten-year lease at the Soviet base at Berbera. Cold War loyalties were a slippery concept in the Third World, often linked more with regional opportunities than to ideological compatibility.

Cold War intrigue also developed in Angola after Portugal granted it independence in 1975. Rebel groups, including the Soviet-backed MPLA (Popular Movement for the Liberation of Angola), and the U.S.-sponsored FNLA (National Front for the Liberation of Angola) and UNITA (National Union for the Total Independence of Angola), headed by the fiery Jonas Savimbi, had been fighting to take over the country since 1961. Henry Kissinger wanted to extend $50 million in covert aid to FNLA and UNITA, but CIA Director William Colby insisted that the plan go to Congress first, where it died. This concern was motivated in part by the pervasive post-Vietnam syndrome in the United States. Congress did not want to support another American mission against Communism in the Third World. Lawmakers instead passed the Clark amendment, which meant no new money for the Angolan operation, and enacted much more stringent provisions for oversight of CIA operations worldwide. The Soviets were not constrained by such considerations and remained active with their Cuban proxy troops in Angola. Savimbi later picked up assistance as a "freedom fighter" during the Reagan administration, and in 1993 plotted against an elected leader, the Soviet-trained Jose Eduardo dos Santos, to take over the country.

President Ronald Reagan placed Somalia, Kenya, and Sudan as pillars in his containment strategy in the strategic Horn, located close to the oil-producing Middle East, and he also supported "freedom fighters" in both Angola and Afghanistan. The waning of the Cold War in 1989 saw Cubans finally depart Angola. It also facilitated an end to the border war between Ethiopia and Somalia. Soviet advisers and money exited Ethiopia, as Moscow grew increasingly disgusted with Mengistu's regime and his treatment of Eritrea, which was suffering from a government-induced famine. The United States helped broker a peace agreement that allowed Eritrea to become independent in 1992. Somalia lost importance after the Soviets left Ethiopia, and the advent of repressive governments in Sudan and Kenya created pressure for terminating U.S. military aid. The rise of Mikhail Gorbachev and *perestroika* in the Soviet Union and the changing tenor of the Cold War had a significant impact on both superpowers' approach to Africa, as many Soviet-supported Marxist regimes lost their legitimacy. In 1989 the Soviet Union finally left Afghanistan.

After Washington stopped funding Somalia's government, Mogadishu erupted in civil war and in 1991 dangerous conditions forced the evacuation of the American embassy. When the U.S. Marines brought in humanitarian aid, a new post–Cold War task for the service, they became enmeshed in an old Cold War responsibility, nation building, and several Marines died before the United States pulled out. African nations, like those of Central America, the Middle East, and Asia, became hotbeds in the Cold War. Ultimately, superpower aid, intervention, and wars distorted their economies and as often propped up oppressive leaders as preserved more benevolent ones. To understand the reasoning behind the interventions is to see the prism and the score sheet by which the Cold War powers measured the rest of the world and their positions in it.

NOTES

1. Quoted in Richard E. Welch, *Response to Revolution: The United States and the Cuban Revolution, 1959–1961* (Chapel Hill: University of North Carolina Press, 1985), 94–95.

2. Richard H. Immerman, *The CIA in Guatemala: The Foreign Policy of Intervention* (Austin: University of Texas Press, 1982), 117; declaration cited in ibid., 146–47.

3. Peurifoy as quoted in Stephen E. Ambrose, *Ike's Spies: Eisenhower and the Espionage Establishment* (Garden City, N.Y.: Doubleday, 1981), 222.

4. Lester Langley, *The United States and the Caribbean in the Twentieth Century*, 4th ed. (Athens: University of Georgia Press, 1989), 191.

5. Immerman, *CIA in Guatemala*, 103. An interpretation that dissents from the view of the Arbenz regime as Communist is Piero Gliejeses, *Shattered Hope: The Guatemalan Revolution and the United States, 1944–1954* (Princeton, N.J.: Princeton University Press, 1991).

6. Richard M. Nixon, *Six Crises* (Garden City, N.Y.: Doubleday, 1962), 215–19.

7. Quotes from Welch, *Response*, 161–63; 167.

8. Welch, *Response*, 57, 104.

9. Quoted in Peter Grose, *Gentleman Spy: A Life of Allen Dulles* (Boston: Houghton Mifflin, 1994), 521.

10. Thomas G. Paterson, "Fixation with Cuba: The Bay of Pigs, Missile Crisis, and Covert War against Fidel Castro," in Paterson, ed., *Kennedy's Quest for Victory: American Foreign Policy, 1961–1963* (New York: Oxford University Press, 1989), 135–36.

11. Zubok and Pleshakov, *Inside the Kremlin's Cold War: From Stalin to Khrushchev* (Cambridge, Mass.: Harvard University Press, 1996), 261.

12. See U.S. Senate, Staff Report of Select Committee to Study Governmental Operations with Respect to Intelligence Activities, *Covert Action in Chile, 1963–1973* (Washington, D.C.: Government Printing Office, 1975), cited in Thomas G. Paterson et al., *American Foreign Policy: A History since 1900*, 3rd ed. (Lexington, Mass.: D. C. Heath, 1991), 589.

13. Quoted in Mark Hamilton Lytle, *The Origins of the Iranian-American Alliance, 1941–1953* (New York: Holmes and Meier, 1987), 208.

14. Peter L. Hahn, *The United States, Great Britain & Egypt, 1945–1956: Strategy and Diplomacy in the Early Cold War* (Chapel Hill: University of North Carolina Press, 1991), 209.

15. Quoted in Frank Costigliola, *France and the U.S.: The Cold Alliance Since World War II* (New York: Twayne Publishers, 1992), 114–115.

16. Nikita S. Khrushchev, *Khrushchev Remembers: The Last Testament*, ed. and trans. Strobe Talbott (Boston: Little Brown, 1974), 431–32, 437.

17. Quoted in Alexander DeConde, *A History of American Foreign Policy*, Volume II: *Global Power (1900 to the Present)*, 3rd ed. (New York: Scribners, 1978), 292.

18. State Department letter quoted in Jeffrey A. Lefebvre, *Arms for the Horn: U.S. Security Policy in Ethiopia and Somalia, 1953–1991* (Pittsburgh: University of Pittsburgh Press, 1991), 72.

19. Lefebvre, *Arms for the Horn*, 98–99; Grose, *Gentleman Spy*, 503.

6

The Final Years: Détente, a New Cold War, and Denouement

Unlike previous administrations, Richard Nixon's did not make "the transformation of Soviet society a precondition to negotiations." Instead, Nixon and his National Security Adviser, Henry Kissinger, worked with Moscow though a policy of détente, or lowering tensions, and "linkage," offering American cooperation in some areas in exchange for Soviet concessions in others. He and Kissinger hoped to foster "a realistic accommodation of conflicting interests" with Russia, as well as with that long-vilified state, Communist China.[1] The American public, however, idealistically saw détente as an agent of change in Russia, whereas Soviet leaders saw it as the means to an end, a demonstration that "history was on their side."[2] These conflicting expectations led Americans to sour on the policy, and by the late Carter and, particularly, Reagan administrations, a new Cold War was underway with Russia. This chapter examines the dramatic events of the last two decades of the East-West relationship, from détente to the denouement of Soviet Communism.

THE SALT TALKS

When Nixon came into office in 1969, containment was undergoing its ultimate debacle in Vietnam. The United States had five hundred thousand troops in Southeast Asia without a plan of winning, and Nixon would use détente to extricate the United States from that morass. One of the first expositions of this new policy was the Nixon Doctrine in July, which "sought to navigate between overextension and abdication" of American power, and declared that allies in Asia would have to defend themselves first, unless threatened by a nuclear-armed nation (Document 13).[3] Nixon also believed that the Soviets, who were North Vietnam's patrons, could help the U.S. leave that country, and in part to enlist their aid, he courted China, opening travel and grain shipments that summer. Three years later, he made a historic trip to mainland China, where he and his Chinese counterparts, Chairman of the Communist Party Mao Zedong and Premier Zhou En-lai (Chou En-lai), announced the beginning of "progress toward the normalization of relations between China and the United States" and declared that "neither should seek hegemony in the Asia-Pacific region, and each is opposed to efforts by any other country" to do so.[4] As hoped, this visit elicited an invitation to the president to come to Moscow.

By 1970 the Russian nuclear arsenal was on a par with that of the United States, and Washington aimed for sufficiency in arms rather than excess. The superpowers relied on the doctrine of Mutually Assured Destruction (MAD): Both sides would be deterred from starting a nuclear war for fear of wreaking world apocalypse. Thus, as Nixon slashed American troop strength by one-third and ended the draft, he also began a series of talks with the Soviet Union, the Strategic Arms Limitation Talks or SALT. The first agreement, SALT I in 1972, limited the development of antiballistic missile systems to two sites for each power, one to protect its capital and the other to defend its ICBMS. This fit the needs of MAD, because most cities remained vulnerable to attack. SALT also kept ICBMs and submarine-launched ballistic missiles (SLBMs) at their current level. The Soviets emerged from SALT with an advantage in missiles, and the United States with more warheads and bombers. SALT II, the next proposed agreement, suggested a comprehensive ceiling on the number and range of weapons delivery systems, but became very controversial as Americans grew distrustful of arms agreements with Russia. Critics, like Senator Henry "Scoop" Jackson (D-Wash.), feared that as the United States scaled back, SALT would give the Soviets a first-strike advantage. While Jackson focused on the sheer number of weapons, the Nixon administration emphasized that Soviet geopolitical influence was the greater worry, and détente was addressing that most effectively.

FOR OR AGAINST DÉTENTE

Yet, as Kissinger notes, détente and its "linkage" concept "challenged American exceptionalism and its imperative that policy be based on the affirmation of transcendent values."[5] Because many Americans had hoped that détente might change Soviet diplomacy, they were keenly disappointed to discover that "it constituted a de facto acceptance of the Brezhnev Doctrine and an American acknowledgment that the USSR was the undisputed military-political policeman in Eastern Europe," Thomas McCormick writes. The policy did yield economic returns, including large grain orders and some high-tech exports, as well as a reduction in military expenditures. By 1976 Communist bloc, or COMECON, trade was beginning to integrate into the global market.[6] Yet COMECON remained a miserable performer; in 1989, for example, the total amount of computers produced by its industrial powerhouse, East Germany, was equal to 2 percent of the number manufactured by tiny Austria.

More significant for détente than growing trade was the role of West German Chancellor Willy Brandt. Brandt practiced *Ostpolitik*, establishing closer links with the East—the Soviet bloc and especially East Germany. The Berlin crisis finally ended as Brandt oversaw mutual recognition of East and West Germany, with access to West Berlin now guaranteed. East-West discussions continued with the Conference on Security and Cooperation in Europe (CSCE) culminating in the Helsinki Accords in 1975. They included a nonaggression pact, enticements for trade and tourism, and greater media access. Most important was the section entitled Basket Three, which required that signatories honor "civil, economic, social, cultural, and other rights and freedoms, all of which derive from the inherent dignity of the human person."[7] These would be used by dissenters in the Communist bloc, including Lech Walesa in Poland and Václav Havel in Czechoslovakia, to put pressure on their governments. At the time, the accords were strongly condemned in the United States because they seemed to legitimize the Soviet sphere. While defending his administration against this charge in 1976, President Gerald Ford made a gaffe when he declared in a presidential debate that there was no Soviet domination of eastern Europe!

Senator Jackson remained the most indefatigable foe of détente. He was particularly concerned with the issue of Jewish emigration from the Soviet Union. Numbers had been increasing thanks to improving Soviet-American relations, from four hundred in 1968 to thirty-five thousand in 1973. But when the Soviets began to tax emigrants, Jackson pushed through an amendment linking Soviet Most Favored Nation (MFN) status to freedom of emigration. Kissinger, Jackson's nemesis, noted wryly that while the United States rushed to leave Vietnam, some of its legislators were ready "to embark on an unlimited agenda of global interventionism on humanitarian issues."[8] With the present generation of leadership in Moscow, change was unlikely. Indeed, so hamstrung was American policy in the late Nixon administration that SALT

II failed, South Vietnam crumbled, and Soviet Jewish emigration stalled while Cubans went to Angola to serve as proxy soldiers for Soviet ends. When the Cambodian Communist Khmer Rouge attacked a U.S. merchant ship, the *Mayaguez*, in 1975, President Ford dispatched the Marines in a tragic rescue attempt in which forty-one soldiers died. Americans, glad for some show of strength, applauded Ford's action. No wonder that by the mid-1970s, in the wake of Vietnam and Watergate, the Soviets believed that an "aggravated crisis of capitalism" had set in.[9]

When Jimmy Carter became president in 1977, like Jackson, his foreign policy idealistically emphasized human rights. His National Security Adviser, Zbigniew Brzezinski, and his Secretary of State, Cyrus Vance, both believed that "détente had been oversold to the American public." Vance wanted to enhance the Soviet-American relationship and Brzezinski to limit the Soviet arms buildup. Both advanced a new SALT agreement. The Carter administration dropped the "linkage" policy, but this undercut its arms control agenda, because the United States was asking the Soviets for both SALT II and respect for human rights. Consequently, it got little. The president meanwhile began a correspondence with Brezhnev on human rights and arms control issues. The aging dictator, who was often in a pill-induced stupor, did not respond well to what he saw as Carter's moralizing. He took a hard-line posture on the new Soviet Backfire bomber and was further piqued that Carter had exchanged letters with Andrei Sakharov, the noted Soviet dissident and Nobel Prize winner. The Soviet leader had little patience for "pseudo-humanitarian slogans."[10]

SETBACKS IN DÉTENTE

In 1979 the United States suffered a serious setback in Iran, long an American client state, when the revolution of the Ayatollah Ruhollah Khomeini led to the capture of American hostages at the U.S. embassy in Teheran. They were held for over a year. Then, on Christmas night, 1979, Russian forces invaded Afghanistan, taking its capital, Kabul, and installing a new president. The United States protested, but Brezhnev responded that the Soviets had been invited. For Carter, the invasion was a great disappointment. He suspended SALT discussions and announced stiff economic sanctions. The United States sent military and economic aid to Pakistan, offered the same to China (with which it now shared full diplomatic relations), and recalled the U.S. Ambassador to Moscow. The United States also protested the Soviet action by boycotting the 1980 Moscow Olympics.

On January 23, the president issued the Carter Doctrine to shore up the U.S. position in the Middle East against Iran and Sovietized Afghanistan and North Africa, and to reassure U.S. allies like Saudi Arabia: "Any attempt by any outside force to gain control of the Persian Gulf region will be regarded as an assault on the vital interests of the United States of America, and such an assault will be repelled by any means necessary, including military force."[11] After a failed military intervention in April 1980 to rescue the hostages in Iran, resulting in eight American casualties, Carter's representatives began negotiations. The hostages were finally freed in the first few days of the Reagan administration in 1981.

Meanwhile, a new crisis was brewing close to the Soviet heartland. Protests over rising meat prices in Poland had led to the creation of an independent workers' movement, Solidarity, in the Gdansk Shipyard in the summer of 1980. The workers were assisted by the support of the Polish Catholic Church and the Polish-born Pope John Paul II. The establishment of such a union in the "workers' utopia" made a mockery of the Communists' class consciousness, and both the Soviet Union and the Polish Commmunist party were alarmed. Soviet Foreign Minister Andrei Gromyko declared in October, "We simply cannot and must not lose Poland," and East German leader Erich Honecker called for action (see Document 14).[12] Troops on the Soviet-Polish border were placed on alert, and East German and Czechoslovak divisions prepared for a possible invasion. But Moscow arranged for General Wojciech Jaruzelski to set up martial law in the fall of 1981. Jaruzelski's hard-nosed regime squashed Solidarity's open movement for the time being, though in the end even he began to accommodate to the popularity of Solidarity and Polish nationalism.

REAGAN DRAWS A HARD LINE

By the early 1980s, the Soviets, their Cuban proxies, and their Marxist allies were not only holding on but were on the march all over the globe, from Africa to Central America to Asia. This imperialism ended most sympathy for détente in the United States, stiffened American resolve, and led to the election of Ronald Reagan as president (1981–1989), who continued and magnified Carter's post-Afghanistan hard line toward the Soviets. Well aware of the American people's penchant for exceptionalism and desire for inspiring rhetoric, Reagan predicted in 1981 that "the West won't contain communism, it will transcend communism."[13] Reagan's relentless focus on the Soviet Union as the source of "all the unrest that is going on" overlooked "complexities," notes historian Michael Sherry. In a more magnanimous interpretation, Kissinger writes that the president "oversimplified America's virtues . . . to convince the American people that the East-West ideological conflict mattered."[14] If his values-based approach lacked nuances, Reagan also brought both the United States and the U.S.S.R. together for talks that would lead to huge reductions in force levels and an end to the Cold War. As Reagan's defenders and critics have both agreed, his rhetoric and his programs allowed for "a more solidly based approach to détente than anything the Nixon, Ford, or Carter administrations had been able to accomplish."[15]

Under the mantra of "peace through our strength," Reagan first conducted an enormous arms buildup. He was convinced that American military weakness had put the United States at risk.[16] During Reagan's first five years the United States spent almost $2 trillion on military expenses, the highest peacetime defense expenditure in history. Much of the spending went to large items like the B-1 and B-2 (Stealth) bomber; cruise, MX, and Pershing missiles; and Trident nuclear submarines. The United States installed 1,500–mile-range Pershing missiles for NATO to compete with the Soviet SS-20s. Although European governments had asked for the Pershings because they were unsure that the United States would fight a Soviet nuclear attack on Europe from the American homeland, many West Germans, especially the young, resisted the new weapons, as did French, Italian, and British activists. In the United States, Reagan's buildup also spurred dissent. On June 12, 1982, seven hundred thousand antinuclear protesters demonstrated in New York City, the largest such gathering in U.S. history. Referenda for a nuclear freeze passed in eight states, and Congress came within two votes of passing its own version. The popular imagination was captivated by fears of nuclear war, in movies like *The Day After* (1983), watched by a television audience of one hundred million.

A NEW COLD WAR SIMMERS

In 1982 Brezhnev was succeeded by Yuri Andropov, who died within a year, as did his successor, Konstantin Chernenko. The new Cold War simmered, and in March 1983, Reagan stoked the fires by identifying the Soviet Union as an "evil empire."[17] He would be vilified for this statement, yet the Soviets seemed to prove him right on August 31, 1983, by shooting down a civilian airliner, Korean Air Lines Flight 007, when it accidentally invaded Soviet airspace. Reagan bombastically blasted "this barbaric act," which he suggested was typical of "totalitarianism."[18] Soviet spokesmen initially made the preposterous argument that the plane was on a spy mission. The shooting was in fact a tragic error that became a defining moment in the renewed Cold War. Despite its being a mistake, what struck many Americans was that the Soviet Union appeared capable of an act of blatant terror, confirming the "evil empire" accusation of the president.

Flippant remarks by U.S. officials who talked about post-nuclear cleanup made easy "with enough shovels" only worsened tensions. Reagan himself joked in what he thought was an off-the-record radio announcement that "The bombing will begin in five minutes."[19] Despite the jocularity, the president was horrified at the prospect of nuclear war, and on March 23, 1983, he announced the Strategic Defense Initiative (SDI), a shield that would make nuclear weapons "impotent and obsolete."[20] By deflecting incoming nuclear weapons with particle beams and lasers, the system represented an alternative to MAD. SDI was derided by critics, however, who called it "Star Wars" and condemned Reagan for furthering the arms race and violating the 1972 antiballistic missile treaty.[21] Yet, paradoxically, some scientists charged that it would not be effective, because its laser shield was vulnerable to saturation. For many, SDI was worth consideration. Although MAD had worked so far, the idea of permanently basing U.S. national security on Americans' vulnerability to destruction seemed untenable.

Reagan also addressed local conflicts with the Reagan Doctrine, which called for support of "freedom fighters" against Communism. The United States sent Stinger antiaircraft missiles to the anti-Soviet Afghan rebels or *mujahideen*. The administration pushed Congress to overturn the Clark Amendment in order to assist Jonas Savimbi, the anticommunist guerrilla leader in Angola. In Latin America, with the exception of the 1983 overthrow of the Marxist New Jewel movement in Grenada, such assistance to anticommunists was not popular. Washington's support of El Salvador's military regime against a left-wing insurrection, and its assistance to the *Contras* fighting the Marxist Sandinista government in Nicaragua, were both widely attacked in the press and in Congress, who saw them as an example of excessive U.S. interventionism. The Nicaraguan entanglement got the Reagan administration in deep trouble in 1986, when the Iran-Contra affair was revealed. Scholars agree that the affair had a role in shifting the tenor of the administration to a softer line against Communism. The scandal led to resignations and firings in the executive branch, and, writes Michael Schaller, "the new team . . . proved far more receptive to the goals of arms control and détente with the Soviet Union."[22]

GORBACHEV AND *GLASNOST*

A new team was also in place in the Kremlin by 1986. A vigorous, urbane Mikhail S. Gorbachev had become General Secretary the year before, and he argued eloquently for reforming and modernizing Soviet society. He wanted both *perestroika*, or economic restructuring of an obsolete command economy, and *glasnost*, political openness in place of authoritarian repression. Gorbachev dropped his government's Marxist-Leninist tenets of the inevitability of class struggle and world revolution. He believed instead that the superpowers' choice lay "between survival and mutual annihilation."[23] Gorbachev wagered that his society and its economy could be reformed and stay Communist—and that the non-Russian republics would want to stay part of a reformed U.S.S.R. He was mistaken.

The initial meeting between Reagan and Gorbachev occurred in November 1985 in Geneva, the first such summit in six years. Nancy Reagan may have played a role in the historic meeting, because her astrologer, Joan Quigley, enlightened Mrs. Reagan that the Soviet president's "Aquarian planet is in such harmony with Ronnie's . . . [that] they'll share a vision." Indeed, at Geneva, Reagan dropped his "evil empire attitude," and Gorbachev came around to Reagan's suggestions.[24] Both leaders expressed a serious interest in arms reduction, with Reagan insisting on SDI as the instrument and Gorbachev advancing the removal of all nuclear weapons by the year 2000.

These plans were amplified at a summit at Reykjavik, Iceland, in October 1986. Reagan and Gorbachev agreed to a 50 percent reduction in strategic forces in five years, and a complete abolition of ballistic missiles by 1996. This breathtaking start to a START (Strategic Arms Reduction Talks) agreement was not to last. The proposal was hastily and bitterly dropped when the Soviets insisted that there be no testing of SDI for ten years—prompting Reagan to walk out of the room. Reykjavik was also problematic for the nuclear-reliant NATO allies Britain and France because it threatened their independent defense posture. Subsequently, negotiators did agree to the 50 percent cut in strategic forces, and in December 1987 Gorbachev and Reagan agreed to dismantle all intermediate-range nuclear missiles (INF) in Europe in a verifiable manner. Although this accord covered only a small percentage of total nuclear forces, it was a great breakthrough. European nations' nuclear forces were left alone, and the discussion of SDI was tabled.

THE BREAKUP OF THE SOVIET UNION USHERS IN THE END OF THE COLD WAR

For Gorbachev, the arms reductions were not fast enough. He tried bravely to reform the creaking Soviet system, but *glasnost* and *perestroika* worked against each other, with openness making opposition to the Soviet system ever more blatant. Soon, Sovietized eastern Europe began coming apart. In Poland, supporters of Solidarity swept elections in June 1989, sharing power with General Wojciech Jaruzelski, the former hard-line president. The Hungarian government held multiparty elections, and began to dismantle its border fence with Austria, allowing East Germans to pour through and into Austria in order to reach West Germany. The most rigidly Stalinist states, like Czechoslovakia and East Germany, refused to reform, however.

Gorbachev was angry with such holdouts, but as he would learn, democracy would make moot the idea of reform Communism anyway. In November 1989, a month after Gorbachev lambasted the recalcitrant East German leader Honecker and praised the virtues of peace as stabilized by the Berlin Wall, Germans at last breached the wall. The Brezhnev Doctrine, which had occasioned Soviet intervention in the Prague Spring in 1968, was not reactivated. Henry Kissinger argues that Gorbachev was "unsuited by temperament" to crack down in the satellites. He was also economically vulnerable to the international ostracization that would have ensued. Thus, "Gorbachev was increasingly facing a choice between political suicide and the slow erosion of his political power."[25] Soon after the wall fell, with the strong support of West German Chancellor Helmut Kohl, East and West Germany unified, with united Germany joining NATO in 1990.

Hard-liners in the Kremlin were unable to recognize that the Soviet Union had overstretched itself. The reforms enacted under Gorbachev only seemed to expedite the decline. In June 1988 the Baltic states, part of the Soviet Union since 1940, began their quest for sovereignty. In the fall of 1989 Azerbaijan and Armenia, in the midst of ethnic conflict with each other, declared independence from the Soviet Union. Other Soviet republics, including Georgia, Moldava, Belorus, and Ukraine followed, calling for national autonomy and respect for local culture and traditions. Gorbachev and his advisers vainly tried to hold back the tide. Making token concessions, the Soviets insisted, for example, that Russian be the primary language, that the Baltics and Soviet Union were irrevocably connected, and that secession was utterly out of the question. But the dissolution of the Soviet Union was outscaling Gorbachev or anyone else's ability to stop it. Gorbachev sent in troops and cut off natural gas supplies to Lithuania in March 1990, but unlike his predecessors, was unprepared to stop the movement.

Not even the Russians wanted to stay in the Union. In May, Boris Yeltsin was elected chairman of the Russian Supreme Soviet, and Russia became a sovereign nation on June 12. Ukraine and Belarus soon followed. In December a nervous Gorbachev sent more troops to Lithuania, as well as to Georgia, Moldavia, and Ukraine. Pressure from the West was minimal.

As former CIA official Robert Gates notes, the administration of George Bush (1989–1993) believed that pushing Gorbachev might bring his conservative opponents to "move against him or might even drive him to join them." Washington and other capitals were then more focused upon the reunification of Germany.[26] To preserve the Union, Gorbachev promoted a new Union Treaty that would provide more autonomy to the republics. In March 1991 a referendum on the plan passed, and in June, after Yeltsin was elected President of Russia, he helped ensure support for the treaty among eight of the republics. Signing of the agreement was set for August 20.

But on August 19, angry hard-liners attempted a coup against Gorbachev, holding him in his dacha on the Black Sea, while Yeltsin and his supporters barricaded themselves inside the Russian parliament building. For a few tense days, peaceful reform looked in grave danger. The Soviet military refrained from attacking the parliament, however. Gorbachev survived the coup, but there was no longer any meaningful part of the Soviet government left—the leaders of the KGB, Army, and the Interior Ministry, who had orchestrated the coup, were all under arrest. Yeltsin banned the Communist party and made all Soviet agencies Russian. The republics declared their independence; and by September, "Gorbachev was all that was left of the Soviet Union."[27] He resigned on Christmas Day, after the leaders of Russia, Ukraine, and Belarus had joined in the so-called Commonwealth of Independent States, a weak and watered-down successor of the U.S.S.R.

Both Gorbachev and Reagan deserve credit for the ending of the Cold War. Gorbachev's creative attempts to reform his society and its repressive gray mien, and his willingness to build a relationship with the West rather than remain wedded to world revolution, were matched by Reagan's flexibility. Resolute in restoring American power and prestige during the bleak early 1980s, and thus forcing the Russians to face the crisis of their crippled economy, the president during his second administration was also sensitive enough to realize that U.S. security would be well served by working with the new boss in the Kremlin.

The end of the Cold War, and the Soviet Union, came as a surprise to most Americans. This outcome, some cracked, would deprive America of a sense of moral purpose: What would it fight for now? Though an oversimplification, it is true that the Cold War and Communism were well matched to the crusading, idealistic nature of American foreign policy. The post–Cold War order presents a more diffuse challenge, and hostilities will require more versatile and more subtle responses. The United States is now the world's leading economic and military power and must bear that responsibility most carefully.

The Russian Federation has not given up its imperial pretensions. In 1997 Yeltsin had troops in Georgia and Armenia, and only recently signed a peace treaty with the breakaway republic of Chechnya. Nationalists like Alexander Zhirinovsky, calling for a reconstituted Soviet Union, have run strongly in recent elections, as have communists. The United States, despite its preeminent position and the beneficence of its checkbook, can hardly dictate Russia's future. That country still occupies an enormously strategic position in Eurasia and has only recently reluctantly acquiesced to some of its former satellites' joining NATO. To keep the peace, many American policymakers acknowledge, the United States will need to work closely with Russia in the future.

NOTES

1. Henry A. Kissinger, *Diplomacy* (New York: Simon and Schuster, 1994), 712.

2. Joan Hoff, *Nixon Reconsidered* (New York: Basic Books, 1994), 184.

3. Kissinger, *Diplomacy*, 708.

4. Ibid., 728–29.

5. Ibid., 742.

6. Thomas P. McCormick, *America's Half-Century: United States Foreign Policy in the Cold War* (Baltimore: Johns Hopkins University Press, 1989), 168–69.

7. *Conference on Security and Cooperation in Europe: Part II*, Hearings before the Subcommittee on International Political and Military Affairs of the [House] Committee on International Relations (Washington, D.C., 1975), 123.

8. Kissinger, *Diplomacy*, 756.

9. Zbigniew Brzezinski, *Power and Principle: Memoirs of the National Security Adviser, 1977–1981* (New York: Farrar, Straus and Giroux, 1985), 148.

10. Ibid., 146, 155.

11. Quoted in John Dumbrell, *The Carter Presidency: A Re-evaluation*, 2nd ed. (Manchester and New York: Manchester University Press, 1995), 200.

12. Mark Kramer, "Cold War Crises: Poland, 1980–81: Soviet Policy during the Polish Crisis," in Cold War International History Project *Bulletin*, Spring 1995, 118.

13. Quoted in John Lewis Gaddis, *The United States and the End of the Cold War: Implications, Reconsiderations, Provocations* (New York: Oxford University Press, 1992), 123.

14. Michael S. Sherry, *In the Shadow of War: The United States since the 1930s* (New Haven: Yale University Press, 1995), 399; Kissinger, *Diplomacy*, 767.

15. See Gaddis, *U.S. and the End of the Cold War*, 123; and the assessment in Michael Schaller, *Reckoning with Reagan: America and Its President in the 1980s* (New York: Oxford University Press, 1992), 176.

16. Reagan, "The Soviet Union is a Serious Threat to the U.S.," March 23, 1983, in William Dudley, ed., *The Cold War: Opposing Viewpoints* (San Diego: Greenhaven Press, 1992), 234.

17. See Document 15.

18. Quoted in Sherry, *Shadow of War*, 403.

19. "Rivals Trade Charges on Security Issues, Economic Policies; Democrat is Linked to 'Failed Policies,' " *Washington Post*, August 25, 1984, p. A1.

20. "Reagan Proposes US Seek New Way to Block Missiles," *New York Times*, March 24, 1983, p. A20, quoted in Kissinger, *Diplomacy*, 778.

21. Richard Barnet, "The Cold War Exacted Great Costs from the U.S.," in Dudley, ed., *The Cold War*, 279.

22. Schaller, *Reckoning with Reagan*, 173.

23. Quoted in Kissinger, *Diplomacy*, 788.

24. Quoted in Schaller, *Reckoning with Reagan*, 171.

25. Kissinger, *Diplomacy*, 793.

26. Robert M. Gates, *From the Shadows: The Ultimate Insider's Story of Five Presidents and How They Won the Cold War* (New York: Simon and Schuster, 1996), 528.

27. Ibid., 525.

7

Legacies of the Cold War

The implications of the Cold War (1946–1991) continue to be felt today, as they will for decades to come. The Cold War ended only in 1991, and so millions who grew up with it, worked under its auspices, and were affected by it—either as supporters, critics, arms-bearers, or victims—are still alive, influencing policies and votes. So too are many of the institutions, ideologies, and other infrastructure, from military bases to academic programs, that made up the Cold War state in the United States, the NATO countries, Russia, the former Warsaw Pact nations, and the Third World. This concluding interpretive chapter examines the political, international, diplomatic, economic, social, and cultural impact and consequences of the Cold War, using the United States as its focus and the lens through which to assess the Cold War's larger meaning.

POLITICAL EFFECTS

Politically, the Cold War created the modern security state. In the United States this meant the agencies authorized under the 1947 National Security Act, including the Department of Defense, the National Security Council, the CIA, and the Air Force. The Defense Department became a huge conduit for spending on military hardware and other defense needs that employed millions of Americans in programs that continue today in scaled-down form. Similar agencies in the Soviet Union with such innocuous names as the Ministry of Medium Machine Building, which directed the production of nuclear weapons and antibacteriological equipment, served the same purpose.

Although the United States no longer keeps planes flying twenty-four hours per day to monitor Russian activity, some Cold War era facilities still operate as if the era never ended. The hardened underground nuclear blast monitoring facility, Cheyenne Mountain Air Station in Colorado, is one example. This headquarters of the North American Aerospace Defense Command (NORAD), which opened in 1966, still operates with 1,100 employees to the tune of $150 million per year, ready to "counter" the Russians.[1]

Each nation spied on the other and covertly attempted to subvert it to serve national security and global interests. Thus, when the Soviet-sponsored international Communist movement conducted political campaigns in Europe against American commercial and cultural influence and the Marshall Plan in the late 1940s, U.S. labor organizations and the CIA responded. American unions sent funds to their noncommunist counterparts fighting a Communist-sponsored strike in France in the fall of 1947, and the CIA coordinated a campaign to defeat the Communist party in Italy's election in 1948. That year, George F. Kennan of the State Department Policy Planning Staff suggested that the CIA expand into the area of covert operations and "political warfare." He later called NSC directive 10/2, which he sponsored to promote covert activities ranging from progaganda to paramilitary forces to resistance groups, "the greatest mistake I ever made" because of its consequences for expanding the scope of American secret involvement abroad.[2] The agency would effect covert missions to bring about governments favorable to U.S. Cold War interests in Iran, Guatemala, Cuba, and Chile during the 1950s, 1960s, and 1970s—actions that remained highly controversial when brought to light. The KGB's secret and often brutal operations took place in an autocratic society, generating less discussion. Both agencies have survived the Cold War. The KGB is now the Russian Intelligence Service, and the CIA has been struggling to reassess its function in a new era as well as to recover from demoralizing spy cases like that of Aldrich Ames, a CIA agent who conducted a massive espionage operation for the Soviet Union and Russia between 1985 and 1994 that gravely damaged U.S. security and resulted in the deaths of several of its agents abroad.

Along with the executive branch, the House Un-American Activities Committee and the Senate Internal Security Subcommittee, among others, amplified the Cold War political atmosphere in the 1950s. The Supreme Court later would overturn some of the legislators' Communist-fighting provisions as unconstitutional, but the threat of public scrutiny for "left-leaning" politics hung heavy for years. The Cold War also affected educational priorities in Congress, particularly after the U.S.S.R. blasted off the first artificial satellite, Sputnik I, in 1957 and legislators made a large appropriation to rectify the situation. Eisenhower created two blue-ribbon panels, the Gaither Commission and the Commission on National Goals, both of which gave such a pessimistic view of American defense weakness that the president stifled them. The link between education and defense readiness remained beyond the Cold War, as President Bill Clinton made clear in his 1997 State of the Union address: "Education is a critical national security issue for our future."[3]

INTERNATIONAL EFFECTS

Internationally, the Cold War created a bipolar world. It was in many ways a competition for the hearts and minds of the peoples of the globe. The Soviets proclaimed themselves the model of social and economic equality, and Americans countered as the exemplar of economic wealth and political freedom. In a February 1946 radio address Stalin declared, "The Soviet social system is a truly popular system, issued from the depths of the people and enjoying its mighty support."[4] Some U.S. policymakers feared that this might be true. Soviet momentum in Europe elicited concerns that America would no longer be a model for the world, and the desire to set a compelling example is expressed by both Kennan, who declared that "[t]he issue of Soviet-American relations is in essence a test of the over-all worth of the United States," and by the authors of National Security Council Paper No. 68, who called for the United States "to demonstrate the superiority of the idea of freedom by its constructive application."[5]

In support of this goal to stand up to the Soviets both militarily and culturally, Harvard President James Conant founded the Committee on the Present Danger (CPD), an organization that pushed for greater defense spending, a mandatory draft, peacetime deployment of troops in Western Europe, and made a strong case to the public "to win a cold war of indefinite duration." The CPD and its luminary membership promoted "a more militaristic, Europe-first Cold War consensus in the upper levels of the American foreign policy establishment," writes Conant's biographer, James Hershberg.[6]

Each side played on its opponent's vulnerabilities. In the United States, racial problems during the Cold War left a bad taste with Africans, Indians, and Asians, who received second-class treatment in some American hostelries and airports, particularly in the South. African-American entertainer Josephine Baker was active in informing her world audiences about the American racial divide, including its lynchings and segregation, in the 1950s. So damaging were her words to the American image that the U.S.

government restricted her travel and performances both domestically and overseas. At the same time, the need for a positive image abroad helped to promote civil rights in the United States. But progress was slow, and American racial problems remained a sore. "Government officials came to realize that if they wished to save Third World countries for democracy, they would have to improve the image of American race relations," writes historian Mary Dudziak.[7] In this case, it was easier to squelch Josephine Baker than it was to change encrusted American attitudes. Still, the appeal to world opinion proved a powerful weapon for civil rights advocates and in part moved otherwise reluctant congressmen to support civil rights legislation by the mid-1960s.

DIPLOMATIC EFFECTS

While the world remained rigidly split into camps, diplomatic relations in the Cold War were accompanied by a series of significant oscillations of high and low hostility between the superpowers, ranging from "the spirit of Geneva" to the Cuban Missile Crisis, from détente to the rhetoric of the Evil Empire. It was thus a sometimes frighteningly polarized relationship, alternating with periodic bursts of ebullience and longer spells of cool and correct interchange. Neverthless, for nearly five decades the two sides kept their allies aligned—the United States by consensus in NATO, the Soviet Union by force in the Warsaw Pact—and at least after the death of Stalin, discussion and negotiation were possible and happened increasingly often between the two camps.

With the demise of the Soviet Union, Cold War tensions ceased, and the "arms race" became a term of the past. The once-mighty Soviet Warsaw Pact defense organization, designed to keep order both within the Soviet camp and without, lost its ability to do so, and the satellites effectively asserted themselves against Kremlin authority. Some of those countries—the Czech Republic, Poland, and Hungary—have now been accepted to join NATO. The oppressive nature of the Communist societies of the East as compared to the freedoms available in the liberal-democratic societies of the West illuminates why the Soviet Union, once Gorbachev had opened his society to internal dissent, did not survive the Cold War.

ECONOMIC CONSEQUENCES

Economically, the Cold War affected nearly all countries of the globe. In the United States, Americans sacrificed to pay for fifty years of defense spending and foreign military and humanitarian aid to limit the spread of Communism, "a sustained commitment to principle that no theorist of popular democracy could have imagined or expected," as one scholar put it.[8] During the conflicts of the Cold War, economic pressures increased immensely. The Korean War led to a national emergency in the United States as Truman enacted price controls, enlarged the army, and increased defense spending. During the Vietnam War, military expenditures combined with the social welfare programs of Lyndon Johnson's Great Society to create painful inflation that lasted for a decade. Throughout this process, the U.S. military-industrial complex burgeoned, and its legacy still has an impact on the American economy. Russia and its former allies in eastern and central Europe continue today to wrestle with the consequences of decades of economic stagnation and oppression, as well as environmental pollution, and their legacies include corruption, crime, fouled air and water, and continued economic and political instability. In the United States, the end of the Cold War allowed American voters to concentrate fully on domestic political issues. For instance, Republicans could no longer play the Cold War card of a supposedly "soft" Democratic party on defense matters.

Economic ideology also became a battleground between East and West during the Cold War. In 1959 Vice President Richard Nixon attended an economic exhibition in Russia where he argued with Khrushchev over the virtues of American washing machines in what came to be called the "kitchen debate," as the Soviet dictator insisted, unconvincingly, that each new apartment in the Soviet Union had one. The Cold War became a proving ground for the military-industrial prowess of each nation. Until 1965, as scholar Aaron Friedberg has noted, both sides "did about equally well" in production of ICBMs and warheads. But this parity in military technical sophistication soon evaporated. Government-sponsored research in the United States helped create the computer industry, where early research in artificial intelligence was perfected and, in an interesting progression, made useful later for the U.S. military. Although both the United States and the U.S.S.R. used public money to expand scientific research with military applications, it was only in the United States that commercial potential was also exploited. As Friedberg suggests, this gave the U.S. "a decided and, ultimately, decisive advantage."[9]

SOCIAL AND CULTURAL EFFECTS

Socioculturally, the Cold War affected all countries under its sway to varying degrees, ranging from mild propaganda to assorted paranoias, fears, and exaggerations. An early example of the "culture wars" was the 1948

Soviet-sponsored "Cultural Conference for Peace" in Breslau (now Wroclau), Poland. Prominent American artists and authors, including novelist Howard Fast and Harvard professor Harlow Shapley, responded to a Soviet-penned "Open Letter to Writers and Men of Culture in the United States" to come to Breslau and unite in response to a "new threat of fascism," which was how the Soviet Union envisioned the Truman Doctrine.[10] The Soviet Union's cultural crusade drew worldwide support from notables such as actor Charlie Chaplin, scientist Albert Einstein, and artist Pablo Picasso, whose peace dove became the movement's motif. The Breslau conveners planned a "Cultural and Scientific Conference for World Peace" in March 1949 at the Waldorf Astoria Hotel, a gala event whose sponsors included Einstein and maestro Leonard Bernstein. Critics of the Soviet Union, such as philosopher Sidney Hook, were barred from addressing the Waldorf conference. In response, the CIA funded organizations like the Congress of Cultural Freedom, made up of European and American anticommunist intellectuals and activists like Hook, actor Robert Montgomery, and novelist Arthur Koestler. The Congress had members in thirty-five countries and sponsored exhibits, conferences, and publications, including the magazine *Encounter*.

More influential in shaping the culture and outlook of average American citizens was the legacy of the atomic bomb. There was fear and gloom at the new destructiveness of the weapon, as well as jingoistic euphoria. NBC radio commentator H. V. Kaltenborn cried in alarm: "For all we know, we have created a Frankenstein! We must assume that with the passage of only a little time, an improved form of the new weapon we use today can be turned against us." But the wide appeal of the Kix Cereal "Atomic 'Bomb' ring," with its "gleaming aluminum warhead," indicated the contrasting excitement with which many saw the bomb.[11] Following the blast-off of a Soviet atomic weapon in 1949, Truman ordered the development of the even more threatening hydrogen bomb. The arms competition would have a tremendous effect on domestic political culture in the United States and the Soviet Union. In the United States, for example, fallout shelters were constructed throughout the country, stocked with food supplies for an attack. Some families built their own shelters. In the 1950s and early 1960s, schoolchildren hid under their desks during air-raid drills. Bert the Turtle told children to "Duck and Cover."[12] The Cold War consciousness was thus ingrained in children, and in their parents, as George Bush recalled (Document 17). By the 1970s, the arms race with the Soviet Union had evolved to mutually assured destruction, with each nation's citizens hostage to the fear of atomic devastation but détente having lessened the danger of imminent attack.

In the civilian realm, atomic energy was hailed initially as the curative for cancer and a source of cheap power. In 1947 *Collier's* magazine pictured a paraplegic emerging from his wheelchair in the haze of a mushroom cloud.[13] A decade later, the first nuclear powered energy plant opened. The Socialist party saw nuclear energy as making possible a higher standard of living for all. As physics professor Freeman Dyson wrote recently about his work with isotopes in the 1950s, "It looked then as if nuclear energy would be the great equalizer."[14]

Even as atomic energy promised benificence in the 1950s and early 1960s, protest movements against the bomb were growing, including the Stockholm Peace Appeal, SANE (the Committee for a Sane Nuclear Policy), and Women Strike for Peace, a group of middle-class mothers concerned about strontium-90 showing up in cow's milk from radioactive fallout. In 1962 a distrustful HUAC called the Women Strike for Peace members to testify in Washington, and these women confirmed that, indeed, they might have a mimeograph machine! HUAC's investigation appeared ludicrous, as a Herblock cartoon demonstrated, with one congressman asking his neighbor, "I came in late; which was it that was un-American—women or peace?"[15]

The Cold War had a strong effect on domestic political culture. In the early years, the constellation of world events convinced American officials that the trend was going against U.S. national interests. But they overreacted to the Soviet threat abroad and exploited it for domestic political purposes. In reaction to this atmosphere, Hollywood made many movies about the Communist threat, including *The Red Menace* (1949), *I Was a Communist for the FBI* (1951), and *Big Jim McLain*, featuring John Wayne in a celebration of HUAC (1952). By the 1960s, Hollywood studios were no longer producing such ham-handed fare; instead, the Cold War ethos was more subtle. The television series *Star Trek*, writes historian Rick Worland, "allegorized the geopolitical Cold War conflict: Captain Kirk and the Federation represent America and 'the Free World' locked in Cold War struggle with implacable ideological enemies—the Klingons and Romulans—analogous to the Soviet Union and Maoist China." During *Star Trek*'s run, which coincided with the height of the Vietnam War, 1966–1969, the series focused on the Federation's fear of " 'Klingonism' " as it "competed militarily and politically for the allegiance and resources of Third World planets." Worland suggests that the mixed-race crew of the starship *Enterprise* represented "the unbridled confidence and optimism of mid-century America." The United States in the mid-1960s was not only the most advanced economic power in the world, it was using this might to fight the

War on Poverty and social injustice *and* bringing the Great Society to Vietnam along with ambitious missions to outer space.[16]

THE EFFECTS OF THE VIETNAM WAR

The containment-inspired Vietnam War had an enormous effect on American political, economic, social, and cultural life. The unquestioned allegiance to the domino theory, liberal internationalism, nation-building arrogance, missionary diplomacy, and credibility led Americans into the war and justified their stay. As Defense Secretary Robert McNamara noted in 1964: "South Vietnam is both a test of U.S. firmness and specifically a test of U.S. capacity to deal with 'wars of national liberation.' . . . U.S. disengagement and the acceptance of Communist domination would have a serious effect on confidence. . . . [A]ny country threatened in the future by Communist subversion would have reason to doubt whether we would really see the thing through."[17]

Vietnam affected the 1968 election, contributed to Watergate, and effectively ended the presidency of Lyndon Johnson. Socioculturally, it underlined a divide in the country between the affluent who could avoid the draft, and the sons of the poor and minorities who went to Vietnam. It further led to questioning of old attitudes and conventions and new developments and outlooks on race, sex, gender, class, art, music, and intellectual pursuits. Questioning American Cold War fears, for example, became Hollywood and TV fare, as in the irreverent series *M.A.S.H.* during the 1970s.

After Vietnam, the United States scaled back its use of military force significantly. Michael Sherry notes that President Ford started a trend in the *Mayaguez* incident (see Chapter 6) that was followed by Reagan with his military intervention in Grenada in 1983 and air strikes against Libya in 1986, of taking a stand "where nuclear confrontation or serious conventional combat was unlikely and where the stakes were limited or largely symbolic." This "gulf" between Cold War "purpose" and the "actual use of American power" was not inappropriate after Vietnam.[18] The United States could no longer claim the mantle of a dominating power. Indeed, the United States and the Soviet Union were in the midst of the era of détente, a policy designed to lessen tensions between the two powers. Yet détente offered mixed returns. Washington was beginning to look like a crippled giant. When Jimmy Carter left the Oval Office in 1981, American hostages were being held in Iran, the U.S. public remained unsure about its role in the world, and the Soviet Union's global influence was on the upswing.

RECENT LEGACIES OF THE COLD WAR

Incoming President Ronald Reagan boldly asserted that the United States had values to impart to the world. "The last pages of communism's sad, bizarre chapter in human history are even now being written," declared the president in 1983 (see Document 15). He did much to restore the nation's confidence, although like his immediate predecessors, he was risk-aversive in the use of American power, as exemplified in the major engagement of his term: the overthrow of the left-leaning New Jewel Movement on the island of Grenada. Meanwhile, the U.S. defense budget experienced its fastest buildup in peacetime history. Some of the more gung ho anticommunists working for him, like Lieutenant Colonel Oliver North of the National Security Council staff, embarrassed his administration, most especially during the Iran-Contra affair, with its illegal selling of weapons to Iran and funneling of U.S. Treasury funds to the Nicaraguan *Contras*.

It was Reagan and Soviet president Mikhail Gorbachev who effected the first real cuts in nuclear arms, as opposed to mere ceilings. These reductions and the better Soviet-American relations that accompanied them helped end the Cold War. As one historian notes, the president "generally meant precisely what he said" in his suggestions for arms reduction, a strong negotiating position, and his hope to create a post-nuclear order—and this strong stand was effective.[19]

Under the doctrine of *glasnost*, the explosion at the Chernobyl nuclear power plant in 1986 forced Soviet officials to deal openly with a large environmental disaster for the first time. Meanwhile, dissent grew against old Soviet ways in foreign policy. In the journal of the Soviet Institute of the World Economy and International Relations, "editors apologized to their readers for years of superficiality and inertia in the journal's treatment of topical issues." With this new thinking in Russia, Gorbachev's star rose in western Europe. Yet NATO's draw remained, with 73 percent of West German poll respondents indicating that they wished the country to stay in the alliance in 1986.[20]

At the same time, the Eastern bloc began to unravel. In 1971 Polish émigré Leszek Kolokowski called for those under Soviet domination to practice "living in truth," following "an ethical life in which we are not silent in the face of knavery, servile to those in authority, or accepting of the petty gifts of our oppressors." This was difficult given the power of the socialist state, but after the Helsinki Accords of 1975, dissident groups like Charter 77 in Czechoslovakia took the moral high ground away from their opponents and, suggests Gale Stokes, "this process, more than any single political, economic, or military event, is what doomed the Communist regimes of Eastern Europe."[21] Beginning with Solidarity in the early 1980s, the liberalizing movement spread quickly after Gorbachev came to power, although there was strong resistance in Stalinist states like East Germany.

In 1988 George Bush, Reagan's vice president, ran for president against Massachusetts governor Michael S. Dukakis in a race still redolent with themes of the Cold War. Bush painted the governor as soft on crime, both through Bush's use of the Willie Horton case, in which Dukakis had furloughed a convicted criminal who had then raped and killed a woman in another state, and by his emphasizing Dukakis's membership in the American Civil Liberties Union. Michael Sherry suggests that both of these accusations were veiled attempts to link Dukakis with softness on Communism. If he let Willie Horton go, what would he do to the Soviets? And as a "card-carrying member" of the civil liberties organization, he was very similar to being a "card-carrying Communist."[22] The Berlin Wall fell and the Cold War ended during Bush's term, and it was his administration that along with the West German government, helped bring about the unification of Germany inside NATO, leaving an important legacy for the post–Cold War world. Russian leaders had not planned for how to deal with the collapse of the World War II lines in Europe, and the Soviet bloc itself fell with little resistance. In 1997 three of the former Soviet bloc states—Hungary, the Czech Republic, and Poland—were authorized to join NATO, in what was described in the founding act of the arrangement signed by both NATO and Russia as an attempt "to achieve greater stability and security in the European-Atlantic area." The Cold War is over, yet the now enlarged NATO, in a position facing Russia, still bears some resemblance to the old order.[23] For the generations who grew up amid the Cold War, the insecurities of a possible "invasion" from the east, or west, linger—a fact that will shape the politics and culture of the United States, Europe, and much of Asia for some time to come.

NOTES

1. *Philadelphia Inquirer*, May 18, 1997, A10.

2. Quoted in Peter Grose, *Gentleman Spy: A Life of Allen Dulles* (Boston: Houghton Mifflin, 1994), 293.

3. *San Francisco Chronicle*, February 5, 1997.

4. Stalin, quoted in *New York Times*, February 10, 1946, in Herbert Feis, *From Trust to Terror: The Onset of The Cold War, 1945–1950* (New York, 1970), 75.

5. Kennan quoted in Frank Costigliola, "'Unceasing Pressure for Penetration': Gender, Pathology, and Emotion in George Kennan's Cold War," *Journal of American History* 83 (March 1997): 1334; see Document 8.

6. James G. Hershberg, *James B. Conant: Harvard to Hiroshima and the Making of the Nuclear Age* (New York: Knopf, 1993), 493–94, 512. The Committee declined in the 1950s but was reformed in 1976 by critics of détente led by Paul Nitze, former head of the Policy Planning Staff and chief author of NSC-68.

7. Mary Dudziak, "Josephine Baker, Racial Protest, and the Cold War," *Journal of American History* 81 (September 1994): 556.

8. Richard Gid Powers, *Not without Honor: The History of American Anticommunism* (New York: Free Press, 1995), 258.

9. Aaron Friedberg, "Science, the Cold War, and the American State," *Diplomatic History* 20 (Winter 1996), 118.

10. Quoted in Powers, *Not without Honor*, 207.

11. Paul Boyer, *By the Bomb's Early Light: American Thought and Culture at the Dawn of the Atomic Age*, rev. ed. (Chapel Hill: University of North Carolina, 1994), 5, 11, 88.

12. Ibid., 353.

13. Ibid., 156.

14. Freeman Dyson, "Can Science Be Ethical?" *New York Review of Books* (April 10, 1997), 46.

15. *Washington Post*, December 11, 1962, quoted in Merry E. Wiesner, Julius R. Ruff, and William Bruce Wheeler, *Discovering the Western Past: A Look at the Evidence*, 3rd ed. (Boston: Houghton Mifflin Company, 1997), 329.

16. Rick Worland, "From the New Frontier to the Final Frontier: *Star Trek* from Kennedy to Gorbachev," *Film and History* 24 (1994): 19–35.

17. Robert S. McNamara, Memorandum to President, January 7, 1964, quoted in *In Retrospect: The Tragedy and Lessons of Vietnam* (New York: Random House, 1995), 107.

18. Michael S. Sherry, *In the Shadow of War: The United States since the 1930s* (New Haven: Yale University Press, 1995), 338–39.

19. John Lewis Gaddis, *The United States and the End of the Cold War: Implications, Reconsiderations, Provocations* (New York: Oxford University Press, 1992), 131.

20. Michael J. Sodaro, *Moscow, Germany and the West from Khrushchev to Gorbachev* (Ithaca, N.Y.: Cornell University Press, 1990), 333, 363.

21. Gale Stokes, *The Walls Came Tumbling Down: The Collapse of Communism in Eastern Europe* (New York: Oxford University Press, 1993), 21–23.

22. Sherry, *Shadow of War*, 434.

23. NATO and Russia Founding Act, White House Press Release of May 27, 1997. See web site http//www.embusa.es/nato/founding.html

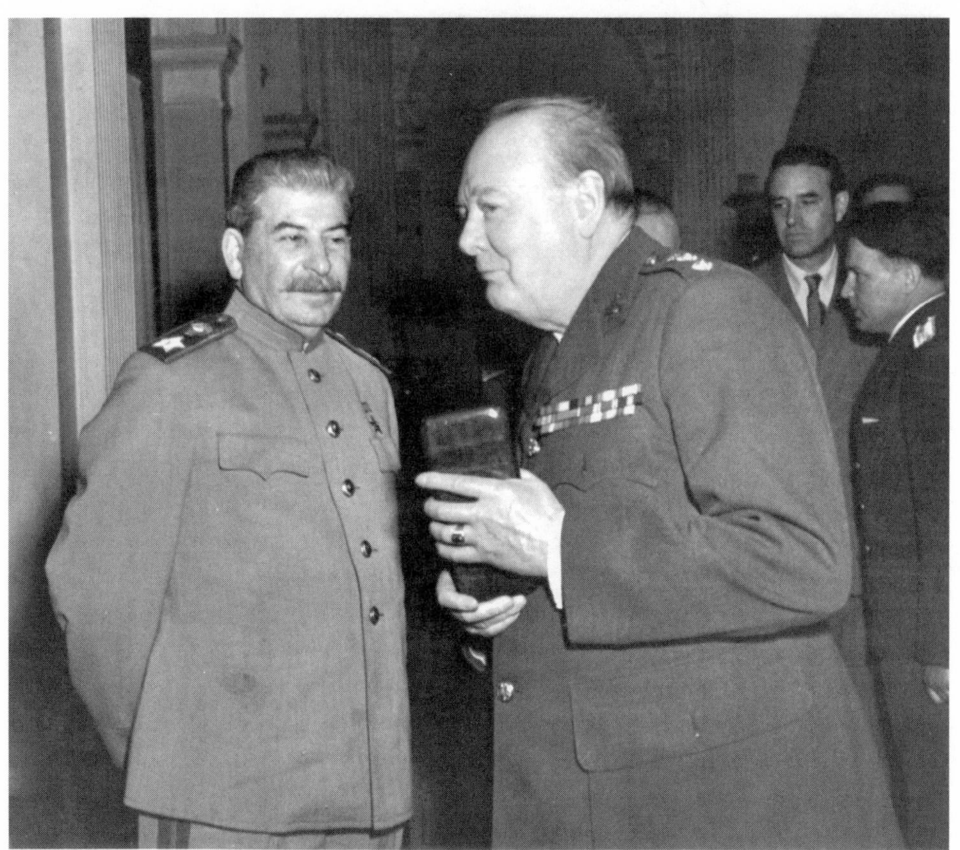

British Prime Minister Winston Churchill and Soviet Marshall Josef Stalin at the Yalta Conference, February 1945. Along with U.S. President Franklin D. Roosevelt, these leaders discussed such issues as Russia's entry into the war against Japan, the formation of the United Nations, and the fate of the liberated governments of Eastern Europe. National Archives

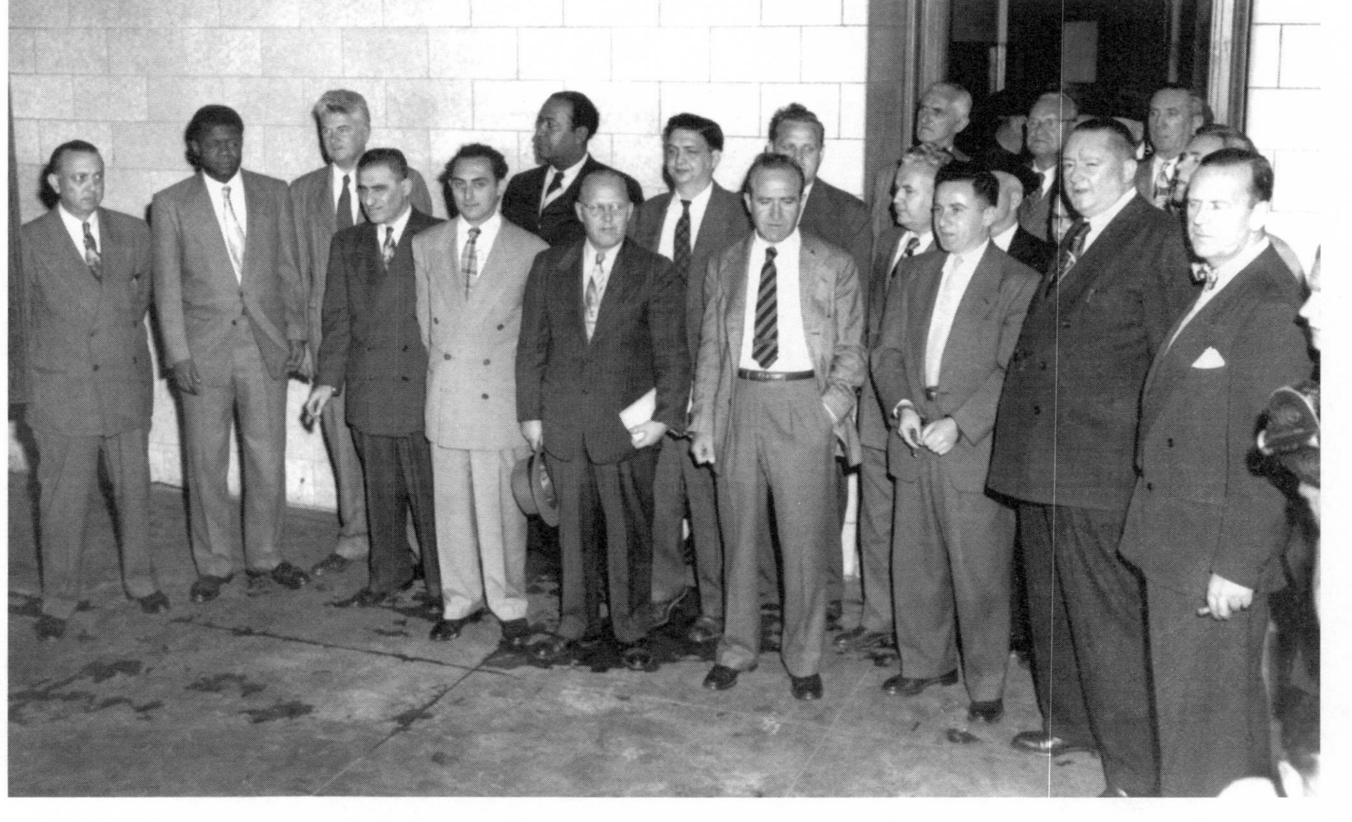

American Communist Leaders charged under the Smith Act, or Alien Registration Act, November 1949. Judge Harold R. Medina found the leaders of the CPUSA guilty of violating the Smith Act, which prohibited the teaching and advocacy of overthrowing the government by force. Seven defendants were sent to prison, as were five of their lawyers who failed to keep them in order. Daily News L. P. Photo.

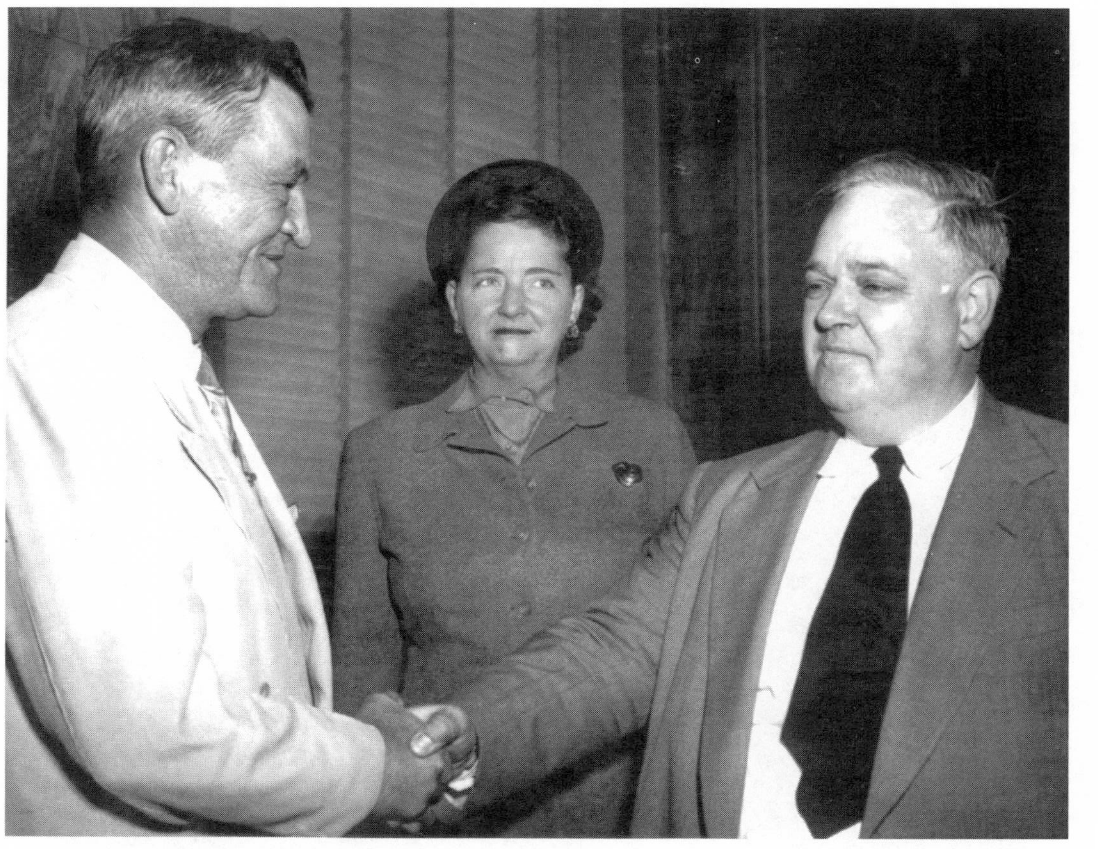

Former Communist spies Whittaker Chambers (right) and Elizabeth Bentley shake hands with Major General Claire Chennault, wartime Air Force Commander in China, before the Senate Internal Security Subcommittee Hearings, May 1952. Used by permission of AP/WIDE WORLD PHOTOS

Senator Joseph McCarthy and his close associate, counsel Roy Cohn, at the Army-McCarthy hearings in 1954, which looked into McCarthy and Cohn's having pressured the Army to grant privileged treatment to G. David Schine, another McCarthy staff member, whose files are in the box. The hearings destroyed McCarthy's career. ABC Photo Division Press Information

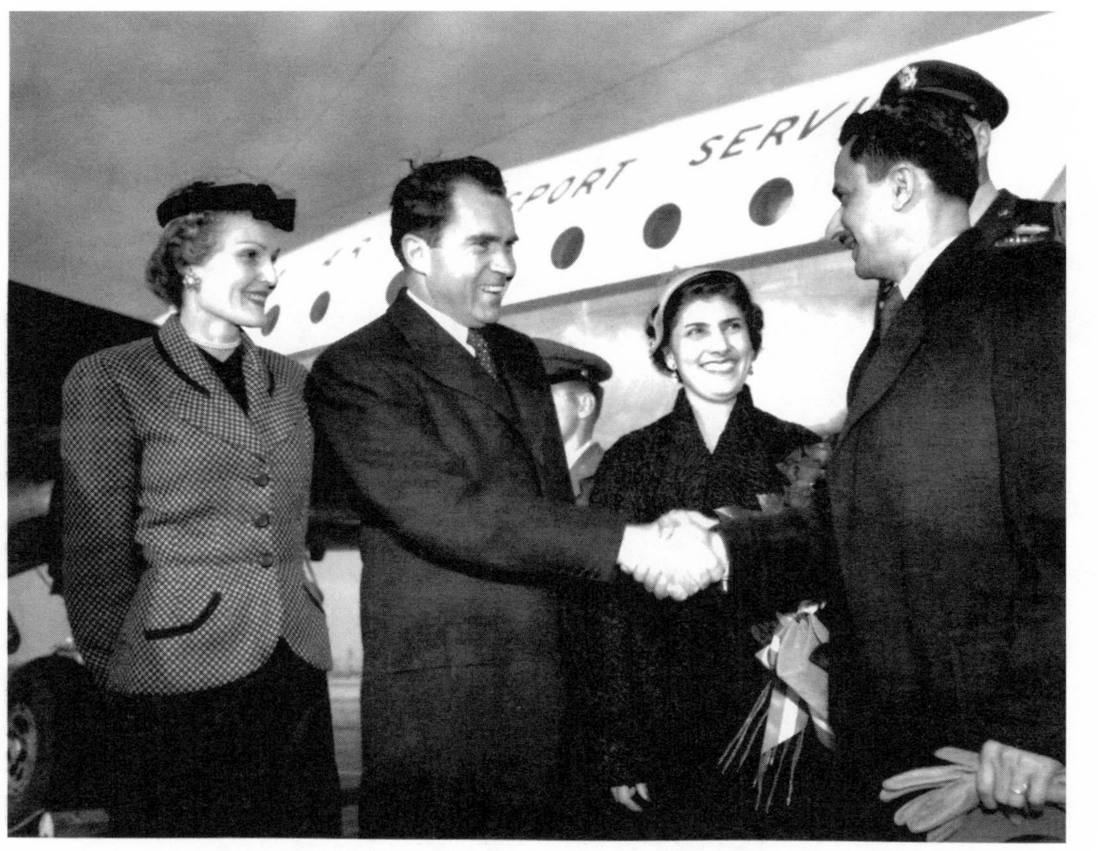

Mrs. Pat Nixon (left) and Vice President Richard Nixon shaking hands with Guatemalan President Carlos Castillo Armas (right) and Senora Armas at National Airport, Washington, D.C., in November 1955 after the U.S.-backed coup that brought Armas into office. USIA/National Archives

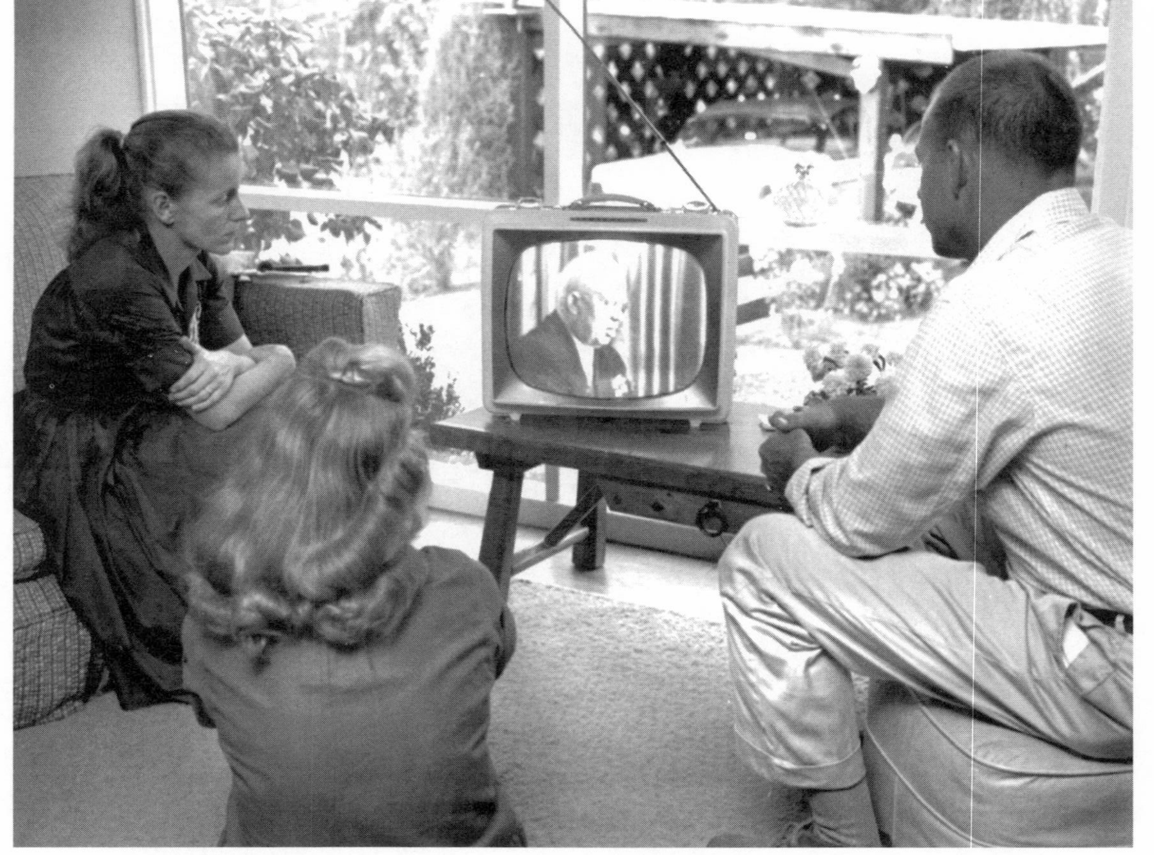

An American family watches Soviet Premier Nikita Khrushchev giving a 45-minute broadcast address during his inaugural visit to the United States, September 27, 1959. USIA/National Archives

Khrushchev, attending sessions of the United Nations, embraces Cuban Premier Fidel Castro on September 20, 1960, at a time when the Eisenhower Administration, convinced Castro was a Communist, had begun trade sanctions against his new revolutionary government and was secretly planning his overthrow. Used by permission of AP/WIDE WORLD PHOTOS

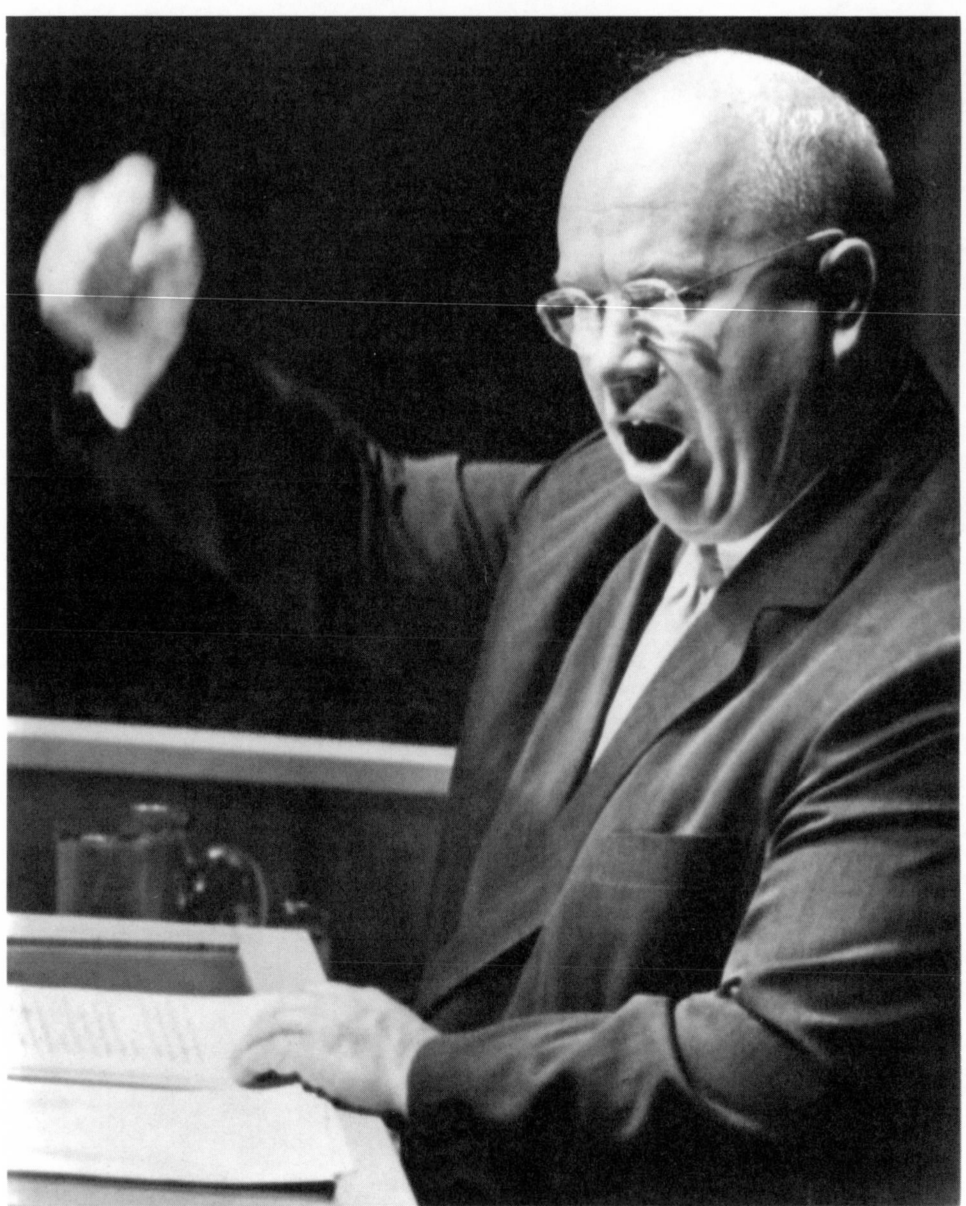

Khrushchev waves his fist at the same 1960 UN session, when he took an angry swipe at both the United States and the United Nations, accusing them of furthering the interests of Western imperialism in the Congo. Later in this session, a furious Khrushchev stunned the delegates by removing one of his shoes and pounding it on the table. Used by permission of Corbis-Bettmann

A Cuban exiles' "club" in Key West, Florida, in 1961, which served as a shelter for immigrants fleeing Cuba for the United States and was run by an organization known as the Christian anti-Communist Group. Michael Rougier, *Life* magazine © Time, Inc.

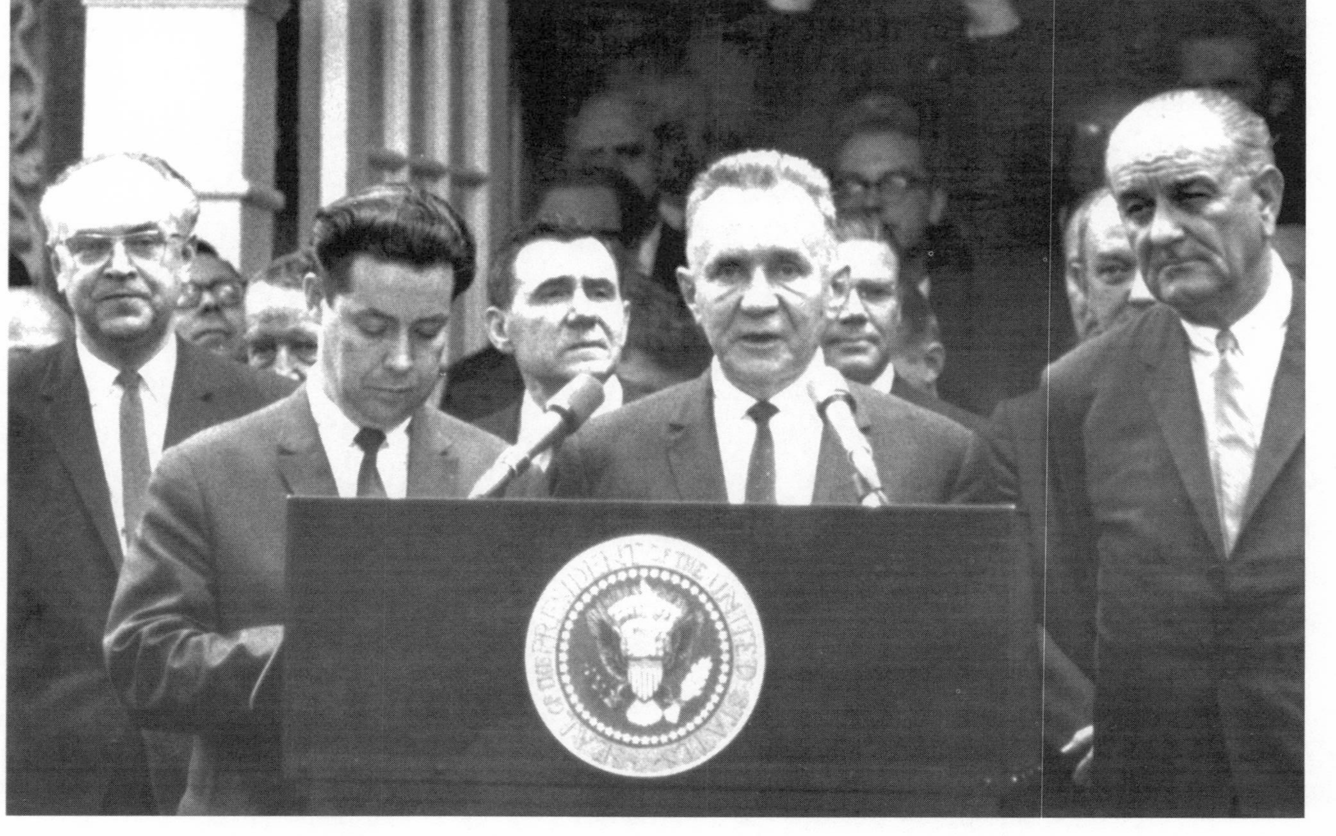

Soviet Premier Aleksei N. Kosygin speaking at Glassboro State College in Glassboro, New Jersey, September 23, 1967, after meeting with President Lyndon B. Johnson (right), a visit that was supposed to herald better relations with the Soviet Union and the Communist bloc; however, the arms race and the Vietnam War continued. White House National Archives

Soviet Colonel General A. M. Mayorov (left) shows Czechoslovakian President Ludvík Svoboda (center) and Communist Party leader Gustáv Husak (right) the busts of Soviet military heroes standing in the compound of the Headquarters of the Central Group of Soviet forces in Milovice, Czechoslovakia, May 1972. National Archives

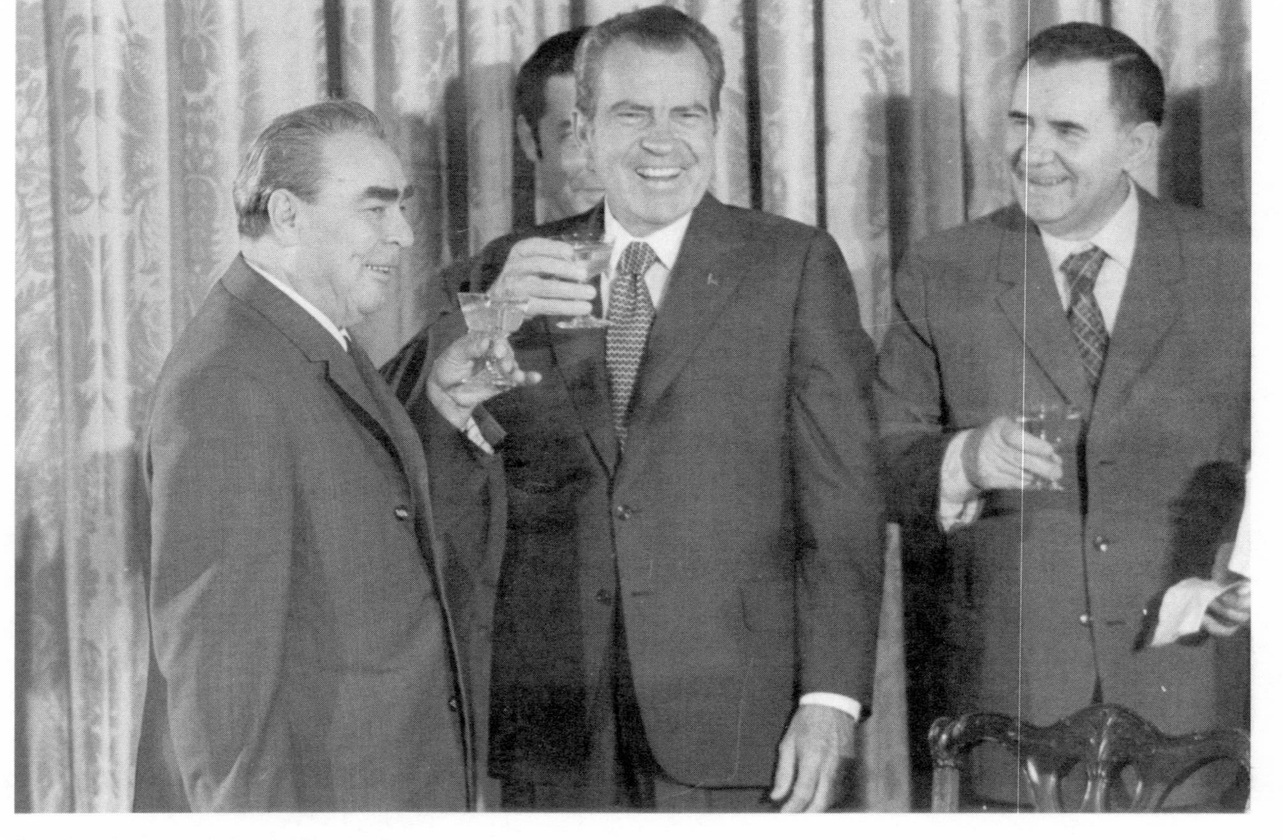

President Nixon with Soviet General Secretary Leonid I. Brezhnev (left) and Soviet Foreign Minister Andrei Gromyko (right) at the Washington Summit, June 1973. This meeting took place at the height of détente following the Paris Peace Accords, and introduced initiatives for economic and cultural exchange as well as a commitment to expedite the SALT II discussions on arms control. Library of Congress

Biographies: The Personalities Behind the Cold War

Dean Acheson (1893–1971)

Secretary of State

Dean Acheson, President Harry S Truman's Secretary of State, was born April 11, 1893, in Middletown, Connecticut, where his father was rector at Holy Trinity Church. He attended Groton, Yale University, and Harvard Law School. He married Alice Stanley in 1917, and after graduation from Harvard, clerked for Supreme Court Judge Louis Brandeis and joined the law firm of Covington and Burling in Washington, D.C.

His public career began in 1933, when he was named Undersecretary of the Treasury, but within a year he departed after a policy dispute with President Roosevelt. In 1941 he returned to the government as Assistant Secretary of State for Economic Affairs, when he and FDR concurred on the need for assisting Britain in the war. In 1945 President Truman named him Undersecretary of State. Acheson hoped to continue a positive relationship with Moscow, but he became increasingly pessimistic with the expansion of the Soviet Union into eastern Europe.

As an internationalist, Acheson strongly believed that U.S. national security required a postwar role in Europe, and shepherded a large reconstruction loan to Britain through Congress. He was instrumental in creating the Truman Doctrine and Marshall Plan, and promoted the reconstruction of West Germany and Japan and their integration into the Western sphere.

In 1949, he became Secretary of State, even as some senators remained suspicious of his internationalism. Acheson promised isolationist senators that no great number of soldiers would go to Europe under NATO and that West Germany would stay disarmed, claims that proved premature. Acheson dismissed the value of negotiating with the Kremlin, and after the Soviet Union blasted off its first atomic weapon in 1949, he believed that the United States should proceed with the H-bomb. This heightened defense posture was enshrined in NSC-68, even as Acheson recognized the limits of Washington's abilities, and for some did not go far enough in fighting the Communist threat.

This became apparent in August 1949, when his department issued a White Paper to explain U.S. China policy, and pointed out that Americans were not responsible for the "fall" of China. Not everyone was convinced (see Document 5). After Mao established the People's Republic of China (PRC) in October, Acheson reckoned that Communist Chinese courting of the Soviets would strain the relationship between the two Communist giants, and he was correct.

Already in trouble over the China issue, Acheson got in deeper water by defending his friend Alger Hiss, the accused spy. Given the temper of the times, and the spy revelations pouring out of Los Alamos and Britain, this position was impolitic, if brave. Then in January 1950 Acheson told the National Press Club that Korea lay beyond the U.S. "defensive perimeter." This speech would come back to haunt him after Communist North Korea invaded the South in June. The invasion and resulting war impressed Acheson that something had to be done about Europe's stability against Communism, and he began actively to press for German rearmament. The French government resisted, and it proved impossible for Germany to be rearmed during Acheson's term. However, he did set the stage for the Germans to join NATO later in the decade by sending American troops to Europe.

After leaving office in 1953, Acheson continued to advocate for a strong U.S. international role. As one of the so-called wise men, he advised President Kennedy during the Cuban Missile Crisis to launch an air strike against Cuba, but this option was nixed as too dangerous. He worked also in the mid-1960s as a State Department consultant on measures to bring the U.S. and Europe closer together. During Vietnam, as a close adviser to Johnson, Acheson began as an all-out supporter of the war. However, by 1968 he changed his mind on Vietnam, and this shift by an old-line Cold Warrior helped convince Johnson to pursue negotiations with the North. Acheson died on October 12, 1971.

Jimmy Carter (1924–)

39th U.S. President

James Earl Carter, U.S. president from 1977 to 1981, was born October 1, 1924, in Plains, Georgia, to Earl and Lillian Carter. His father was a successful peanut farmer, and had a great deal of influence on Jimmy, who idealized the man. After graduation from Plains High School, Carter was accepted into the Annapolis Naval Academy in 1943, where he studied naval engineering.

He married Rosalynn Smith, also of Plains, one month after graduation in July 1946, and spent part of the early Cold War stationed off the coast of China during its civil war. After his father died in 1953, Carter left the service to return to Plains, from which he hoped to pursue a boyhood dream to become governor of Georgia. He served on the Sumter County School Board from 1956 until 1962, when he was elected state senator, but failed in his bid for governor in 1966.

The disappointment led Carter, encouraged by his sister Ruth, to renew his religious faith. He was elected governor in 1970, having become a strong advocate for civil rights. Six years later, Carter gained support as an outside-the-beltway presidential candidate. He promised that he would aim the U.S. ship of state toward different goals from his predecessors, and human rights became a hallmark.

Carter's presidency coincided with an important period in the Cold War. At first, he continued the spirit of détente with the Soviet Union, while promoting human rights abroad. Carter believed that the United States no longer could claim global sweep and that the Soviet Union had ceased to be an expansive power. Both his National Security Adviser, Zbigniew Brzezinski, and his Secretary of State, Cyrus Vance, initially downplayed anticommunism in U.S. foreign policy. By the end of his presidency, however, Brzezinski had become a hawk, and so too had Carter.

Carter's emphasis on reining in expectations—delegitimizing the diplomatic ambitions that led to the Vietnam debacle, and calling for economic belt-tightening—did not sit comfortably with Americans. His human rights message, however, had universal appeal. In February 1977, Carter wrote a letter of support to Soviet dissident Andrei Sakharov, and urged that organizations like Radio Free Europe promote humanitarian aims. He attempted to free Soviet dissident Natan Shcharansky in exchange for releasing Soviet spies in the United States. Yet four hundred Soviet dissidents were sentenced between 1975 and 1980—Shcharansky himself receiving a fourteen-year term. Leonid Brezhnev was not interested in what he saw as Carter's intrusive humanitarianism.

In line with his policy of scaling back the American role abroad, Carter ended imperialistic legacies like the U.S. control of the Panama Canal, and even considered taking U.S. troops out of South Korea. His administration formally recognized the People's Republic of China, and ended diplomatic relations with Taiwan. Carter also ushered in a major peace treaty between Israel and Egypt.

The worst crisis of the Carter administration occurred during the Iranian revolution, when revolutionaries seized the American embassy and fifty-two hostages in November 1979, vilifying the United States for three decades of support to the deposed shah. The hostages were held for over a year. Carter's one rescue attempt was sadly botched, in what appeared further confirmation to many of the inability of his administration to deal with the difficulties facing the country, including economic problems and an increasingly ascendant Soviet Union. Carter identified a "national malaise" as being at the root of these problems, but convinced few Americans that they, rather than their president, were responsible for this.

Even though Carter's human rights policy helped to discredit oppressive leaders like Nicaraguan dictator Anastasio Somoza, it could not prevent a surge of new Marxist regimes in the late 1970s, including Somoza's successors, the Sandinistas. At the same time, Cuban troops served Soviet ends in Angola and Somalia. These developments appeared part of an ominous pattern only amplified by the Soviet invasion of Afghanistan in December 1979, to which the administration responded with sanctions and by freezing the SALT II process. U.S. officials expedited plans for the deployment of intermediate range nuclear missiles to Europe. Carter also announced the Carter Doctrine to protect U.S. interests in the Middle East, and strongly protested the Kremlin's crushing of the Polish Solidarity movement in 1980. Carter thus laid the groundwork for the Reagan administration's hard-line approach to the Soviet Union.

Carter was not reelected. In his postpresidential years, his human rights concerns have continued to preoccupy him, and he has been active in monitoring elections in emerging democracies like Nicaragua, Panama, and Haiti, and also participated in the peace settlement between Ethiopia and Eritrea. In the United States, he has been very active in charitable projects, including Habitat for Humanity.

Whittaker Chambers (1901–1961)

Witness against Communism and Alger Hiss

Whittaker Chambers, the accuser of Alger Hiss during the famous Hiss-Chambers spy case of the early Cold War, was born on April 1, 1901, and grew up in Lynwood, Long Island, a pudgy outcast dominated by his eccentric mother. He entered Columbia University in 1920, where he discovered that he had great talent for poetry and politics. Yet Chambers dropped out of Columbia and discovered a new and compelling cause—

bolshevism. He saw in Lenin's writings the roots of his family's struggles. Chambers' parents' marriage was falling apart, and his only brother would commit suicide in 1926.

Chambers became a Communist and began writing for party organs like the *Daily Worker*. In 1931 he married Esther Shemitz, whom he had met at a textile strike. The following year he became editor of *The New Masses*. He also joined the Communist underground and served as a spy in the U.S. Government for Soviet intelligence for the next six years. But he began to grow disillusioned with Communism in the wake of Stalin's purges and in April 1938 he left the party. After a period of hiding, he secured a position at *Time* as a book review writer.

Chambers told his story to government representatives, but nothing was done with it until May 1945, when he was interviewed by the FBI. Reluctant to be labeled an "informer," three years later, he appeared before HUAC and named as one of his sources Alger Hiss, poised and polished State Department lawyer and head of the Carnegie Endowment for International Peace. Hiss denied the charges, but Congressman Richard Nixon (R-Calif.) pursued the matter. Chambers knew an inordinate amount about Hiss—from the rare birds he'd spotted to the kennel his dog was housed in. After both men had spoken in front of HUAC in August 1948, Hiss sued Chambers, and Chambers responded with his cache of State Department documents that Hiss had supplied him from 1937 to 1938, the so-called "pumpkin papers." The documents were not highly classified, but obtaining them would have assisted the Soviets to decipher other coded documents.

Hiss was indicted by a grand jury for perjury in December 1948. Though his first trial ended in a hung jury in 1949, the Soviet bomb and the "fall" of China made the case against him more compelling a year later, when a jury found him guilty, a decision that helped Richard Nixon's career. Drawing adherents on both sides, the Hiss-Chambers case became a seminal controversy of the Cold War. Hiss went to his grave denying his guilt. Many believed him, but the consensus of scholarly opinion now is that he was culpable.[1]

Having left *Time* owing to the notoriety of the case, Chambers assisted Senator Joseph McCarthy in defeating Maryland Senator and McCarthy foe Millard Tydings in 1950. He began writing his best-selling autobiography *Witness* (1952), a confession of his life as a Communist and then a defector from the cause. Chambers changed his views about McCarthy by 1953, yet he never publicly denounced the senator.

Chambers began writing for William F. Buckley's new conservative magazine, *National Review*, after McCarthy died in 1957. He also returned to *Time*. Increasingly ill owing to his weight, he enrolled at Western

Maryland State College to finish his degree in Romance languages. Toward the very end of his life, having second thoughts about Soviet-American détente, Chambers ended his connection with *National Review*, opposed to its criticism of Khrushchev's visit to the United States as well as its support of the arms race. He died in 1961 of a coronary.

Allen Welsh Dulles (1893–1969)

Director of Central Intelligence

Allen Dulles, who as Eisenhower's Director of Central Intelligence was chiefly responsible for creating the CIA in its Cold War form, was born to a Presbyterian minister and his wife in Watertown, New York, on April 7, 1893, into a family that included several diplomatic luminaries, among them three secretaries of state. Two years after graduation from Princeton in 1914, he joined the foreign service. He served as an intelligence officer in Vienna and Berne, and along with brother John Foster, joined the American delegation at the 1919 Paris Peace Conference. The following year, he married Clover Todd, and in 1926 followed his brother to the law firm of Sullivan and Cromwell.

Dulles maintained a strong interest in foreign events, joining the board of the Council of Foreign Relations in 1927, and briefly served as an envoy in Germany for President Franklin Roosevelt. In 1941 he became chief of the Office of Strategic Services (OSS) in Switzerland, the foreign espionage agency, where he closely followed German dissidents' plans for the assassination of Hitler. He returned to practice law in Washington in 1945, and two years later, Secretary of Defense Forrestal asked him to compile a survey of U.S. intelligence operations. Dulles recommended that these activities be centralized, and thus became one of the chief proponents of the Central Intelligence Agency, which would succeed the OSS in 1947. Dulles also urged that the agency engage in covert activities.

Following Truman's victory in the 1948 election, Dulles, a Republican, had to give up his dreams of being secretary of state, a position he had been promised by Truman's defeated opponent, Thomas E. Dewey. Nevertheless, he kept busy fighting the Cold War, forming the Free Europe Committee, which created Radio Free Europe. After the outbreak of the Korean War, Dulles joined the government as Deputy Director of Operations at the CIA. In January 1953 Eisenhower named Dulles CIA director, and he would bring the agency into great prominence in fighting Communism during its heyday in the 1950s. When Dulles took over, the CIA was using East European émigrés to infiltrate behind the Iron Curtain for intelligence gathering and subversive activity, to little effect. Dulles steered the CIA to its greatest success outside Europe, where it acted covertly to overthrow two governments, in Iran (1953) and in Guatemala (1954). Such efforts imbued the agency's staffers with feelings of arrogance and invincibility, leading to the Bay of Pigs disaster in 1961. Under Dulles, the CIA also conducted unorthodox biological and chemical research. The program resulted in the death of at least one man from an LSD overdose, and continued to administer drugs to as many as fifty unwitting subjects until 1963. Other, less fatal experiments included a tunnel dug fifteen feet underneath Berlin to tap secret Soviet intelligence communications. Although the tunnel was discovered in 1955, both it and Dulles's clandestine U-2 spy plane project yielded enormous amounts of intelligence.

Following Khrushchev's secret speech denouncing Stalinism in 1956, the CIA sent edited versions of it abroad in order to destabilize foreign Communist parties. The Hungarian revolution that followed de-Stalinization drew great interest from the CIA, although the agency did little to help the revolutionaries. Still, émigré broadcasters at Radio Free Europe were enthusiastic onlookers, and the CIA was criticized for allowing expectations to be raised unjustifiably. Meanwhile, the President's Board of Consultants on Foreign Intelligence Activities examined the CIA and blasted its excessive zeal in covert operations, declaring that in countering the Soviets, "almost any action can be, and is being, justified."[2]

This report was prophetic. Dulles, who lost some of his zest for life after his brother died in 1959, did not follow the CIA's Bay of Pigs planning closely, and the U.S.-sponsored Cuban invasion was a disaster. He had to resign from office. He continued working as a consultant for the government, traveling to South Vietnam in 1962. Five years later, however, Dulles was a critic of the war, if a discreet one. He died on January 29, 1969, of complications brought on by pneumonia.

Mikhail Sergeyevich Gorbachev (1931–)

General Secretary and President of the Soviet Union

Mikhail S. Gorbachev was born in Privolnoe, Stavropol, Southern Russia, on March 2, 1931, to a peasant family. The 1930s were difficult times for peasants in Russia, and Gorbachev's paternal grandfather was sent to Siberia during collectivization, accused of not sowing enough grain. Gorbachev's maternal grandfather, however, became chairman of a collective farm.

While his father was away fighting in World War II, young Gorbachev worked in the fields. His exemplary agricultural work got him a spot at Moscow State University, where he enrolled in legal studies. He became a leader in the Communist Youth League or Komsomol, and joined the party in 1952. Three years later, he graduated with the Kalinin Prize, awarded to the second-best student in the school, and married Raisa Maximovna Titorenko. Just as Khrushchev had done before him, he returned home to begin the climb upward in Stavropol. Gorbachev was a strong believer in his country's economic and political system, but was no mere party hack. In the mid-1960s, unlike most provincial party men, he traveled to Europe, where he was impressed with the life-style and demeanor of Western peoples. Gorbachev's belief in the system would drive him to attempt to improve it once he got in power.

In 1970 Gorbachev became first secretary of the Party in Stavropol, a powerful position but one that he did not abuse. His outgoing personality and touting of his region's achievements helped him shine. Gorbachev's contribution to the successful harvest in Ipatovsky in 1978 landed him on the front page of *Pravda.* He also introduced some mild reforms during his term. Meanwhile, he cultivated a powerful mentor, Yuri Andropov, chairman of the KGB, who vacationed near Stavropol.

In 1978 Andropov brought Gorbachev to Moscow as secretary of the Central Committee in charge of agriculture, and he soon ascended to full member status in the Politburo. At the same time, Soviet agricultural output plummeted from 237 million tons in 1978 to 158 million three years later, aggravated by bad weather. As was typical in Soviet cultivation, crops rotted in the field and never got to market because of transportation and storage problems. Gorbachev's call for more private plots was not heeded.

Andropov became General Secretary upon the death of Brezhnev in 1983, and asked Gorbachev to examine the struggling Soviet economy with an eye to instituting some reforms. Andropov died in 1984, however, and was replaced by the rigidly Communist Konstantin Chernenko, Brezhnev's closest aide. It was only after the death of Chernenko, in March 1985, that Gorbachev—as General Secretary of the Communist Party—could effect reform.

Gorbachev identified the source of the country's endemic economic problems and technological backwardness in its culture. Yet *perestroika,* his economic program of restructuring, did not work. While meat and grain production increased, so did appetites, and more food had to be imported than ever before. Though *perestroika* did allow for more variety in consumer goods and offered limited opportunities for entrepreneurship, the Soviet people were not appreciative, perhaps because as part of his reforms, Gorbachev made it more difficult to buy liquor. As for *glasnost,* Gorbachev's initiative for openness to enable Soviet citizens to criticize the existing order, it was implemented only slowly. After the Chernobyl disaster in 1986, for example, the Soviet authorities were stingy with information.

As *glasnost* became more of a reality, it encouraged questioning of the system and destabilized the Soviet government.

Gorbachev required a period of peace to effect his program, and pursued a new relationship with U.S. President Ronald Reagan in order to lessen Cold War tensions. Beginning with their first meeting in 1985, the two leaders made important breakthroughs and in late 1987 agreed to dismantle all intermediate range nuclear missiles in Europe. Gorbachev also pulled out of Afghanistan in 1989, and in a profound break with his predecessors, ended the Soviet sphere in eastern Europe. When the Solidarity union in Poland toppled the Communist regime, he did not send in the Red Army. The other satellites followed, liberating themselves from Communist control at lightning speed.

At the same time, non-Russians in the Soviet Union began their struggle for independence. Soviet troops failed to quell the revolts. The Communist party lost its monopoly on power in 1990 after the first democratic election in Soviet history, and Gorbachev had to change his title to President of the Soviet Union. He survived a coup attempt in August 1991 by Soviet hard-liners who rejected his reforms and his "losing" of the empire. Yet Gorbachev's undying faith in Communism made him unpopular with Russians, who rallied behind Boris Yeltsin instead. Yeltsin had left the party in 1990 and become president of the newly sovereign Russian republic in June 1991, under a treaty that devolved power to the Soviet republics. Lacking a country, Gorbachev resigned on Christmas Day 1991.

If the demise of the Soviet Union was not something he had aimed for, Gorbachev had certainly made a signal contribution to ending the Cold War. Also key to undoing the Soviet empire were its overreaching global ambitions, its sclerotic political system, and the cost of waging the new technological Cold War, as heightened by Reagan's defense buildup. Gorbachev's *perestroika* could not reverse the years of decline, and *glasnost* allowed people to vote in free elections, where they did not choose Communists. Today, Gorbachev is still a sought-after speaker, especially in the West. He remains very unpopular in Russia, where he ran for president in 1996 and only garnered half a percentage point of the vote.

J. Edgar Hoover (1895–1972)

FBI Director

John Edgar Hoover, director of the FBI for nearly half a century, was born on New Year's Day, 1895, in Washington, D.C. He and his mother, Annie, were very close, and he lived with her until she died. After receiving his law degree at Georgetown University in 1917, Hoover went to work for the Justice Department, where he began pursuing left-wing subversives during the postwar Red Scare. After an anarchist blew up Attorney General A. Mitchell Palmer's house in 1919, Palmer created the Bureau of Investigation and put Hoover in charge of a crusade to round up domestic radicals, a pivotal step in his career path.

In 1921 Hoover was made Assistant Director of the Bureau, and three years later, became director of a new Federal Bureau of Investigation (FBI). In reaction to Red Scare excess, the agency did not pursue domestic radicals, and remained quiet until the 1930s, when the kidnapping of the Lindbergh baby created legislation that changed the agency's role from investigation to fighting crime. In 1936 Clyde Tolson became Hoover's chief of staff; he remained until 1972. The two were inseparable, sharing a "spousal relationship," but it is not known if this extended to a more intimate bond.[3] During this period, the director greatly expanded the Bureau's secret investigations of suspected subversives.

Hoover's Cold War role is perhaps his best known. He devoted an inordinate amount of energy to the fight against domestic Communism, neglecting other compelling problems, like organized crime. Hoover attacked Truman's approach to domestic security, and particularly his loyalty program. The FBI chief was much more comfortable with Eisenhower, who agreed with his emphasis on security concerns over civil liberties.

The order Hoover sought to maintain at the Bureau became part of his own routine. When his weight ballooned to two hundred pounds, he went on a diet—and then insisted that all of his agents meet the lower figure for their weight on the Metropolitan Insurance height/weight chart. His professionalism and dedication inspired many followers at the Bureau; he became synonymous with its works. Yet Hoover's position also gave him power over all Americans, and this power corrupted him. In 1964 and 1965, he used confidential information gained from wiretaps of Martin Luther King, Jr., to accuse the civil rights leader of being a "moral degenerate." By using such information, the man whose job it was to enforce federal law was breaking it. During the Vietnam War, radical elements of the antiwar movement helped expose and disgrace his repressive tactics. Hoover died on May 2, 1972, of natural causes.

Lyndon Baines Johnson (1908–1973)

36th U.S. President

Lyndon B. Johnson, U.S. President from 1963 to 1969, was born in Blanco, Texas, on August 27, 1908, son of a farmer-legislator and his cultured wife. Although Johnson's mother had the greater influence on him as a boy, he developed the habits of his father, with a penchant for rough speech and a distrust of intellectuals. After attending Southwest Texas State Teachers College, he became a school teacher in Cotulla—where the poverty he saw made a lasting impact on him—and in Houston. After participating in several local campaigns, he came to Washington in 1931 on the staff of Congressman Richard Kleberg. Three years later, he met and married Claudia "Lady Bird" Taylor. They would have two daughters. In 1935 Johnson became Texas' state director of the National Youth Administration, and in 1937 was elected congressman from his home state. After the Japanese attack on Pearl Harbor, he became the first congressman to join the Navy.

President Roosevelt quickly recalled him, along with all other congressmen in the service, but not before the Japanese shot at a plane Johnson was flying in. The war remained a pivotal experience in his life, and Johnson absorbed "the lesson of Munich" well—appeasement was a mistake, whether of Nazis or Communists. Johnson ran for the Senate in 1948 and won by just eighty-seven votes out of nine hundred thousand, which most historians regard as almost certainly a fraudulent victory. Skillfully working his way through the ranks, he became majority leader in 1955. Johnson had excellent political instincts and could extract information from people while making them feel privileged to share it.

In response to the launching of the Soviet satellite Sputnik in 1957, he helped create the National Aeronautics and Space Administration (NASA), and he also contributed to passage of the 1957 Civil Rights Act, which was mandated in part by Cold War priorities abroad. Although the bill did not enable any more Southern black Americans to vote, it set an important precedent for civil rights legislation.

Johnson became Kennedy's vice president in 1961, a position ill-suited to his ambitious nature, though he did some useful work in civil rights and space exploration in this post. After Kennedy's assassination in November 1963, Johnson entered the presidency. His interest in curbing poverty led him to implement the Great Society and its programs, including Medicare, Medicaid, urban aid, and job training. Along with the landmark civil rights and voting rights acts of 1964 and 1965, such measures made Johnson's administration memorable for its contributions to social reform in the United States.

Johnson was just as ambitious in fighting Communists in Vietnam. He wanted to emphasize the Great Society over the war, but declared, "If we let Communist aggression succeed in taking over South Vietnam, there would follow in this country an endless national debate . . . that would shatter my presidency, kill my administration, and damage our democracy."[4] Indeed, this was precisely what happened—*while* fighting Communism. Johnson sent 543,000 Americans to Vietnam, while downplaying this escalation and dissembling to the American people about its successes, thus fueling the divisive debate he had predicted.

As the preservation of South Vietnam became an increasingly questionable proposition and a symbol of the failure of containment, Johnson received conflicting counsels from his close advisers. In the wake of the North Vietnamese Tet offensive in January 1968, Johnson's support among the American people sank to 26 percent.[5] Continuous antiwar protests and the vote tallies from the early 1968 primaries demonstrated Johnson's unpopularity with both war supporters and opponents, and the president dropped out of the race unexpectedly on March 31, 1968. After he left office, Johnson returned to his Texas ranch, wrote his memoirs, and died on January 22, 1973.

George F. Kennan (1904–)

Diplomat and Author

George F. Kennan, the prominent U.S. diplomat who wrote the "Long Telegram" (see Document 2), was born February 16, 1904, in Milwaukee. Kennan's mother died shortly after his birth, and Kennan was raised by his strict Protestant father. He grew up a quiet, intellectual child, with an outlook of superior detachment to others and to the common culture that has remained with him through his life. He matriculated at Princeton University and joined the diplomatic service in 1926 to become the first bona fide specialist on Russia. Kennan married Norwegian Annelise Sorenson in 1931. The couple would have three children.

From 1933 to 1936 Kennan joined William Bullitt, the first U.S. ambassador to the Soviet republic, at the American embassy in Moscow. He returned in 1944 as minister-counselor of the embassy, aiming a critical eye at Soviet moves in eastern Europe. After the war, on February 22, 1946, Kennan wrote his "Long Telegram" to explain Soviet behavior. This influential document greatly enhanced Kennan's stature, and he went on to head the State Department's Policy Planning Staff (PPS). From that perch, Kennan wrote "The Sources of Soviet Conduct," which appeared pseudonymously in *Foreign Affairs* in July 1947. It called for a new approach—containment of the Soviet threat. But Kennan also endorsed diplomatic negotiations with Russia as long as they were "hard boiled."[6] He was an advocate of realism in foreign policy, and saw national power and interests as more important than idealistic concerns. He had little patience for public opinion.

The United States adopted containment as official policy, yet Kennan disagreed with the way it was put into practice, especially in the Third World. His views increasingly diverged from those of Secretary of State Dean Acheson. He opposed the development of NATO, because he favored German reunification and did not want to see a permanent division of Europe. He rejected the development of the hydrogen bomb, as he thought nuclear technology should be shared. And he was especially critical of NSC-68, which seemed to him to be based on worst-case projections. In early 1950 he was replaced as head of Policy Planning by Paul Nitze, who spearheaded the implementation of NSC-68, bringing one million more men under arms and close to $50 billion in spending.

Kennan went to the Institute for Advanced Studies at Princeton, but after the outbreak of the Korean War, he conducted discussions with Soviet envoy Jacob Malik to bring about an end to the conflict. In April 1952 he became U.S. ambassador to the Soviet Union, hoping to continue these negotiations, but an anti-American campaign in Moscow undermined his efforts. Kennan publicly criticized the Soviet government and became *persona non grata* in Moscow. Secretary of State John Foster Dulles, who felt Kennan's views were insufficiently hard-line, did not offer him another job.

Returning to the United States in the midst of the McCarthy period, Kennan was further convinced of the baleful effects of public opinion and considered leaving the country. Yet he continued to serve as a government consultant, though disagreeing with such initiatives as Germany's inclusion in NATO. To further his convictions, he made an abortive run for Congress in 1954, and then worked for the presidential candidacy of Adlai Stevenson in 1956. In the late 1950s, Kennan became an even more outspoken critic of Cold War diplomacy in a series of BBC lectures that called for German reunification, a negotiated settlement leading to the superpowers pulling out of Europe, and an end to nuclear weapons on the continent. Kennan's writing on these topics impressed John F. Kennedy, who made the diplomat ambassador to Yugoslavia in 1961. But after Josip Broz Tito's arrest of dissident Milovan Djilas, Congress enacted sanctions against Yugoslavia. Kennan resigned in disgust, and he never served the government again.

Although he initially supported U.S. intervention in Vietnam, in 1966 Kennan testified against it in the Senate. Many Americans came to agree with him as Vietnam ended the consensus over containment policy. In his later years, Kennan continued to support détente, oppose the arms race, and press for the United States to mind its domestic concerns. In his nineties, Kennan remains a prolific author and an irascible observer.

Nikita Sergeyevich Khrushchev (1894–1971)

First Party Secretary of the Communist Party and Premier of the Soviet Union

Nikita Khrushchev, leader of the Soviet Union from 1953 to 1964, was born in Kalinovka, Kursk, in Ukraine to a miner and his wife. Trained as a metal fitter, he joined the Bolsheviks after the revolution, and served in the civil war. He became Party Secretary in Yuzovka (now Donetsk) in 1925, and conducted party activity at the Stalin Industrial Academy in Moscow from 1929 to 1932, ostensibly while studying metallurgy. While in Moscow, he worked on the Metro subway system, before going home to take the post of Chairman of the Ukrainian Council of Ministers in 1944.

Five years later he returned to Moscow to lead the party organization, joining Stalin's closest confidants, who included Lavrenty Beria, Georgii Malenkov, Nikolai Bulganin, and himself. After Stalin's death in 1953, Khrushchev helped engineer the destruction of the scheming and ruthless Beria to become the effective leader of the Soviet Union, and in 1958 he was named both First Secretary and Premier. Emphasizing improvements in agricultural output, he conducted a massive "virgin lands" campaign to cultivate the steppes of Kazakhstan, planning to surpass the United States in butter and meat output by 1960–1961.

Despite such rivalry, Soviet-American relations improved under Khrushchev. In 1955 Khrushchev and his American counterpart, Dwight D. Eisenhower, held their first summit, in Geneva. Notwithstanding the rhetoric of a new "spirit of Geneva" between the two superpowers, the conference's results were limited.

Khrushchev is best known for his "Secret Speech," given at the Twentieth Party Congress in 1956. For the first time, a Soviet leader attacked Stalin's crimes, marking an end to the wide-scale executions in Russia characteristic of Stalin's reign. The resulting blow to Stalinist credibility decimated the ranks of foreign Communist parties, and upset Chinese leader Mao. Khrushchev also encouraged a "thaw" that allowed dissenters like Alexander Solzhenitsyn to publish. The prison gulag, however, continued until the 1980s.

In 1958 Khrushchev declared that Berlin must be incorporated into East Germany, launching the Berlin Crisis, which continued for the next three years. Despite the tension, Khrushchev traveled to the United States in 1959, where he was favorably impressed with Midwestern farms but found actress Shirley McLaine's dancing too decadent. U.S. Vice President Richard M. Nixon also visited Moscow that year to attend the Moscow Exhibition, and engaged in a famous debate with the Soviet premier over the quality and availability of American appliances.

These clashes over popular culture and economic prowess were benign, however, compared to the crisis that followed the Soviet shoot-down of Francis Gary Powers's U-2 spy plane on May Day, 1960. Eisenhower dissembled about the nature of the flight, and a furious Khrushchev canceled a planned summit. At the same time, he also attacked Mao at a conference in Budapest, as the rupture between the two Communist giants grew.

At the Vienna summit with President Kennedy in June 1961, Khrushchev again pronounced that he would sign a separate peace with the East German government to stop the exodus of its people to the West. The United States resisted, and in August, Khrushchev responded by building the Berlin Wall. The Soviet leader was aware that year that the Kennedy administration, after failing at the Bay of Pigs, was plotting to have Cuban leader Fidel Castro assassinated. For Khrushchev these schemes and the continuing Berlin issue only showed Washington's disrespect for Soviet prestige. Thus, in 1962 he installed forty nuclear missiles in Cuba to prevent another invasion and to preserve an ally and Communist showcase in the Caribbean. A U-2 plane spotted the missiles on October 15, leading to the Cuban missile crisis—the most hazardous encounter of the Cold War. After several rushed telegrams and a blockade, the United States got Moscow to dismantle the missiles in return for promising never to invade Cuba again. Khrushchev had avoided a deadly confrontation, but Castro seethed, as—for different reasons—did certain Kremlin officials. One of them groused, "Ask any one of our marshals or generals, and they will tell you that plans for the military 'penetration' of South America were gibberish, fraught with the enormous danger of war."[7] Owing to such sentiments, Khrushchev was ousted from power in 1964. He died seven years later.

Henry Kissinger (1923–)

Assistant to the President for National Security Affairs and Secretary of State

Henry Kissinger, President Nixon's and President Ford's National Security Adviser and Secretary of State, was born in Furth, Germany, on May 27, 1923. His family emigrated to New York when Henry was fifteen. He was drafted by the U.S. Army in 1943 and after the war attended Harvard on the G.I. Bill. He married Anneliese Fleischer in 1949. They had two children, but the marriage later ended in divorce. In 1954 Kissinger received his Ph.D. from Harvard, writing a thesis on Metternich and Castlereagh, two nineteenth-century diplomats and practitioners of "realpolitik"—the idea that power, rather than morality, is the key determinant of relationships among competing states.

At Harvard, Kissinger began working as a consultant for the U.S. Government, and led the CIA-funded International Seminar for scholars. At the invitation of philanthropist Nelson Rockefeller, he also began coordinating a Council on Foreign Relations study group that was researching ways to cope with the Soviet challenge in 1955. The outcome was *Nuclear Weapons and Foreign Policy*, a study that questioned the then-prevalent doctrine of massive retaliation, arguing that limited nuclear war could be fought and won. Kissinger's best-selling book generated much controversy and got him tenure at Harvard.

He hoped that his ideas would win over the Kennedy and Johnson administrations, for whom he served as a consultant, but his influence was marginal. From the sidelines, Kissinger critiqued American diplomacy as reactive, responding to crises as they happened rather than guided by a theory or system, and not taking sufficient account of the relative strength of other states. In 1968 he joined New York Governor Nelson Rockefeller's presidential campaign as foreign policy guru, calling for an opening to China and the Soviet Union as a way of detaching from the Vietnam War, and argued for negotiations with Hanoi.

Rockefeller failed to get the nomination, but the president-elect, Richard M. Nixon, hired Kissinger in November 1968. Kissinger overcame an aversion to Nixon, whom he thought was a hothead, to sign on as Assistant to the President for National Security Affairs. His and Nixon's views were indeed compatible; both men looked to détente for ending the Vietnam War and creating the framework for a new foreign policy.

Kissinger's prominence grew with his first visit to China in July 1971 and his meetings with North Vietnamese negotiator Le Duc Tho in Paris in 1972, the same year that he and Nixon traveled to China to open relations with that country. The following year, Soviet leader Leonid Brezhnev came to Washington, completing the diplomatic triangle. Kissinger became Secretary of State in August 1973, while remaining National Security Adviser. He dealt effectively with the Yom Kippur War that October, getting supplies to Israel, and subsequently began a shuttle diplomacy to the Middle Eastern capitals to restore peace and improve relations. In March 1974, he married Nancy Sharon Maginnes.

By the last year of the Nixon administration, détente was growing increasingly unpopular, as many Americans thought it was benefiting the Soviet Union more than the United States. As détente's key advocate, Kissinger was roundly blamed, yet he stayed on into the Ford administration as Secretary of State, though no longer National Security Adviser after October 1975. In April 1975 America's global position took a beating in

Southeast Asia, with the victory of the murderous Khmer Rouge in Cambodia and the North Vietnamese invasion of South Vietnam.

Kissinger had wanted to continue aid to South Vietnam, but Congress was not interested. Neither was the legislature keen to finance an American role in Angola, where a Marxist group was attempting a takeover after the Portuguese pullout. Kissinger had more success in Rhodesia, where he assisted in the negotiations for blacks' eventual accession of power from the white government in that country, now called Zimbabwe.

Since he left the White House in 1977, Kissinger has made a successful career as an international business consultant. During the Republican Convention in 1980, he briefly flirted with the notion of being Secretary of State for a Reagan-Ford ticket, but Reagan correctly surmised that Kissinger had "a lot of baggage" and chose George Bush, not Ford, as his vice president.[8]

Kissinger's successes in American diplomacy, including the improved relations with China and the Soviet Union, made him one of the greatest American diplomats of this century, despite the catastrophic end of the Vietnamese peace agreement. Yet his willingness to overlook the prerogatives of morality in diplomacy allowed him to nod at such initiatives as the expansion of the Vietnam war into Cambodia and the CIA intervention in Chile, and damaged his legacy.

Joseph Raymond McCarthy (1908–1957)

Wisconsin Senator

Joseph McCarthy, the Wisconsin senator whose name is indelibly linked with the excesses of the anticommunist crusade of the early 1950s, was born November 14, 1908, in Grand Chute, Wisconsin, to an Irish-Catholic farming family. He attended law school at Marquette University, and was remembered as a very likable, almost obsequious, young man, as well as an ambitious one. After graduation in 1935, McCarthy practiced law in Waupaca, Wisconsin, but upset many of its citizens by freely granting divorces; he maintained his living by poker playing. In 1936 he entered the district attorney's race in Shawano, Wisconsin, as an avid New Dealer. Defeated, he ran three years later for circuit judge, in what is universally described as a "dirty campaign" against a well-respected incumbent, Edgar Werner. Yet Werner was also an imperious judge, disliked by many younger attorneys, and McCarthy capitalized on this to win the race.[9]

After the war broke out, McCarthy became a first lieutenant with the Marine Corps. He spent most of the war in the Pacific as an intelligence officer, as well as an occasional volunteer gunner in combat missions. His combat record expanded with his age, from fourteen missions in 1944 to thirty-two in 1951.[10] In 1944, with the newly burnished image of a brave fighter (he would receive a host of medals, including the Distinguished Flying Cross) while in the South Pacific, he ran for the Senate as a Republican. Defeated, he ran again in 1946, this time crushing veteran Wisconsin politician Robert La Follette. He was proud of his reputation as an average "Joe," with his vices of drinking, gambling, and women. But his overexaggerated masculine image would become plain bullying before long.

McCarthy cultivated a circle of prominent anticommunist friends, including the Jesuit priest Edmund Walsh of Georgetown University, and J. Edgar Hoover, who was a gambling partner. He became nationally prominent in February 1950 when he gave a famous speech in Wheeling, West Virginia, charging the State Department with hiding 205 Communists said to be influencing the Department's policies toward the Soviet Union. McCarthy had no proof for his accusations, which were cobbled together from lists of suspected "security risks," and his repetition of them simply amounted to a strategy of the big lie. Yet for a time he enjoyed the support of powerful friends like Hoover. McCarthy garnered wide enthusiasm for alerting Americans to the Communist menace in the wake of the Hiss case, Rosenberg convictions, and the start of the Korean War. One of his key targets was a State Department adviser named Owen Lattimore, whom McCarthy insisted was a Communist agent. Lattimore, an expert on Asia, had been a sympathizer toward past Soviet policies, but he was no spy. Lattimore debunked McCarthy's attacks in Senate hearings, but to little effect. The senator only continued his outrageous smears.

McCarthy even tried to impugn the motives of Defense Secretary and war hero George C. Marshall, accusing him in 1951 of being part of "a great conspiracy" and comparing him with Stalin. Owing to McCarthy and others like him in government, many Americans lost their jobs, accused of aiding the Communist cause. It was risky to attack McCarthy, because he was popular among many segments of the American population—as an anticommunist, as a populist, and as an Irish Catholic.

In 1952 he was reelected and became chairman of the Permanent Subcommittee on Investigations. This prominent position would lead him to overstep himself, however, when his committee investigated Communist infiltration in the Army during 1953–1954. The Army in turn charged McCarthy with asking special favors for a staff member, G. David Schine, and the Senate held hearings on the matter. In the end, McCarthy's career was wrecked by the hearings, which resulted in his censure by the Senate. This turn of events was propelled by McCarthy's inept hiring of staff, the exposure of his methods by TV journalist Edward R. Murrow, and the extremely effective performance of the Democrats' attorney, Joseph Welch, in the hearings in 1954. By then, the senator's reckless accusations made even Hoover blanch. His ambitions had gotten the better of him, and he had few friends left.

Despite the censure, McCarthy considered a run for president in 1956. On May 2, 1957, four years after marrying Jean Kerr and less than a year after they had adopted a baby girl, McCarthy died of hepatitis, exacerbated by excessive alcohol consumption. He was just forty-eight years old. By then, Americans were beginning to lose interest in domestic Communists, whose number had shrunk to three thousand.

McCarthy lives on, however, because his name identifies an era and the excesses carried out in the name of fighting Communism in that period. These included the state and federal hearings and trials of suspected Communists in Hollywood, in schools and universities, and in many other walks of American life. McCarthy, more than anyone else, made anticommunism a term of opprobrium in America, and contributed as well to the polarization of American political life for the rest of the Cold War.

Richard M. Nixon (1913–1994)

37th U.S. President

Richard Milhous Nixon, U.S. President from 1969 to 1974, was born to a Quaker grocer and his wife in San Clemente, California, on January 9, 1913. Nixon grew up in difficult circumstances (two of his brothers died of tuberculosis), attended Whittier College and Duke University law school, and married teacher Pat Ryan. They had two daughters. He practiced law in Whittier, and after service in World War II, ran for Congress in 1946. He defeated his opponent, incumbent Jerry Voorhis, a former socialist and strong labor supporter, in a viciously anticommunist race.

Nixon was a strong supporter of the Truman Doctrine and Marshall Plan aid. A member of the influential House Un-American Activities Committee, in 1948 he coauthored the Mundt-Nixon bill to require all Communist and Communist-front groups to register in the United States. Nixon also doggedly pursued Whittaker Chambers' accusations against Alger Hiss when many of his colleagues wanted to drop the case (see Chambers' biography earlier), and this effort paid off when Hiss was found guilty of perjury.

In 1950 Nixon was elected to the Senate, using the anticommunist sword to impugn his opponent, Helen Gahagan Douglas. Two years later, he became Eisenhower's running mate, though he almost lost his position on the ballot owing to suspected financial misdealings. In a nationally televised speech, he held up his dog Checkers (a gift from a supporter), and pointed out that Pat wore only a "Republican cloth coat" because of their impoverished status. The Checkers speech and its origins were emblematic of Nixon's difficult relationship with the press. Nixon felt compelled to counter his foes in the media, and seemed unable to laugh at himself.

Nixon remained vice president through both of Eisenhower's terms and ran for president in 1960, losing by under 120,000 votes. In 1968 he made a comeback, and was elected president on a pledge to get out of the Vietnam War "with honor" and preserve law and order at home. Nixon, the hard-line anticommunist, chose to pursue détente with the Communist bloc in order to get out of Vietnam. At home, though his administration's rhetoric was anti–Great Society, it actually continued many of LBJ's social programs and created several new ones, like the Environmental Protection Agency and the Consumer Product Safety Commission, as well as expanded Affirmative Action policies.

Nixon quickly took steam out of the antiwar movement by ending the draft and beginning troop pullouts. However, many Americans were outraged to learn in 1970 that he had widened the war into Cambodia, and a protest at Kent State University led to tragedy that May. Subsequently, the antiwar movement diminished as Nixon's policy of Vietnamization won over most Americans. Neverthless, Nixon remained obsessed with his political opponents, using "dirty tricks" including harassment, wiretapping, and IRS investigations. During his reelection campaign in 1972, Nixon's staff broke into the headquarters of the Democratic National Committee at the Watergate complex. At first Nixon was able to squelch the story, but devastating revelations convinced a congressional committee to charge Nixon with obstructing justice and abusing his power to hurt domestic opponents. A White House tape showed that Nixon had been involved with the coverup of burglary from the beginning.

Nixon had two presidencies. One was a complete disaster, characterized by a man who betrayed the country's trust and sought to "get" his enemies. But there was also a statesmanlike presidency, and here Nixon's greatest achievement was reshaping U.S. foreign policy toward the Soviet Union and China. In the spirit of détente, he also wished to end the American role as global policeman, as expressed in his Nixon Doctrine (Document 12), as well as to replace the Cold War bipolar order with cooperation between the major economic powers of the world. But détente's legacy of lessened tensions did not last and generated much opposition domestically.

Rapprochement with the two Communist powers did assist the United States to exit from Vietnam, but the Vietnam peace agreement lasted barely two years. In the rest of the Third World, Nixon's diplomacy typically subordinated local interests to superpower concerns. In Chile, his administration helped overthrow the elected government of Marxist Salvador Allende in 1973. In the Middle East, the United States and Israel grew closer in ways that limited the Soviet role in the region. Iran became ever more dependent on American military aid. Thus, Nixon's methods were not a fundamental break with containment, and when détente proved disappointing, the Cold War continued more intensely than before.

The Watergate scandal led to Nixon's resignation from office on August 9, 1974. In his retirement, he wrote several books and traveled abroad as a goodwill ambassador for the United States. When Nixon died on April 22, 1994, he was mourned by many. The passage of time had significantly enhanced his reputation.

Ronald Wilson Reagan (1911–)

40th U.S. President

Ronald Reagan, U.S. president from 1981 to 1989, was born on February 9, 1911, in Tampico, Illinois, and grew up in nearby Dixon, the son of a devoted, religiously involved mother and an alcoholic shoe-salesman father. He discovered his talent for acting in high school. In 1932 he graduated from Eureka College, and became a strong Democrat after his father got a job in a New Deal program. While covering baseball spring training as a sportscaster in California in 1937, he took a successful screen test at Warner Brothers. He went on to star in such movies as *Knute Rockne-All American* and *King's Row*. After marrying actress Jane Wyman in 1940, he spent the war years making Army films.

Reagan first became aware of Communist influence in Hollywood during the war, and his concerns drove him to serve as an FBI informant. He also became active in the Screen Actors Guild, serving as its president from 1947–1952, where he purged Communists from its ranks. Reagan saw the Communists as a foreign conspiracy, and began carrying a gun to protect himself. Although he testified during the HUAC hearings in the 1950s, he did not name names.

He and Wyman divorced in 1949, and Reagan married Nancy Davis three years later. In 1954 he began working for General Electric as a goodwill ambassador, delivering homilies on the merits of free enterprise and the disadvantages of socialism, themes that he identified with throughout his life, and he became a Republican. The company dropped him in 1962, after he had spoken to the far-right John Birch Society. His acting career had also dried up by then.

Two years later, Reagan delivered a powerful address for the Republican presidential candidate, Senator Barry Goldwater, which sent $1 million into the Goldwater coffers. This new prominence led to Reagan's election as governor of California in 1966. He served two terms. In 1976 he ran for president but failed to gain the nomination. Four years later he was nominated and elected, and became one of the most popular presidents of the twentieth century.

In his foreign policy, Reagan followed in the path of the late Carter administration toward the Soviet Union. However, Reagan's optimistic personality and his abilities as the "Great Communicator" made for a sharp contrast with his dour predecessor. He sheathed his hard-line policy in inspiring idealistic rhetoric. The Soviet Union was to Reagan the embodiment of totalitarianism, particularly during the late Brezhnev era, when the United States and the Soviet Union seemed to be moving toward a new Cold War. In March 1983, Reagan identified the Soviet Union as "the focus of evil in the modern world."[11] He was convinced that American military weakness had put the United States at risk, and pushed through the largest peacetime buildup in American history, at a cost of almost $2 trillion during his first five years. His defense outlays and hawkish rhetoric spurred a nuclear freeze movement in 1982–1983. Reagan opposed the freeze, but also was uncomfortable relying on the deterrent of mutually assured nuclear destruction to protect the U.S. from Soviet attack. He proposed the controversial Strategic Defense Initiative, a shield against nuclear war designed to make atomic weapons obsolete. He also proved ready to make extraordinary concessions with the new Soviet leader, Mikhail Gorbachev, who came to power in 1985.

In Latin America, Reagan's policy was oriented toward the East-West conflict, and included intervention in Grenada in 1983; aid to the Nicaraguan *Contras*, an anticommunist insurgency, during the mid-1980s; the related Iran-Contra scandal in 1986, in which U.S. treasury funds were illegally diverted to the *Contras*; and the provision of $5 billion in military and economic aid to El Salvador, where Washington supported a right-wing government.

During Reagan's second term, especially in the wake of the Iran-Contra crisis, his posture moderated to some degree, a shift expedited by the arrival of Gorbachev. The two leaders made significant reductions in their respective nuclear arsenals, although the United States preserved its SDI option. In 1987 Reagan called for Gorbachev to tear down the Berlin Wall, and two years later, Germans dismantled it—after nearly three decades of serving as the most potent symbol of the Cold War. Though many scholars are rightly critical of Reagan for the Iran-Contra scandal and some of his domestic economic policies, he—along with Gorbachev—deserves a good deal of credit for ending the long Cold War.

After leaving the White House in 1989, Reagan oversaw the construction of his library in Simi Valley, California. But his hopes for enjoying an active retirement on his horse ranch were not met, because for the last few years he has been ill with Alzheimer's disease.

Josef Stalin (1879–1953)

General Secretary of the Communist Party of the Soviet Union

Leader of the Soviet Union from 1928 until his death in 1953, Josef Stalin was born on December 21, 1879, in the small town of Gori, Georgia, in the Russian Empire. Forced to attend a seminary, he soon rebelled and joined the Bolshevik wing of the Social Democratic Party. After the Bolsheviks came to power under the leadership of V. I. Lenin, Stalin became general secretary of the Communist Party, and emerged as sole leader by 1928.

He soon implemented a brutal economic program, which involved forced collectivization of agriculture and rapid industrialization. Millions died, and his oppressive treatment led his second wife, Nadezhda Alliluyeva, to kill herself in despair in 1932. A few years later, Stalin oversaw a monstrous purge, with the secret police arresting and executing old Bolsheviks, army officers, and Politburo members, among thousands of others. The Soviet effort in World War II represented a vital contribution for the Allies and left the Red Army in much of Eastern Europe, where the Soviets established satellite regimes. They also sponsored Communist movements in France and Italy, whose success was prevented by the CIA.

Yet Stalin was not reckless. In 1946, at Western insistence, he removed his forces from Iran and stopped pressuring Turkey for territory, and in 1948 he backed off when the Berlin blockade failed. Moreover, he did not send his troops into the Korean War, but urged Zhou En-lai of China to do so instead. He did not press where Western vital interests lay.

Nevertheless, on March 10, 1952, Stalin made an attempt to settle matters on the continent with a "Peace Note" that would have provided for a peace treaty for Germany, negotiated by a unified, neutral German state with all foreign powers leaving the country. Both U.S. Secretary of State Dean Acheson and West German Chancellor Konrad Adenauer feared that Stalin was trying to derail the Western alliance and its tight link to West Germany, and thus to weaken containment. Acheson responded to the note by calling for free elections for a unified German government, which the Soviets rejected.

Stalin died on March 5, 1953, from a stroke. The Soviet leadership continued to follow many of his legacies. It was xenophobic, obsessed with secrecy, and loyal to the dessicated Marxist dogma of revolution and anti-imperialism. The Communist party itself was made up of an encrusted elite. Nevertheless, the ruthless power of Stalin was never again duplicated. For most Russians, Stalin's reputation remains in the dustbin, romanticized only by those who see him as a leader who knew how to pull the country together, if brutally.

Mao Zedong (Mao Tse-tung) (1893–1976)

Chairman of the Communist Party of the People's Republic of China

Mao Zedong, founder and leader of Communist China for nearly three decades, was born to a prosperous farming family in Hunan province on December 26, 1893. Although his father forced him into marriage at fourteen, young Mao escaped and in 1915 enrolled in Teachers Training School in Changsha. He became a physical cultist, jumping into freezing ponds as his contribution to strengthening China, then constricted by foreign influence and internal weakness. These endurance swims later became a motif of his rule.

After the May 4th revolutionary student movement in 1919, and on the heels of the Soviet Bolshevik revolution, Mao participated in the secret first congress of the Communist Party of China in 1921. To others at the Congress, he appeared an unkempt and long-haired man from the country, though clearly highly intelligent. At that time, both the Communists and the Nationalist or Kuomintang party, led by Jiang Jieshi (Chiang Kai-shek), had unified to reform China, and Mao ran the Nationalists' Peasant Institute.

In 1927, however, the Chinese Communists suffered a terrible rout at the hands of the Nationalists, and Mao was fortunate not to be among the tens of thousands killed. Mao organized an army from the remnant. Soon, however, the Nationalists drove his forces out of their base in Jiangxi, and their Long March began to Yenan, six thousand miles away. This journey propelled Mao to become leader of the Chinese Communist Party in 1935. The chief problem for China then was the Japanese occupation, and Mao again united with the Nationalists against the foreign foe. Meanwhile, his Army grew to four hundred thousand men, and the party to two hundred thousand by 1940.

Mao began to acquire cultlike status among his followers, as he and Jiang returned to their previous hostility. Mao's troops had more success in drawing in peasants than did the city-based Jiang's, and after World War II a full-blown civil war broke out. By 1949, Mao's forces had driven the

Nationalist troops to Taiwan, and the Communist People's Republic of China was established on October 1. Mao's revolution would completely restructure this ancient society and send millions of Chinese to their deaths.

The United States refused to recognize Mao's government, and the Chinese leader asked Stalin for help. But he got only $300 million in credits—less than Russia gave to Poland. Insults continued, and Mao did not attend Stalin's funeral in 1953, the only Communist head of state not to do so. The following year he met with Khrushchev, who was alarmed in the wake of the Korean War at Mao's seeming eagerness to launch another conflict with the United States.

The differences between Mao and Khrushchev widened after Khrushchev attacked Stalin in 1956. Mao insisted that Stalin's mistakes were his own, not those of Communism. In 1958 he launched the Great Leap Forward, forcing five hundred million peasants into collectives and introducing a number of failed experiments, including backyard blast furnaces. Mass starvation ensued. Khrushchev thought that Mao's agricultural communes were harebrained, and by 1961 the Soviet leader pulled out his advisers. This slowed down China's nuclear program, and Beijing did not test its first A-bomb until 1964. The H-bomb followed three years later.

After the disaster of the Great Leap Forward, Mao allowed the economy to be freed up somewhat under the tutelage of Deng Xiaoping. Meanwhile, Mao prepared for a new crusade, the Cultural Revolution, in 1965, which recruited youths into the Army's Red Guards to attack the party as well as perceived bastions of privilege like the universities. The Red Guards soon were out of control, and millions died in the manic atmosphere before the leader reined in the Guards. He decided that universities were needed after all, if only for "science and engineering."[12]

Mao emerged from the Cultural Revolution with even more of a cult of personality—and his old associate Deng was purged, though still alive. Then, in the midst of a border war with Russia, Mao decided to end his hostile attitude toward the United States. President Richard Nixon was moving in the same direction. In 1972 Nixon and Henry Kissinger came to Beijing and met the Chairman and Zhou En-lai, his closest confidante. It was an amazing turn of events. The resulting relationship made it possible for China to enter the UN, taking Nationalist China's place on the Security Council, and also fostered Soviet-American détente, even if it did not appreciably alter the settlement reached in Vietnam.

Mao died on September 9, 1976, having unified a diverse country against incredible odds as well as completely reshaped its society and economy. Despite the opposing ambitions of Mao's wife, who thought that Deng

Xiaoping was "an international capitalist agent," Deng Xiaoping took over. He did indeed allow capitalism to flourish. But the country retains its stultifying political atosphere, and today Mao is again feted in a cult of personality.[13]

NOTES

1. See, for example, Allen Weinstein, *Perjury: The Hiss-Chambers Case* (New York: Knopf, 1978).

2. Quoted in Peter Grose, *Gentleman Spy: The Life of Allen Dulles* (Boston: Houghton Mifflin, 1994), 446.

3. Richard Gid Powers, *Secrecy and Power: The Life of J. Edgar Hoover* (New York: Free Press, 1987), 173.

4. Doris Kearns, *Lyndon Johnson and the American Dream* (New York: Harper and Row, 1976), 252.

5. See Melvin Small, *Johnson, Nixon, and the Doves* (New Brunswick: Rutgers University Press, 1989), 134–35.

6. Quoted in David Mayers, *George Kennan and the Dilemmas of U.S. Foreign Policy* (New York: Oxford University Press, 1988), 112.

7. Quoted in Aleksandr Fursenko and Timothy Naftali, *"One Hell of a Gamble": Khrushchev, Castro & Kennedy, 1958–1964* (New York: W. W. Norton, 1997), 353.

8. Quoted in Walter Isaacson, *Kissinger: A Biography* (New York: Simon & Schuster, 1992), 719.

9. Quoted in David M. Oshinsky, *A Conspiracy So Immense: The World of Joe McCarthy* (New York: Free Press, 1983), 22.

10. Oshinsky, *McCarthy*, 31.

11. See Document 15.

12. Quoted in Dick Wilson, *Mao: The People's Emperor* (London: Hutchinson, 1979), 403, 420.

13. Quoted in Wilson, *Mao*, 442.

Primary Documents of the Cold War

Document 1
WARTIME OUTLOOK ON POSTWAR EUROPE

This excerpt illuminates the State Department outlook in the waning months of World War II. At the time, Germany's defeat was nearly certain, even though several more bloody months would be required to assure it. The report predicted accurately that at war's end, the Soviet army would sit astride much of Europe, but the State Department was less prescient in its reckoning of the U.S. role. It suggested that the American position in the postwar world would be a limited one, with no troops in the Middle East, no position east of Italy, as well as no ideological role "which would give rise to great influence in Europe," a supremely wrong prediction! Instead, in the Middle East and eastern Europe, the major players were expected to be the Soviet Union and Britain. In itself, this outcome was not objectionable to Washington, but the United States looked on disapprovingly at the *way* in which the two powers jockeyed for position. In Washington's pre–Cold War thinking, *both* Russia and Britain were "ruthless," playing a "nauseating" game of power politics in the eastern Mediterranean.

The version of events delineated here is both strikingly at odds with the eventual outcome in the region, as well as surprisingly accurate. Contrary to the scenario painted in what follows, the United States did indeed pick up the British pieces in the Middle East after the war, and found Soviet attempts at entrenchment in the region to be of more concern than British "economic exclusiveness." Most significantly, the U.S. role in the postwar world would not be the limited one that the

State Department predicted. However, the statement is more prescient for eastern Europe, where many of the countries highlighted in the document did fall under Soviet influence, although the pattern of "friendly" governments generally meant puppet regimes, rather than the "good neighbor" model of U.S. client states in Latin America, and the United States turned out to be far less comfortable with the Soviet "sphere of influence" than this document would suggest.

Upon the German collapse, the following assumptions seem warranted:

1) The Soviet Army will be the most powerful on the European continent, and will occupy Europe up to a line which is substantially the longitude of Berlin and running south to the border between Yugoslavia and Italy. The southern limit of this occupation will probably be from the southern boundary of Bulgaria westward to the Adriatic, possibly dividing Albania.

2) The Army of the United States will be the second most powerful on the continent of Europe but, aside from the zone of occupation agreed upon in Germany, will have physical occupation only of lines of communication and ports. . . .

Politically, the Soviet government will have governments acting in substantial compliance with their desires in Poland, Rumania, Bulgaria, Czechoslovakia and Hungary. Such governments may also exist in Yugoslavia, Austria and Greece. On the collapse of Finland, a like government will exist in Finland, possibly also in Norway and Denmark, although the degree of influence in both places will be far less than in the other countries named. . . . These and other similar political arrangements will expand the Soviet influence far beyond the areas in which she could exert actual military force.

6) The British will be able to secure a large measure of compliance from the Governments of the Netherlands and Belgium, Denmark, Portugal and Greece. . . .

7) The degree of American influence in the situation will tend to diminish, though it will be maintained for a time through the hope of economic assistance. The United States has not yet become the protagonist of any set of ideas or set of policies which would give rise to great influence in Europe on doctrinaire grounds. . . .

THE UNDERLYING PROBLEM: THE EASTERN MEDITERRANEAN AND THE MIDDLE EAST

. . . From intelligence and other data at hand the conclusion seems warranted that:

The Soviet Union proposes to extend her influence south to the Persian gulf throughout its entire length, and westward to the Mediterranean, roughly as far west as Cairo. . . . They propose to have an influence analogous to that which the British now have in Iraq and the Levant states, and to extend their influence in Turkey. . . .

This must be taken in connection with the Soviet policy of extending its sphere of influence to the Adriatic through Rumania, Bulgaria, and Yugoslavia; and the probability that they will secure by some method an entry into the Aegean sea, either through Turkish territory, or through Thrace. As long as the latter was done through friendly agreement, few problems would be raised; but the Soviet doctrine that the governments must be "friendly" is still obscure. If it is meant that these governments must not engage in intrigue against the Soviet Union there could be no possible objection; if it is meant that, by subsidizing guerrilla or other movements, virtual puppet governments are to be established, a different situation would prevail.

The foregoing has set up an unresolved conflict between the Soviet aspirations and the British aspirations. The British see a threat to the empire life line, cutting them off from their Far Eastern interests including India, and reducing Britain from the status of a world power to the status of a strong Atlantic power. . . .

It may likewise be assumed that the British attempt to exclude the United States from the Middle East will continue, which is presently going on despite official denials in Whitehall and perhaps contrary to the personal policy of Winston Churchill. . . . The British assumption appears to be that in any major conflict arising out of this region, the United States necessarily will come to the support of Britain, irrespective of the fact that we shall have been excluded from the area (save perhaps a grudging acceptance of our oil interests in Saudi Arabia). . . .

[T]he policies and the measures must be adopted so that the United States shall be in the best position to deal with the situation should the unsolved conflict between the British and Soviet Union reach an open issue. . . . [T]he solid fact is that despite the negotiations in progress at Dumbarton Oaks, there is no visible diminution of the moves and countermoves on the ground, or of the tenacity with which both sides are pursuing nationalist objectives. Power politics is continuing between these countries today in the pattern made nauseatingly familiar by the Axis in 1935-1939.

THE AMERICAN POLICY

1. The General Objective. Accepting, without discussion, the self-limitations placed on the use of American force and the American influence east of Italy, it seems that we have to draw a careful line of policy based on the tools we shall actually have in hand. . . .

A Soviet "sphere of influence" in these areas operated in somewhat the same fashion as we have operated the good neighbor policy in Mexico and the Caribbean area would be no threat to anyone, and would raise no essential conflicts since it would not conflict with the basic interests of the peoples of these countries, nor with the operation of the British life line and the only casualty would be the attempt at economic exclusiveness sought by certain elements in the British Government. In this aspect it would make relatively little difference to us or perhaps to anyone else who had the dominant position. . . . [T]he basic concept behind such a policy is first the elimination of these countries as a center of power politics, and second a basic concern for the rights and situation of the populations of the countries involved.

Source: "Principal Problems in Europe." State Department Policy Committee, September 16, 1944. Author(s) unknown. (Adolf Berle Papers, box 70, State Department Subject File, FDR Library.)

Document 2
LONG TELEGRAM: THE CHARGÉ D'AFFAIRES IN THE SOVIET UNION (GEORGE F. KENNAN) TO THE SECRETARY OF STATE, MOSCOW, FEBRUARY 22, 1946

Perhaps the most important single primary source on the Cold War, this assessment of Soviet psychology, history, and conduct, and the recommended American response to it, has acquired near-legendary status, as has Kennan's subsequent pseudonymously authored article in *Foreign Affairs*, "The Sources of Soviet Conduct," which developed from the telegram and for the first time publicly called for "long-term, patient but firm and vigilant containment of Russian expansive tendencies."[1] Written in response to a query from the Treasury Department as to why the Soviets were not joining the International Monetary Fund or the World Bank, the telegram appeared at a pivotal moment, just as American policy toward the Soviet Union was becoming more openly critical, in a four-week period that included Winston Churchill's "Iron Curtain" speech and the U.S. demand that Soviet troops leave Iran (in perhaps the first application of the containment thesis). The Long Telegram both foreshadowed and influenced the harder line toward the Soviet Union that followed.

Kennan called here for "a more positive and constructive picture of [the] sort of world we would like to see than we have put forward in past," and a re-energized, morally strong, and disciplined American society to effect this, thus turning away from the passive and nonideological approach of Document 1, and underlining what he saw as the close connection between domestic and foreign policy.

Despite Kennan's repeated attempts to distance himself from the actual practice of containment that developed from his policy points that follow here, Kennan has become indelibly linked with this practice. Containment actually represented a more limited approach toward Russia than some in the American Congress wanted, because it accepted the current extent of Soviet power and called for evolutionary change rather than a rollback of this influence. It also seemed to concede the initiative to the Soviet Union, placing the United States in the reactive position. During the Korean War, General Douglas MacArthur rebelled against the limitations of containment doctrine in Asia and called for a more aggressive stance against Communism, but he was overruled.

Kennan's telegram, in sharp distinction to Document 1, attributes to the Soviet Union alone the status of threatening force, with Britain now part of the "Western World." Frank Costigliola has pointed out that by using "tropes of gender and pathology"—the Soviet Union described as a "rapist" bent on "penetration" and suffering from "psychosis"—Kennan's telegram "convinced many that the Soviet government was a monstrous force, fanatically committed to destroying the United States and the American way of life."[2] Ironically and unwittingly, perhaps, Kennan contributed to the very "hysterical anti-Sovietism" in the United States that he sought to mitigate.

At bottom of Kremlin's neurotic view of world affairs is traditional and instinctive Russian sense of insecurity. Originally, this was insecurity of a peaceful agricultural people trying to live on vast exposed plain in neighborhood of fierce nomadic peoples. To this was added, as Russia came into contact with economically advanced West, fear of more competent, more powerful, more highly organized societies in that area. . . .

It was no coincidence that Marxism, which had smoldered ineffectively for half a century in Western Europe, caught hold and blazed for first time in Russia. Only in this land which had never known a friendly neighbor or indeed any tolerant equilibrium of separate powers, either internal or international, could a doctrine thrive which viewed economic conflicts of society as insoluble by peaceful means. . . . In this dogma, with its basic altruism of purpose, they found justification for their instinctive fear of outside world, for the dictatorship without which they do not know how to rule, for cruelties they did not dare not to inflict, for sacrifices they felt bound to demand. In the name of Marxism they sacrificed every single ethical value in their methods and tactics. Today they cannot dispense with it. It is fig leaf of their moral and intellectual respectability. Without it they would stand before history, at best, as only the last of that long succession of cruel and wasteful Russian rulers who have relentlessly forced country on to ever new heights of military power in order to guarantee external security of their internally weak regimes. . . .

The Soviet regime is a police regime par excellence, reared in the dim half world of Tsarist police intrigue, accustomed to think primarily in terms of police power. This should never be lost sight of in gauging Soviet motives.

In summary, we have here a political force committed fanatically to the belief that with U.S. there can be no permanent *modus vivendi*, that it is desirable and necessary that the internal harmony of our society be disrupted, our traditional way of life be destroyed, the international authority of our state be broken, if Soviet power is to be secure. This political force has complete power of disposition over energies of one of world's greatest peoples and resources of world's richest national territory, and is borne along by deep and powerful currents of Russian nationalism. In addition, it has an elaborate and far flung apparatus for exertion of its influence in other countries, an apparatus of amazing flexibility and versatility, managed by people whose experience and skill in underground methods are presumably without parallel in history. Finally, it is seemingly inaccessible to considerations of reality in its basic reactions. For it, the vast fund of objective fact about human society is not, as with us, the means against which outlook is constantly being tested and re-formed, but a grab bag from which individual items are selected arbitrarily and tendenciously to bolster an outlook already preconceived. This is admittedly not a pleasant picture. Problem of how to cope with this force in [is] undoubtedly the greatest task our diplomacy has ever faced and probably greatest it will ever have to face. . . . I cannot attempt to suggest all answers here. But I would like to record my conviction that problem is within our power to solve—and that without recourse to any general military conflict. And in support of this conviction there are certain observations of a more encouraging nature I should like to make:

1) Soviet power, unlike that of Hitlerite Germany, is neither schematic nor adventuristic. . . . [I]t is highly sensitive to logic of force. For this reason it can easily withdraw—and usually does—when strong resistance is encountered at any point. . . .

2) Gauged against Western World as a whole, Soviets are still by far the weaker force. Thus, their success will really depend on degree of cohesion, firmness and vigor which Western World can muster. . . .

3) Success of Soviet system, as form of internal power, is not yet finally proven. . . . In Russia, party has now become a great and—for the moment—

highly successful apparatus of dictatorial administration, but it has ceased to be a source of emotional inspiration. Thus, internal soundness and permanence of movement need not yet be regarded as assured. . . .

For these reasons I think we may approach calmly and with good heart problem of how to deal with Russia. . . .

1) Our first step must be apprehend, and recognize for what it is, the nature of the movement with which we are dealing. We must study it with the same courage, detachment, objectivity, and same determination not to be emotionally provoked or unseated by it, with which doctor studies unruly and unreasonable individual.

2) We must see that our public is educated to realities of Russian situation. I cannot over-emphasize importance of this. Press cannot do this alone. It must be done mainly by Government, which is necessarily more experienced and better informed on practical problems involved. In this we need not be deterred by [ugliness?] of picture. I am convinced that there would be far less hysterical anti-Sovietism in our country today if realities of this situation were better understood by our people. . . .

3) Much depends on health and vigor of our own society. World communism is like malignant parasite that feeds only on diseased tissue. This is point at which domestic and foreign policies meet. Every courageous and incisive measure to solve internal problems in our own society, to improve self-confidence, discipline, morale and community spirit of our own people, is a diplomatic victory over Moscow worth a thousand diplomatic notes and joint communiqués. . . .

4) We must formulate and put forward for other nations a much more positive and constructive picture of sort of world we would like to see than we have put forward in past. It is not enough to urge people to develop political processes similar to our own. Many foreign peoples, in Europe at least, are tired and frightened by experiences of past, and are less interested in abstract freedom than in security. They are seeking guidance rather than responsibilities. We should be better able than Russians to give them this. And unless we do, Russians certainly will.

5) Finally we must have courage and self-confidence to cling to our own methods and conceptions of human society. After all, the greatest danger that can befall us in coping with this problem of Soviet Communism, is that we shall allow ourselves to become like those with whom we are coping.

Source: From U.S. Department of State, *Foreign Relations of the United States 1946* (Hereafter *FRUS*) Vol. VI: *The Soviet Union* (Washington: Government Printing Office, 1969), 699–709 *passim*.

Document 3
IRON CURTAIN SPEECH, WINSTON CHURCHILL, MARCH 5, 1946

"From Stettin in the Baltic to Trieste in the Adriatic, an iron curtain has descended across the Continent." These immortal words were spoken by British Prime Minister Winston Churchill in an address at Westminster College in Fulton, Missouri, on March 5, 1946. World War II with its Grand Alliance of the United States, Great Britain, and the Soviet Union, had not even been over a year. The speech foreshadowed the imminent shift in U.S. policy toward a posture critical of the Soviet Union. Churchill called his speech "The Sinews of Peace," but the "Iron Curtain" moniker has stuck.

He admonished his audience that Western weakness had encouraged Hitler's aggression in the 1930s, a mistake not to be repeated. This use of the Munich metaphor to stir the Western public to take a stand against Communist expansion would be duplicated by American policymakers all the way into the Vietnam War. Highlighting the pace at which eastern and central European governments had become Communist or were in the "Soviet sphere," Churchill called for unified Western resistance—predicting the containment theory that George F. Kennan would spell out a year later. Churchill dismissed the notion of preserving international security through a balance of power, which he thought would only offer "temptation" to an aggressor, and instead called for an "overwhelming" show of Western strength. U.S. policymakers would agree and enshrine this objective in NSC-68 in 1950 (see Document 15), though a balance of power in a bipolar framework was what kept the peace in the Cold War.

Despite his pessimism about the power of international organizations, Churchill still believed that an alliance of the Western democracies, supporting the United Nations Charter's principles of self-determination, was necessary to avoid "catastrophe." His romantic view here of the unity of "English-speaking" peoples was a direct pitch for an Anglo-American alliance to prevent further Soviet inroads, just as such a union, in conjunction with the Soviet Army as he gratefully recognized here, had helped defeat Hitler in World War II.

Neither President Harry Truman nor the American people were ready for such a security pact in early 1946. Nevertheless, Churchill's speech, coming just two weeks after Document 2, and amplified by Iranian protests that the Soviets had overstayed their wartime occupation in that Middle Eastern country, soon convinced Truman to turn in this direction. The United States extended a large low-interest loan to Britain in 1946, and followed this with Marshall Plan aid to Britain and other European countries, and created a formal Western alliance, NATO, in 1949.

A shadow has fallen upon the scenes so lately lighted by the Allied victory. Nobody knows what Soviet Russia and its Communist international organization intends to do in the immediate future, or what are the limits, if any, to their expansive and proselytizing tendencies. I have a strong admiration and regard for the valiant Russian people and for my wartime comrade, Marshal Stalin. There is deep sympathy and good will in Britain—and I doubt not here also—toward the peoples of all the Russias and a resolve to persevere through many differences and rebuffs in establishing lasting friendships. We understand the Russian need to be secure on her western frontiers by the removal of all possibility of German aggression. We welcome Russia to her rightful place among the leading nations of the world. We welcome her flag upon the seas. Above all, we welcome constant, frequent, and growing contacts between the Russian people and our own people on both sides of the Atlantic. It is my duty, however, for I am sure you would wish me to state the facts as I see them to you, to place before you certain facts about the present position in Europe.

From Stettin in the Baltic to Trieste in the Adriatic, an iron curtain has descended across the Continent. Behind that line lie all the capitals of the ancient states of central and eastern Europe. Warsaw, Berlin, Prague, Vienna, Budapest, Belgrade, Bucharest, and Sofia, all these famous cities and the populations around them lie in what I must call the Soviet sphere, and all are subject in one form or another, not only to Soviet influence, but to a very high and, in many cases, increasing measure of control from Moscow. Athens alone—Greece with its immortal glories—is free to decide its future at an election under British, American, and French observation. The Russian-dominated Polish government has been encouraged to make enormous and wrongful inroads upon Germany, and mass expulsions of millions of Germans on a scale grievous and undreamed of are now taking place. The Communist parties, which were very small in all these eastern states of Europe, have been raised to pre-eminence and power far beyond their numbers and are seeking everywhere to obtain totalitarian control. Police governments are prevailing in nearly every case, and so far, except in Czechoslovakia, there is no true democracy. . . .

I have felt bound to portray the shadow which, alike in the west and in the east, falls upon the world. I was a high minister at the time of the Versailles Treaty and a close friend of Mr. Lloyd George, who was the head of the British delegation at Versailles. I did not myself agree with many things that were done, but I have a very strong impression in my mind of that situation, and I find it painful to contrast it with that which prevails now. In those days there were high hopes and unbounded confidence that the wars were over, and that the League of Nations would become all-powerful. I do not see or feel that same confidence or even the same hopes in the haggard world at the present time. . . .

From what I have seen of our Russian friends and Allies during the war, I am convinced that there is nothing they admire so much as strength, and there is nothing for which they have less respect than for weakness, especially military weakness. For that reason the old doctrine of a balance of power is unsound. We cannot afford, if we can help it, to work on narrow margins, offering temptations to a trial of strength. If the Western democracies stand together in strict adherence to the principles of the United Nations Charter, their influence for furthering those principles will be immense and no one is likely to molest them. If however, they become divided or falter in their duty and if these all important years are allowed to slip away, then indeed catastrophe may overwhelm us all.

Last time I saw it all coming and cried aloud to my own fellow countrymen and to the world, but no one paid any attention. Up till the year 1933 or even 1935, Germany might have been saved from the awful fate which has overtaken her and we might all have been spared the miseries Hitler let loose upon mankind. There never was a war in all history easier to prevent by timely action than the one which has just desolated such great areas of the globe. It could have been prevented, in my belief, without the firing of a single shot, and Germany might be powerful, prosperous, and honored today; but no one would listen, and one by one we were all sucked into the awful whirlpool. We surely must not let that happen again. This can only be achieved by reaching now, in 1946, a good understanding on all points with Russia under the general authority of the United Nations Organization and by the maintenance of that good understanding through many peaceful years, by the world instrument, supported by the whole strength of the English-speaking world and all its connections. There is the solution which I respectfully offer to you in this address, which I have given the title "The Sinews of Peace."

Let no man underrate the abiding power of the British Empire and Commonwealth. Because you see the forty-six millions in our island harassed about their food supply, of which they only grow one half even in wartime, or because we have difficulty in restarting our industries and export trade after six years of passionate war effort, do not suppose that we shall not come through these dark years of privation as we have come through the glorious years of agony, or that half a century from now, you will not see seventy or eighty millions of Britons spread about the world and united in defense of our traditions, our way of life, and of the world causes which you and we espouse. If the population of the English-speaking Commonwealths be added to that of the United States, with all that such co-operation implies in the air, on the sea, all over the globe, and in science and industry, and in moral force, there will be no quivering, precarious balance of power to offer its temptation to ambition or adventure. On the contrary, there will be an overwhelming assurance of security. If we adhere faithfully to the Charter of the United Nations and walk forward in sedate and sober strength, seeking no one's land or treasure, seeking to lay no arbitrary control upon the thoughts of men; if all British moral and material forces and convictions are joined with your own in fraternal association, the highroads of the future will be clear, not only for us, but for all, not only for our time, but for a century to come.

Source: From Houston Peterson, ed. *A Treasury of the World's Great Speeches* (New York: Simon & Schuster, 1954), pp. 804–6.

Document 4
SPECIAL MESSAGE TO THE CONGRESS ON GREECE AND TURKEY: THE TRUMAN DOCTRINE, MARCH 12, 1947, AS DELIVERED BEFORE A JOINT SESSION

When the Truman Doctrine was announced and Congress implemented it in the Greek-Turkish aid bill of 1947, for the first time the United States was backing up the containment policy with both cold cash and warm bodies. With the British no longer able to support Greece and Turkey, two of their former clients in the British Mediterranean/Middle Eastern sphere alluded to in Document 1, Washington stepped into the breach and provided nearly half a billion dollars and a significant number of advisers at the request of the Greek and Turkish authorities. The Greek government, a reactionary and oligarchic regime, was threatened by what the United States considered as a worse alternative—Communist partisans. The United States believed that Stalin was behind the insurrection, but it was in fact chiefly backed by Yugoslavia's Josip Broz Tito. Over 350 American officers traveled to assist Athens against the Greek National Liberation Front (EAM). Turkey, meanwhile, was resisting Soviet demands to allow Russian access to the Black Sea and to internationalize the straits, a plan that the United States had originally supported but now saw as a dangerous concession to Soviet expansion, and U.S. aid and advisers would go to Turkey to aid in reconstruction. Truman drew a close connection between the existence of totalitarian regimes and American national security. Both

Greece and Turkey became part of the Western orbit and eventually joined NATO.

But the Truman Doctrine was more than a symbol of containment, for it also formed part of the policy of European economic reconstruction that the Marshall Plan would greatly augment with its implementation. American officials believed that this aid was necessary to fight Communism. Because Europeans badly wanted "security," whether supplied by capitalist West or socialist East, as Kennan had noted in Document 2, so too Truman saw that totalitarian regimes "spread and grow in the evil soil of poverty and strife," and he set out to limit those breeding grounds. Neither the Greek nor the Turkish government was democratic, as Truman concedes, but because they represented alternatives to Communist rule or Communist domination, Truman justified the program as part of an American effort to "help free peoples to maintain their free institutions."

The United States has received from the Greek Government an urgent appeal for financial and economic assistance. Preliminary reports from the American Economic Mission now in Greece and reports from the American Ambassador in Greece corroborate the statement of the Greek Government that assistance is imperative if Greece is to survive as a free nation. . . .

When forces of liberation entered Greece they found that the retreating Germans had destroyed virtually all the railways, roads, port facilities, communications, and merchant marine. More than a thousand villages had been burned. Eighty-five percent of the children were tubercular. Livestock, poultry, and draft animals had almost disappeared. Inflation had wiped out practically all savings.

As a result of these tragic conditions, a militant minority, exploiting human want and misery, was able to create political chaos which, until now, has made economic recovery impossible. . . . The very existence of the Greek state is today threatened by the terrorist activities of several thousand armed men, led by Communists, who defy the government's authority at a number of points, particularly along the northern boundaries. . . . Meanwhile the Greek government is unable to cope with the situation. The Greek army is small and poorly equipped. It needs supplies and equipment if it is to restore authority to the government throughout Greek territory.

Greece must have assistance if it is to become a self-supporting and self-respecting democracy.

The U.S. must supply this assistance. . . .

There is no other country to which democratic Greece can turn. . . . The British Government, which has been helping Greece, can give no further financial or economic aid after March 31. Great Britain finds itself under the necessity of reducing or liquidating its commitments in several parts of the world, including Greece. . . .

The Greek government has been operating in an atmosphere of chaos and extremism. It has made mistakes. The extension of aid by this country does not mean that the U.S. condones everything that the Greek Government has done or will do. We have condemned in the past, and we condemn now, extremist measures of the right or the left. . . .

Greece's neighbor, Turkey, also deserves our attention.

. . . Since the war Turkey has sought additional financial assistance from Great Britain and the United States for the purpose of effecting that modernization necessary for the maintenance of its national integrity. That integrity is essential to the preservation of order in the Middle East. The British Government has informed us that, owing to its own difficulties, it can no longer extend financial or economic aid to Turkey. . . .

I am fully aware of the broad implications involved if the United States extends assistance to Greece and Turkey, and I shall discuss these implications with you at this time.

One of the primary objectives of the foreign policy of the United States is the creation of conditions in which we and other nations will be able to work out a way of life free from coercion. This was a fundamental issue in the war with Germany and Japan. Our victory was won over countries which sought to impose their will, and their way of life, upon other nations. To impose the peaceful development of nations, free from coercion, the United States has taken a leading part in establishing the United Nations. . . . We shall not realize our objectives, however, unless we are willing to help free peoples to maintain their free institutions and their national integrity against aggressive movements that seek to impose upon them totalitarian regimes. This is no more than a frank recognition that totalitarian regimes imposed upon free peoples, by direct or indirect aggression, undermine the foundations of international peace and hence the security of the United States.

The peoples of a number of countries of the world have recently had totalitarian regimes forced upon them against their will. The government of the United States has made frequent protests against coercion and intimidation, in violation of the Yalta agreement, in Poland, Rumania, and Bulgaria. I must also state that in a number of other countries there have been similar developments.

At the present moment in world history nearly every nation must choose between alternative ways of life. The choice is too often not a free one.

One way of life is based upon the will of the majority, and it distinguished by free institutions, representative government, free elections, guarantees of individual liberty, freedom of speech and religion, and freedom from political oppression. The second way of life is based upon the will of a minority forcibly imposed upon the majority. It relies upon terror and oppression, a controlled press and radio, fixed elections, and the suppression of personal freedoms.

I believe that it must be the policy of the U.S. to support free peoples who are resisting attempted subjugation by armed minorities or by outside pressures. . . .

We must take immediate and resolute action.

I, therefore, ask the Congress to provide authority for assistance to Greece and Turkey in the amount of $400,000,000 for the period ending June 30, 1948. . . .

In addition to these funds, I ask the Congress to authorize the detail of American civilian and military personnel to Greece and Turkey, at the request of those countries, to assist in the tasks of reconstruction, and for the purpose of supervising the use of such financial and material assistance as may be furnished. . . .

This is a serious course upon which we embark.

I would not recommend it except that the alternative is much more serious.

The United States contributed $341,000,000,000 toward winning World War II. This is an investment in world freedom and world peace.

The assistance that I am recommending for Greece and Turkey amounts to little more than one-tenth of 1 percent of this investment. It is only common sense that we should safeguard this investment and make sure that it was not in vain.

The seeds of totalitarian regimes are nurtured by misery and want. They spread and grow in the evil soil of poverty and strife. They reach their full growth when the hope of a people for a better life has died.

We must keep that hope alive.

Source: Public Papers of the Presidents: Harry S. Truman, 1947 (Washington: Government Printing Office, 1963), pp. 176–80.

Document 5
MARSHALL PLAN

Secretary of State George C. Marshall spoke at Harvard University's commencement in June 1947. In a departure from American policy after World War I, Marshall's remarks emphasized the need for U.S. assistance to war-torn Europe, in a logical progression from the Truman Doctrine. The United States was best able to provide this assistance;

the Europeans were in the optimum position to know what they needed. Though not mentioning the Soviets by name, Marshall hinted at the possibility that some "political parties" would profit from the weakness in Europe, and vowed opposition to their approach. He clearly identified here the devastation that Kennan and Truman had both alluded to in their "diseased tissue" and "evil soil" metaphors. As approved by Congress, his plan provided for $12 billion to rebuild Europe, restore trade, and lower inflation, as well as to create greater stability and unity in Europe, under the auspices of the European Recovery Plan (ERP) and its administration. As a result of the ERP, the United States transferred American liberal values to Europe, including, as historian Michael Hogan notes, "practical plans for liberalizing trade and payments, building central institutions of coordination and control, and . . . public-private partnerships."[3] The United States invited the Soviet Union and its satellites to join, but the requirements of affiliation (a willingness to allow MP officials to monitor and exert influence over the recipient country's economy) was not something the Soviets would contemplate. They further forbade their satellite countries from becoming part of the plan.

I need not tell you gentlemen that the world situation is very serious. That must be apparent to all intelligent people. I think one difficulty is that the problem is one of such enormous complexity that the very mass of facts presented to the public by press and radio make it exceedingly difficult for the man in the street to reach a clear appraisement of the situation. Furthermore, the people of this country are distant from the troubled areas of the earth and it is hard for them to comprehend the plight and consequent reactions of the long-suffering peoples, and the effect of those reactions on their governments in connection with our efforts to promote peace in the world.

In considering the requirements for the rehabilitation of Europe the physical loss of life, the visible destruction of cities, factories, mines and railroads was correctly estimated, but it has become obvious during recent months that this visible destruction was probably less serious than the dislocation of the entire fabric of European economy. For the past 10 years conditions have been highly abnormal. The feverish preparations for war and the more feverish maintenance of the war effort engulfed all aspects of national economies. Machinery has fallen into disrepair or is entirely obsolete. Under the arbitrary and destructive Nazi rule, virtually every possible enterprise was geared into the German war machine. Long-standing commercial ties, private institutions, banks, insurance companies and shipping companies disappeared, through the loss of capital, absorption through nationalization or by simple destruction. In many countries, confidence in the local currency has been severely shaken. The breakdown of the business structure of Europe during the war was complete. Recovery has been seriously retarded by the fact that two years after the close of hostilities a peace settlement with Germany and Austria has not been agreed upon. But even given a more prompt solution of these difficult problems, the rehabilitation of the economic structure of Europe quite evidently will require a much longer and greater effort than had been foreseen. . . .

The town and city industries are not producing adequate goods to exchange with the food-producing farmer. . . . The farmer or the peasant cannot find the goods for sale which he desires to purchase. So the sale of his farm produce for money which he cannot use seems to him an unprofitable transaction. . . . Meanwhile people in the cities are short on food and fuel. So the governments are forced to use their money and credits to procure these necessities abroad. This process exhausts funds which are urgently needed for reconstruction. Thus a very serious situation is rapidly developing which bodes no good for the world. The modern system of the division of labor upon which the exchange of products is based is in danger of breaking down.

The truth of the matter is that Europe's requirements of the next three or four years of foreign food and other essential products—principally from America—are so much greater than her present ability to pay that she must have substantial additional help, or face economic, social and political deterioration of a grave character.

The remedy lies in breaking the vicious circle and restoring the confidence of the European people in the economic future of their own countries and of Europe as a whole. . . .

Aside from the demoralizing effect on the world at large and the possibilities of disturbances arising as a result of the desperation of the people concerned, the consequences to the economy of the United States should be apparent to all. It is logical that the United States should do whatever it is able to do to assist in the return of normal economic health to the world, without which there can be no political stability and no assured peace. Our policy is directed not against any country or doctrine but against hunger, poverty, desperation, and chaos. Its purpose should be the revival of a working economy in the world so as to permit the emergence of political and social conditions in which free institutions can exist. Such assistance, I am convinced, must not be on a piece-meal basis as various crises develop. Any assistance that this Government may render in the future should provide a cure rather than a mere palliative. Any government that is willing to assist in the task of recovery will find full cooperation, I am sure, on the part of the United States Government. Any government which maneuvers to block the recovery of other countries cannot expect help from us. Furthermore, governments, political parties or groups which seek to perpetuate human misery in order to profit therefrom politically or otherwise will encounter the opposition of the United States.

It is already evident that, before the United States Government can proceed much further in its efforts to alleviate the situation and help start the European world on its way to recovery, there must be some agreement among the countries of Europe as to requirements of the situation and the part those countries themselves will take. . . . It would be neither fitting nor efficacious for this Government to undertake to draw up unilaterally a program designed to place Europe on its feet economically. This is the business of the Europeans. The initiative, I think, must come from Europe. The role of this country could consist of friendly aid in the drafting of a European program and of later support of such a program so far as it may be practical for us to do so. The program should be a joint one, agreed to by a number, if not all European nations.

An essential part of any successful action on the part of the United States is an understanding on the part of the people of America of the character of the problem and remedies to be applied. Political passion and prejudice should have no part. With foresight and a willingness on the part of our people to face up to the vast responsibility which history has clearly placed upon our country, the difficulties I have outlined can and will be overcome.

Source: FRUS 1947: V. 3: *The British Commonwealth; Europe* (Washington: Government Printing Office, 1972): 237–39.

Document 6
ENTERTAINMENT AND THE COLD WAR

As the containment doctrine was carried out abroad through such measures as the Truman Doctrine and Marshall Plan, anticommunist sentiment was heating up at home in 1947. In Congress, the House Un-American Activities Committee began hearings on Communist influence in American entertainment, calling forth a series of witnesses and sending some artists to jail. Though some witnesses refused to speak, using their Fifth Amendment rights against self-recrimination, Ayn Rand was among those who served as friendly witnesses for the committee. She testified about the film, *Song of Russia*, which as a World War II vehicle cast Soviet Russia and its collective farms in a decidedly idealized light.

Rand, the former Alissa Rosenbaum, was a Russian émigré who came to the United States in the 1920s, was an extra and then a screenwriter in Hollywood, and went on to found the Objectivist movement, an ideology with an emphasis on individualism and human achievement that distinguished itself most sharply with all forms of socialism and collectivism, even the New Deal, as her emphatic defense of capitalism and the profit motive indicates in what follows. She wrote several works glorifying ambitious men who fulfilled their achievements alone, unfettered by any state interference or meddlesome altruists, in such novels as *The Fountainhead* (1943) and *Atlas Shrugged* (1957) as well as in many polemical tracts. Here she defends the free enterprise system, which she argues is as much a part of "Americanism" as are civil liberties and free speech, and this was also reflected in her criticism of the movie *The Best Years of Our Lives* (1946), which portrayed a banker in an unsympathetic way. Rand emphasized that the Communist agenda in movies could be very subtle—so that even an attack on the motives of businessmen or a glorifying of the poor served the Communists in her telling. Rand was prominent in her attempts to keep movies "clean" of such influences. Her pamphlet, "Screen Guide for Americans," would be published on the front page of the *New York Times* entertainment section.[4]

It is the avowed purpose of the Communists to insert propaganda into movies. Therefore, there are only two possible courses of action open to you, if you want to keep your pictures clean of subversive propaganda:

1. If you have no time or inclination to study political ideas—then do not hire Reds to work on your pictures.

2. If you wish to employ Reds, but intend to keep their politics out of your movies—then study political ideas and learn how to recognize propaganda when you see it. . . .

Don't pretend that Americanism and the Free Enterprise System are two different things. They are inseparable, like body and soul. The basic principle of inalienable individual rights, which is Americanism, can be translated into practical reality only in the form of the economic system of Free Enterprise. . . . You may preach any other form of economics, if you wish. But if you do so, don't pretend that you are preaching Americanism. . . . Throughout American history, the best of American industrialists were men who embodied the highest virtues: productive genius, energy, initiative, independence, courage. . . . Yet all too often industrialists, bankers, and businessmen are presented on the screen as villains, crooks, chiselers, or exploiters. . . . It is a basic American principle that each man is free to work for his own benefit and to go as far as his ability will carry him; and his property is his—whether he has made one dollar or one million dollars. . . . If you do not see the difference between wealth honestly produced and wealth looted—you are preaching the idea of Communism. You are implying that all property and all human labor should belong to the State. . . . It is the proper wish of every decent American to stand on his own feet, earn his own living. . . . get as rich as he can by honest exchange. Stop insulting him and stop defaming his proper ambition. Stop giving him—and yourself—a guilt complex by spreading unthinkingly the slogans of Communism. Put an end to that pernicious modern hypocrisy: everybody wants to get rich and almost everybody feels he must apologize for it. . . .

If what you mean, when you denounce [the profit motive] is a desire to make money dishonestly or immorally-then say so. . . . Make it clear that you are denouncing evildoers, not capitalists. . . .

There are many forms of success: spiritual, artistic, industrial, financial. . . . Don't permit any disparagement or defamation of personal success. It is the Communists' intention to make people think that personal success is somehow achieved at the expense of others. . . . It is the Communists' aim to discourage all personal effort and to drive men into a hopeless, dispirited, gray herd of robots who have lost all personal ambition, who are easy to rule, willing to obey, and willing to exist in selfless servitude to the state. . . .

Don't present all the poor as good and all the rich as evil. In judging a man's character, poverty is no disgrace—but it is no virtue either; wealth is no virtue—but it is certainly no disgrace. . . .

Remember that America is the country of the pioneer, the non-conformist, the inventor. . . . Remember that all the great thinkers, artists, scientists were single, individual, independent men who stood alone and discovered new directions of achievement—alone. . . .

Of all current questions, be most careful about your attitude toward Soviet Russia. You do not have to make pro-Soviet and anti-Soviet pictures, if you do not wish to take the stand. But if you claim that you wish to remain neutral, don't stick into pictures casual lines favorable to Soviet Russia. . . . Don't suggest to the audience that the Russian people are freed, secure, and happy, that life in Russia is just about the same as in any other country—while actually the Russian people live in constant terror under a bloody, monstrous dictatorship. Look out for speeches that support whatever is in the Soviet interests of the moment, whatever is part of the current Communist party line. . . .

The principle of free speech does not require that we furnish the Communists with the means to preach their ideas, and does not imply that we owe them jobs and support to advocate our own destruction at our own expense. The Constitution guaranty of free speech reads: "Congress shall pass no laws. . . ." It does not require employers to be suckers.

Source: "Screen Guide for Americans," by Ayn Rand, with assistance from the Editorial Board of the Motion Picture Alliance for the Preservation of American Ideals, *Plain Talk* (November 1947), republished in Isaac Don Levine, ed., *Plain Talk: An Anthology of the Leading Anti-Communist Magazine of the 40s* (New Rochelle, N.Y.: Arlington House, 1976), pp. 387–93.

Document 7
WHO LOST CHINA?

In August 1949, after several years of ineffective American aid to the Nationalist forces in China, Secretary of State Dean Acheson wrote a lengthy analysis known as the China White Paper, stating in essence that the United States had done all that it could and that the fate of China was up to the Chinese themselves to decide. By then, Mao Zedong's (Mao Tse-tung) Communists were clearly dominating the field, and their People's Republic of China was established the following month. Despite the weakness and corruption of Jiang Jieshi's (Chiang Kai-shek) Nationalist regime, many Americans were outraged by Acheson's statement, believing that more could have been done and seeing the State Department as facilitating the "fall" of China to Communism. Evocation of the "China myth," that the United States had a special responsibility to rescue China dating back to the nineteenth century, is clear in what follows. Isaac Don Levine, editor of *Plain Talk*, a conservative journal of opinion in the late 1940s, here takes issue with Acheson's assessment that China's fate was a Chinese problem, driven by Chinese developments, and that the United States and other powers stood outside and could not affect these developments.

Levine's response to the White Paper reflects his view of the importance of Asia to American security, as well as his keen opposition to China's fate. He and other anticommunist activists (sometimes called the "China lobby") were greatly disturbed at what they perceived as a less than rigorous approach to Asian Communism in comparison to that in Europe—there was no Marshall Plan for Asia, for instance. He even gets in a swipe at the Marshall Plan ("Dollars and more dollars") as lacking sufficient "vision." His broad concept of American defense—"wherever the Communist power is"—underlay the thinking that led the United States into such ambitious military missions as Vietnam.

China's "fall" became an issue that made some officials, like Owen Lattimore and John Stewart Service, targets of McCarthyist attack—as hinted in Levine's cutting remarks about "experts" in the following. Levine compares the U.S. State Department here unfavorably with both Stalin and Mussolini. China's turn to Communism was seen as yet another domino in the Soviet monolith. Yet the Communist Chinese soon were at odds with the Soviets, who treated them patronizingly and gave them insufficient aid. Within a decade, the two powers had suffered a nasty split. The United States, meanwhile, maintained ties with the Nationalist Chinese on Taiwan and did not open relations with mainland China until 1972.

When Secretary of State Acheson declared before the Senate Foreign Relations and Armed Services Committees that America's "first line of defense is still in Europe," he exposed the chaos which underlies our foreign policy. . . .

With the deluge of the Second World War behind us, our first line of defense is wherever the Communist power is. That should be the keystone of any foreign policy. But if we must deal with geographic concepts in relation to our defense, let us at least deal with postwar realities.

It is arguable whether the people of the United States would go to war should there be a Soviet seizure of power, on the order of the Czechoslovak coup, in Finland or in Norway. But most sober observers would agree that a Communist coup in the Philippines, resulting in the establishment in Manila of a Soviet regime, would drive the American people into a war of national defense. . . .

First and foremost is the question: Why the White Paper now? . . . [T]he position of Nationalist China at the beginning of August, on the eve of the release of the White Paper, was grave but not hopeless. . . .

It is known that China's ambassador in Washington, Dr. Wellington Koo, had called at the White House weeks before the White Paper was issued and posed the following questions, in effect, before President Truman:

"Why should the United States strike a finishing blow with its White Paper at the Nationalist forces while they are desperately struggling to hold the surging Communist armies? Was it the intent of the U.S. to speed the victory of the Communist elements? And was not the U.S. officially committed to a policy of containing and combating Soviet aggression and Communist expansion throughout the world?" . . .

How and why President Truman came to yield to the Far Eastern "experts" in the State Department will undoubtedly make fascinating reading at some future date. But the step taken by Secretary Acheson has climaxed our unsavory record of Teheran, Yalta, and Potsdam with a leaf from the book of rapacious despots. There was far more justification for Stalin's last-minute attack on Japan and even more extenuation for Mussolini's stab in the back of France than there was for our using at this hour the dagger of the White Paper on sick China. . . .

At best our present course of 'normalization' is calculated to achieve a stalemate, with Moscow in control of nearly half of Western Europe and most of Asia. Such a state of affairs condemns the world to chronic crises, to economic and political fits, and puts a fatal burden upon America.

Instead of re-arming a crippled western Europe, let us disarm the Red Army. This can be achieved at a fraction of the cost of the new arms program by encouraging, through inducements to resettlement, the mass desertion of soldiers and able-bodied men from the Soviet zones which would undermine the Soviet edifice from within.

Let us boldly pick up the banner of Asian liberation and independence. With Japan extinct as a sea power and in our camp, we can wield a weapon against the Soviets in China which would make the Kremlin aggressors run to cover in no time. General MacArthur, moved from Tokyo to Formosa or Chungking, could turn the Japanese weapon to most effective use.

The White Paper is a denial of the existence of a will to save Asia. The White Paper is at best a testimonial to spinelessness and a confession of guilty conduct in the past. . . . It is one more alarming token of a colossus adrift, of an America guided abroad by men who would buy precarious peace piecemeal with dollars and more dollars rather than steer the world toward a stable peace with vision, with initiative, with courage, with honor.

Source: "Our First Line of Defense," by Isaac Don Levine, *Plain Talk* (September 1949), in Don Levine, ed., *Plain Talk: An Anthology of the Leading Anti-Communist Magazine of the 40s* (New Rochelle, N.Y.: Arlington House, 1976), pp. 45–50.

Document 8
NSC-68 (NATIONAL SECURITY COUNCIL PAPER #68)

After the Soviet atomic bomb blast and the success of the Communists in China, Truman called for action. In January 1950 he issued a directive to the State and the Defense Departments "to undertake a reexamination of our objectives in peace and war and of the effect of these objectives in our strategic plans, in the light of the probable fission bomb capability of the Soviet Union."[5]

Paul Nitze, Kennan's successor as director of the Policy Planning Staff at State, and other officials recommended a strong response in their National Security Council Paper 68. The report inaccurately and simplistically painted a Communist monolith bent on world conquest, embroidering the Soviet threat to an inordinate degree and explicitly calling for systematic economic and military measures to frustrate the Kremlin "by the strategy of the cold war." The document called for both creating a "healthy international community" and for containment—and negotiations, too, once a "start" had been made toward those goals. It recommended a huge new outlay in arms. The Korean War, which began in June 1950, provided the justification for the increase.

Unlike Kennan's Long Telegram, which had expressed doubt that the Soviets were reckless enough to attack and noted their respect for counterforce, the NSC-68 authors were less interested in Soviet intentions than in Soviet capabilities—which they magnified in order to create the impetus for increased spending. As John Lewis Gaddis writes, this exaggeration was part of an ethos in the government that "in periods of mortal peril [traditionally acceptable] standards could not stand in the way of whatever seemed required to defend national security." The safety of the United States and "of an external environment conducive to it" meant that "anything," including an egregious overestimation of the Soviet threat, both domestically and abroad, was appropriate as long as it contributed to supporting containment.[6] NSC-68 was not shy to cite "ideological considerations" in promoting its vision in American foreign policy, calling for the United States "to build a successfully functioning political and economic system in the free world." This document thus continued the path toward activist diplomacy launched with the Long Telegram.

Two complex sets of factors have now basically altered th[e] historical distribution of power. First, the defeat of Germany and Japan and the decline of the British and French Empires have interacted with the development of the United States and the Soviet Union in such a way that power has increasingly gravitated to these two centers. Second, the Soviet Union, unlike previous aspirants to hegemony, is animated by a new fanatic faith, antithetical to our own, and seeks to impose its absolute authority over the rest of the world. . . . With the development of increasingly terrifying weapons of mass destruction, every individual faces the ever-present possibility of annihilation should the conflict enter the phase of total war. . . .

[U]nwillingly our free society finds itself mortally challenged by the Soviet system. No other value system is so wholly irreconcilable with ours, so implacable in its purpose to destroy ours, so capable of turning to its own uses the most dangerous and divisive trends in our own society, no other so skillfully and powerfully evokes the elements of irrationality in human nature everywhere, and no other has the support of a great and growing center of military power. . . .

Practical and ideological considerations therefore both impel us to the conclusion that we have no choice but to demonstrate the superiority of the idea of freedom by its constructive application, and to attempt to change the world situation by means short of war in such a way as to frustrate the Kremlin design and hasten the decay of the Soviet system. . . .

Our overall policy at the present time may be described as one designed to foster a world environment in which the American system can survive and flourish. It therefore rejects the concept of isolation. . . . This broad intention embraces two subsidiary policies. One is a policy which we would probably pursue even if there were no Soviet threat. It is a policy of attempting to develop a healthy international community. The other is the policy of "containing" the Soviet system. . . .

[Containment] seeks by all means short of war to (1) block further exposure of Soviet power (2) expose the falsities of Soviet pretensions (3) induce a retraction of the Kremlin's control and influence and (4) in general, so foster the seeds of destruction within the Soviet system that the Kremlin is brought at least to the point of modifying its behavior to conform to generally accepted international standards.

It was and continues to be cardinal in this policy that we possess superior overall power in ourselves or in dependable combination with other like-minded nations. One of the most important ingredients of power is military strength. . . .

At the same time, it is essential to the successful conduct of a policy of "containment" that we always leave open the possibility of negotiation with the USSR. A diplomatic freeze—and we are in one now—tends to defeat the very purposes of "containment" because it raises tensions at the same time that it makes Soviet retractions and adjustments in the direction of moderated behavior more difficult. . . .

We have failed to implement adequately these two fundamental aspects of "containment." In the face of obviously mounting Soviet military strength ours has declined relatively. . . . [W]e now find ourselves at a diplomatic impasse with the Soviet Union, with the Kremlin growing bolder, with both of us holding on grimly to what we have and with ourselves facing difficult decisions. . . .

It is quite clear from Soviet theory and practice that the Kremlin seeks to bring the free world under its dominion by the methods of the cold war. The preferred technique is to subvert by infiltration and intimidation. Every institution of our society is an instrument which it is sought to stultify and turn against our purposes. . . . The doubts and diversities that in terms of our values are part of the merit of a free system, the weaknesses and the problems that are peculiar to it, the rights and privileges that free men enjoy, and the disorganization and destruction left in the wake of the last attack on our freedoms, all are but opportunities for the Kremlin to do its evil work. . . .

The immediate goal of our efforts to build a successfully functioning political and economic system in the free world backed by adequate military strength is to postpone and avert the disastrous situation which, in light of the Soviet Union's probable fission bomb capability and possible thermonuclear bomb capability might arise in 1954 on a continuation of our present programs. By acting promptly and vigorously . . . we would permit time for the process of accommodation, withdrawal and frustration to produce the necessary changes in the Soviet system. . . .

The analysis shows that this will be costly and will involve significant domestic financial and economic adjustments.

The execution of such a build-up . . . requires that the United States have an affirmative program beyond the solely defensive one of countering the threat posed by the Soviet Union. This program . . . must envisage the political and economic measures with which and the military shield behind which the free world can work to frustrate the Kremlin design by the strategy of the cold war. . . . The only sure victory lies in the frustration of the Kremlin design by the steady development of the moral and material strength of the free world and its projection in the Soviet world in such a way as to bring about an internal change in the Soviet system. . . .

After a decision and a start on building up the strength of the free world has been made, it might then be desirable for the United States to take an initiative in seeking negotiations in the hope that it might facilitate the process of accommodation by the Kremlin to the new situation. . . .

The whole success of the proposed program hangs ultimately on recognition by this Government, the American people, and all free peoples, that the cold war is in fact a real war in which the survival of the free world is at stake.

Source: "A Report to the President Pursuant to the President's Directive of January 31, 1950," April 7, 1950, in *FRUS 1950* Vol. 1 (Washington: Government Printing Office, 1977), 237–92.

Document 9
THE COMMUNIST BLOC AND THE KOREAN WAR

The following five documents are recently declassified and translated cables from the Soviet Foreign Ministry from the period leading up to the Korean War and including the first year of that conflict. They include the transmissions of the U.S.S.R.'s ambassador to North Korea, T. F. Shtykov, to his Soviet superiors before the war began, reporting the needs and Chinese contacts of Kim Il Sung, Chairman of the Cabinet of Ministers of the Korean People's Democratic Republic, as well as Stalin's comforting words to Kim in the midst of military setbacks. These sources reveal the close ties between the Soviet government and its North Korean clients, showing the financial and military arrangements each side worked out with the other and the strong support that Stalin provided to Kim. They are further evidence that the North Korean attack on South Korea did not occur in a vacuum but was aided by the Soviet Union and China, both of which provided support for Kim's attempt to reunite the Koreas. South Korean president Syngman Rhee, who had also wanted to unite the two Koreas under his auspices, never got such backing from the United States, despite the fourth document's allegation that he and his American friends were the aggressors in the conflict. Mao's dismissal of putative American involvement in "such a small territory" demonstrates that his government perhaps had been convinced by Dean Acheson's "defensive perimeter" speech of January 1950 (see Chapter 4) of a limited American interest in Asia. Stalin's sometimes patronizing approach to Mao (Document 5) reveals the inequality of that relationship as well as foreshadows some of the later tensions the two nations would have with each other.

T. F. SHTYKOV TO SOVIET FOREIGN MINISTER ANDREI VYSHINSKY, MARCH 9, 1950, TRANSMITTING NOTE FROM KIM IL SUNG TO SOVIET GOVERNMENT

The cabinet of Ministers of the Korean People's Democratic Republic reports to you about the following:

In 1950 the Korean People's Democratic Republic, in order to strengthen the people's army and to fully equip it with arms, ammunition and technical equipment asked the Soviet government to send to Korea military-technical equipment in the amounts of 120–150 million rubles, in accordance with an application made earlier to the Government of the USSR.

The Korean People's Democratic Republic correspondingly will deliver to the Soviet Union this year:

9 tons of gold—53,662,900 rubles

40 tons of silver—1,887,600 rubles

15,000 tons of monazite concentrate—79,500,000 rubles

In all a sum of 133,050,500 rubles.

Korea is interested in the soonest possible receipt of the goods indicated in this application.

I ask you to inform the Soviet government of our request.

Kim Il Sung

Chairman of the Cabinet of Ministers of the Korean Peoples' Democratic Republic.

T. F. SHTYKOV TO VYSHINSKY RE MEETING WITH KIM IL SUNG, MAY 12, 1950

At the request of Kim Il Sung, on May 12 I had a meeting with him and [Foreign Minister] Pak Hon Yong. During the conversation Kim Il Sung reported to me that upon his return from Moscow he received a letter from Li Zhou-yuan (ambassador to China), in which he reported about a meeting that took place with Mao Zedong and [PRC Foreign Minister] Zhou Enlai. During this meeting the question of the necessity of a meeting between Kim Il Sung and Mao Zedong was discussed. Zhou Enlai proposed that the meeting have an official character. Mao, turning toward Li as if asking when you intend to begin the unification of the country, without waiting for an answer stated that if you intend to begin military operations against the south in the near future, then they should not meet officially. In such a case the trip should be unofficial.

Mao Zedong added further that the unification of Korea by peaceful means is not possible, solely military means are required to unify Korea. As regards the Americans, there is no need to be afraid of them. The Americans will not enter a third world war for such a small territory. . . .

Kim Il Sung reported to me that they intend to discuss roughly the following questions with Mao Zedong:

1. To inform about their intentions about unifying the country by military means and to report about the results of the discussion on this question in Moscow.

2. To exchange opinions on the question of the conclusion of a trade agreement between Korea and China. . . .

3. To inform Mao . . . about the establishment of closer communications between the Central Committee of the labor party of Korea and the Communist party of China. . . .

Kim further asked my advice, about what kind of questions he should raise before Mao Zedong from the point of view of assistance in the intended operation. I declined to answer, stating that it is clearer to him, what he has insufficiencies in and what the Chinese can help him with. . . . He stated that he doesn't have more requests for Mao about assistance, since all his requests were satisfied in Moscow. . . .

Kim Il Sung reported to me . . . that his wish is to begin the operation in June, but he is still not convinced that they will manage it in this period.

[On May 13, Kim and Pak Hon Yong flew to Beijing.]

FYN-SI (STALIN) TO KIM IL SUNG, VIA SHTYKOV, AUGUST 28, 1950

Verbally transmit the following to Kim Il Sung. . . .

1. The CC VKP (b) [Central Committee, All-Union Communist Party (bolshevik)] salutes Comrade Kim Il Sung and his friends for the great liberational struggle of the Korean people which comrade Kim Il Sung is leading with brilliant success. CC VKP (b) has no doubt that in the soonest time the interventionists will be driven out of Korea with ignominy.

2. Comrade Kim Il Sung should not be embarrassed by the fact that he does not have solid successes in the war against the interventionists. . . . In such a war continuous successes do not occur. The Russians also did not have continuous successes during the civil war and even more during the war with Germany. The greatest success of the Korean people is that Korea has now become the most popular country in the world and has turned into the banner of the movement in Asia of liberation from the imperialist yoke.

SHTYKOV TO MINISTRY OF FOREIGN AFFAIRS, MOSCOW, SEPTEMBER 13, 1950

In connection with the forthcoming session of the [UN] General Assembly, we consider it advisable to recommend to the government of the Korean People's Democratic Republic to send a statement to the General Assembly and the Security Council, in which, on the basis of documents found in the archives of the Rhee Syngmann (South Korean] government, to show how the clique of RHEE SYNGMANN prepared an attack on the north, to set forth once again the position of the government of the Korean People's Democratic Republic on the question of the illegality of the American intervention in Korea, to illuminate the barbaric acts of the American armed forces in Korea and to demand the adoption of measures for the immediate cessation of the American intervention and the withdrawal from Korea of the troops of the foreign interventionists.

FILIPPOV (STALIN) TO MAO ZEDONG, DEC. 1, 1950

Comrade MAO ZEDONG!

. . . I thank you for the information about the state of affairs in China, in connection with the successful offensive of the Chinese Peoples Liberation Army in Korea. . . .

Allow me to greet from the soul you and your friends in the leadership, the People's Liberation Army of China and the entire Chinese people in connection with these enormous successes in their struggle against the American troops.

I have no doubt that in the war against the up-to-date and well-armed American army the Chinese army will receive great experience in contemporary warfare and turn itself into a fully up-to-date, well-armed, formidable army, just as the Soviet Army in the struggle with the first-class-armed German army received experience in contemporary warfare and turned into an up-to-date well-equipped army.

I wish you further successes.

Source: From Kathryn Weathersby, author and translator, "New Evidence on the Korean War," Cold War International History Project *Bulletin* 6–7 (Winter 1995/1996), 37–51.

Document 10
"OLD SOLDIERS NEVER DIE . . ." ADDRESS OF GENERAL OF THE ARMY DOUGLAS MACARTHUR, APRIL 19, 1951

In April 1951, at the height of the Korean War and after a period of increasing insubordination toward his Commander-in-Chief President Harry Truman, General Douglas MacArthur, Supreme Commander for the Allied Powers in the Pacific during World War II, occupation commander in Japan, and commander of Allied Forces in Korea, was fired. After his amazingly successful amphibious attack at Inchon earlier the previous summer, which did so much to reverse a disastrous situation for the Allies in the south, MacArthur had been emboldened to take the war north, over the 38th parallel and close to the Chinese border. This had brought the response of hundreds of thousands of Chinese soldiers joining the North Koreans, which MacArthur had not bargained for. Although he continued to insist that all would be well (note here his insistence that China has mustered all her power already, and that the Soviets are nothing to worry about), the United States did not want to risk a war with either major Communist power. MacArthur was tolerated for as long as he was because of his mystique as a larger-than-life, highly effective general who had worked miracles in Japan as well as in Korea. Yet the septuagenarian was beginning to show signs of unbalance. He compared his own country to a Communist state, where political commissars interfered in military actions—ignoring the fact that civilian control of the military has always been a part of American governance. He had to go—but Truman's decision was extremely unpopular.

Half a million people greeted the old soldier on his return to San Francisco. The general's subsequent speech to a joint session of Congress, excerpted here, won a standing ovation. Of course, MacArthur's popularity had long eclipsed the president's, which only exacerbated the situation. In the speech, many of the themes of anticommunism and the importance of Asia that Isaac Don Levine raised in 1949 appear. MacArthur's emphasis on the bravery of the Korean people mirrors Stalin's extolling them as "the banner . . . of liberation" in Asia in his telegram to Kim Il Sung. Clearly, the Koreans, whether northern or southern, were a very potent symbol for their respective backers. Most especially, his speech is a rejection of containment and of the "cold war" idea—his "no substitute for victory" refrain is one that would not sit well with the carefully deliberative planners of NSC-68.

After the popular outcry at MacArthur's firing, the Senate investigated MacArthur's recall, but the hearings did not produce evidence that helped his cause. In fact, other military leaders took the opportunity to point out the flaws in the general's thinking. For example, his desire to bring in the Nationalist Chinese to fight in North Korea, Omar Bradley noted, would lead to the United States joining "in the wrong war, at the wrong place, at the wrong time and with the wrong enemy."[7]

Subsequent to the speech, MacArthur went on a speaking tour and then faded into a quiet life as chairman of the board of the typewriter and defense equipment maker, Remington Rand.

I do not stand here as advocate for any partisan cause, for the issues are fundamental and reach quite beyond the realm of partisan consideration. They must be resolved on the highest plane of national interest if our course is to prove sound and our future protected. I trust, therefore, that you will do me the justice of receiving that which I have to say as solely expressing the considered viewpoint of a fellow American. I address you with neither rancor nor bitterness in the fading twilight of life with but one purpose in mind, to serve my country. [Applause]

The issues are global and so interlocked that to consider the problems of one sector, oblivious to those of another, is but to court disaster for the whole.

While Asia is commonly referred to as the gateway to Europe, it is no less true that Europe is the gateway to Asia, and that broad confluence of the one cannot fail to have its impact upon the other.

There are those who claim our strength is inadequate to protect on both fronts, that we cannot divide our effort. I can think of no greater expression of defeatism. [Applause] If a potential enemy can divide his strength on two fronts, it is for us to counter his effort.

The Communist threat is a global one. Its successful advance in one sector threatens the destruction of every other sector. You cannot appease or otherwise surrender to communism in Asia without simultaneously undermining our efforts to halt its advance in Europe. [Applause] . . .

Prior [to the past war], the western strategic frontier of the U.S. lay on the littoral line of the Americas with an exposed island salient extending out through Hawaii, Midway, and Guam to the Philippines. That salient proved not an outpost of strength but an avenue of weakness along which the enemy could and did attack. . . .

All this was changed by our Pacific victory. Our strategic frontier then shifted to embrace the entire Pacific Ocean which became a vast moat to protect us as long as we hold it. We control it to the shores of Asia by a chain of islands extending in an arc from the Aleutians to the Mariannas held by us and our free allies.

From this island chain we can dominate with sea and air power every Asiatic port from Vladivostok to Singapore and prevent any hostile movement into the Pacific. . . .

The holding of this littoral defense line in the western Pacific is entirely dependent upon holding all segments thereof. . . .

For that reason I have strongly recommended in the past as a matter of military urgency that under no circumstances must Formosa fall under Communist control. [Applause] Such an eventuality would at once threaten the freedom of the Philippines and the loss of Japan, and might well force our western frontier back to the coasts of California, Oregon, and Washington. . . .

While I was not consulted prior to the President's decision to intervene in the support of the Republic of Korea, that decision from a military standpoint proved a sound one [applause] as we hurled back the invaders and decimated his forces. Our victory was complete and our objectives within reach when Red China intervened with numerically superior ground forces. This created a new war and an entirely new situation . . . which called for new decisions in the diplomatic sphere to permit the realistic adjustment of military strategy. Such decisions have not been forthcoming. [Applause]

While no man in his right mind would advocate sending our ground forces into continental China and such was never given a thought, the new situation did urgently demand a drastic revision of strategic planning if our political aim was to defeat this new enemy as we had defeated the old. [Applause]

Apart from the military need as I saw it to neutralize the sanctuary protection given to the enemy north of the Yalu, I felt that military necessity in the conduct of the war made mandatory:

1. The intensification of our economic blockade against China;
2. The imposition of a naval blockade against the China coast;
3. Removal of restrictions on air reconnaissance of Chiang's coastal areas and of Manchuria; [applause]

4. Removal of restrictions on the forces of the Republic of China on Formosa with logistical support to contribute to their effective operation against the common enemy. [Applause]

For entertaining these views all professionally designed to support our forces committed to Korea and bring hostilities to an end with the least possible delay and at a saving of countless American and allied lives, I have been severely criticized. . . .

I called for reinforcements, but was informed that reinforcements were not available. I made clear that if not permitted to destroy the build-up bases north of the Yalu; if not permitted to utilize the friendly Chinese force of some 600,000 men on Formosa; if not permitted to blockade the China coast to prevent the Chinese Reds from getting succor from without; and if there were to be no hope of major reinforcements, the position of the command from the military standpoint forbade victory. We could hold in Korea by constant maneuver and at an approximate area where our supply advantages were in balance with the supply line disadvantages of the enemy, but we could hope at best for only an indecisive campaign, with its terrible and constant attrition upon our forces if the enemy utilized his full military potential. I have constantly called for the new political decisions essential to a solution. Efforts have been made to distort my position. It has been said, in effect, that I am a warmonger. Nothing could be further from the truth. I know war as few other men now living know it, and nothing to me is more revolting. I have long advocated its complete abolition as its very destructiveness on both friend and foe has rendered it useless as a means of settling international disputes. . . .

But once war is forced upon us, there is no other alternative than to apply every available means to bring it to a swift end. War's very object is victory—not prolonged indecision. [Applause] In war, indeed, there can be no substitute for victory. [Applause]

There are some who for varying reasons would appease Red China. They are blind to history's clear lesson. For history teaches with unmistakable emphasis that appeasement but begets new and bloodier war. It points to no single instance where the end has justified the means—where appeasement has led to more than a sham peace. . . . China is already engaging with the maximum power it can commit and the Soviet [Union] will not necessarily mesh its actions with our moves. . . .

The tragedy of Korea is further heightened by the fact that as military action is confined to its territorial limits, it condemns that nation, which it is our purpose to save, to suffer the devastating impact of full naval and air bombardment, while the enemy's sanctuaries are fully protected from such attack and devastation. Of the nations of the world, Korea alone, up to now, is the sole one which has risked its all against communism. The magnificence of the courage and fortitude of the Korean people defies description. [Applause] They have chosen to risk death rather than slavery. Their last words to me were "Don't scuttle the Pacific." [Applause] . . .

I am closing my 52 years of military service. [Applause.] When I joined the Army even before the turn of the century, it was the fulfillment of all my boyish hopes and dreams. . . . I since remember the refrain of one of the most popular barrack ballads of that day which proclaimed most proudly that—"Old soldiers never die; they just fade away." And like the old soldier of that ballad, I now close my military career and just fade away—an old soldier who tried to do his duty as God gave him the light to see that duty.

Good-by.

Source: Congressional Record 1951 (Washington: Government Printing Office, 1951), pp. 4123–25.

Document 11
COLD WAR ANTICOMMUNISM

J. Edgar Hoover, director of the Federal Bureau of Investigation for nearly fifty years, was perhaps the most famous bureaucrat in the American government, and in the 1950s his agency was certainly among the most well known and highly respected of all government offices. The FBI even was glamorized in a weekly television show starring bold and handsome agents. Hoover's legacy, however, has hardly been so positive. Owing to the excesses that were uncovered in the 1960s and 1970s (spying on John F. Kennedy, Martin Luther King, Jr., and numerous antiwar groups), the FBI and its leader fell into serious disrepute. His long failure to uncover, or even to acknowledge, a major threat in the United States—organized crime—was another reason for the FBI's fall from favor.

Hoover is excerpted here from his best-seller on American Communism, a subject that the Bureau clearly overemphasized as much as it overlooked organized crime. He calls for average Americans to join the fight, but even more strongly does he appeal to intellectuals to do their part to "convince men that communism is evil." Hoover was at his prime during the Eisenhower administration, "the best and happiest years he ever had," when the president consulted him regularly and trusted him in a way that the Truman administration and its officials had not.[8]

Historically, it is not surprising that Hoover was very interested in Communism—his investigating roots traced to being A. Mitchell Palmer's assistant during the earlier Red Scare of 1919. But what is

> perhaps more interesting here is his strongly expressed distaste for McCarthyite tactics. Hoover notes the importance of American civil liberties—the FBI is responsible for protecting them—and declares that they must not be trampled by "misguided" citizens who don't like those who are "different." Ironically, he and his agency became caught up in the same pattern of targeting dissenters and hunting them down—and it was this very activity and its spying that contributed to the Bureau's loss of credibility. Hoover clearly forgot his mandate to protect the civil liberties of others, from civil rights leaders to antiwar protesters.

The responsible person who gains an understanding of communism knows that such understanding should lead to the question: "But what can I do about it?" My answer is that we can do a lot. . . .

Of course it is a job for the FBI, one given it by Presidential directives, acts of Congress, and rulings of the Attorney General. But the FBI can't do it all alone. The FBI has jurisdiction over more than 140 violations of federal law, and in a country with over 170 million inhabitants there are fewer than 6200 agents of the FBI. Hence, all of these agents are not available for the investigation of subversive activities. We need the help of all loyal Americans. . . .

Therefore, those individuals who place information they have regarding the communist conspiracy into the proper hands are making a contribution of great value to the security of their country. . . .

As we have seen, identifying communists is not easy. They are trained in deceit and trickery and use every form of camouflage and dishonesty to advance their cause. For this reason we must be absolutely certain that our fight is waged with full regard of the historical liberties of this great nation. *This is the fundamental premise of any attack against communism.* Too often I have seen cases where loyal and patriotic but misguided Americans have thought they were "fighting communism" by slapping the label of "Red" or "communist" on anybody who happened to be different from them or to have ideas with which they did not agree.

Smears, character assassination, and the scattering of irresponsible charges have no place in this nation. They create divisions, suspicion, and distrust among loyal Americans—just what the communists want—and hinder rather than aid the fight against communism.

Another thing. Time after time in this book I have mentioned that honest dissent should not be confused with disloyalty. A man has a right to think as he wishes; that is the strength of our form of government. Without free thought our society would decay. Just because a man's opinion is unpopular and represents a minority viewpoint or is different he is not necessarily disloyal. Hence, one should have the facts before accusing anyone of propagating the party line.

One of the chief jobs of the FBI, fully as important as tracking down spies, is to protect the civil rights of individuals. . . .

Our best weapons are facts and the truth. . . . Don Whitehead in his book, *The FBI Story,* in concluding his study of the FBI and its problems stated the case most accurately when he said:

"The top command of the FBI have no illusions that communism can be destroyed in the United States by the investigation, prosecution and conviction of Communist Party leaders who conspire to overthrow the government by force and violence. That is merely one phase of the job to be done in a world-wide struggle."

The FBI knows that the bigger job lies with the free world's intellectuals—the philosophers, the thinkers wherever they may be, the professors and scientists and scholars and students. These people who think, the intellectuals if you please, are the ones who can and must convince men that communism is evil. The world's intellectuals themselves must see that communism is the deadliest enemy that intellectualism and liberalism ever had. They must be as willing to dedicate themselves to this cause as the Communists have been to dedicate themselves to their cause.

Source: "What Can You Do?" by J. Edgar Hoover, *Masters of Deceit: The Story of Communism in America and How to Fight It* (New York: Holt, 1958) pp. 309–16 *passim.*

Document 12
EARLY VIETNAM AND THE DOMINO THEORY

Both of these documents—one a letter from National Security Council staffer Robert Komer to National Security Adviser McGeorge Bundy, the other a memo from William P. Bundy, Assistant Secretary of Defense for International Security Affairs (and brother of McGeorge)—show that officials were already facing the Vietnam dilemmas in the first year of the Kennedy administration that would emerge much more acutely for the Johnson administration after 1965. Problems that would face the Kennedy administration itself—the autocratic nature of Ngo Dinh Diem, the need for a greater number of American servicemen to help—are also already clear. Despite his making perfunctory pokes at the domino theory, Komer's analysis is the less subtle of the two. He believes that intervention is inevitable and thus expresses the consensus of Defense officials in the still overheated anticommunist climate of the mid–Cold War. Emphasized repeatedly by both analysts is the caveat against suffering "another defeat" (after the neutralization of Laos) that would provide a demonstration "that we would not stand up" to the Communist world. These credibility issues would be key reasons for U.S. action later, despite the fact that South Vietnam is here dismissed as a "squalid, secondary theatre," remote from U.S. interests. Instead of hearing this important precaution, officials proceeded as if Vietnam was as important as MacArthur had imagined North Korea to have been a decade before.

Intervention would not be sufficient to meet U.S. goals in the region, analysts acknowledged, but would provide time, which Kennedy and Johnson administration officials believed would help turn the tide. It didn't, of course. Instead, the American effort became exactly what Bundy, in the second of the two documents, predicted: "a road that has almost no end in sight" and "a wasting asset and an eyesore that would greatly hamper all our relations worldwide," a remarkably prescient prediction yet not one that was heard loudly enough to stop the American intervention. The cavalier way in which Soviet and/or Chinese intervention is addressed here belies the extreme care that Washington took to prevent this outcome—care that in fact prevented a full-scale pursuit of the war.

ROBERT KOMER TO MCGEORGE BUNDY, OCTOBER 31, 1961

Though no admirer of domino theory, I doubt if our position in SEA [South East Asia] could survive "loss" of S. Vietnam on top of that of Laos. Moreover, could Administration afford yet another defeat, domestically?

Perhaps there are alternatives to sending U.S. troops which would have a fair chance of doing the job. But I doubt it. And if the alternatives fail, we still face the question of sending troops—at a later and less satisfactory time.

The case for acting now is that in the long run it is likely to be the most economical. True, we may end up with something approaching another Korea, but I think the best way of avoiding this is to move fast now before the war spreads to the extent that a Korean type commitment is required.

Sending troops now would also lead to much recrimination and some risks of escalation, *but both risks and recriminations would be much greater, say, a year from now* when the whole situation is a lot more heated up. [Emphasis in original]

Admittedly, intervention alone does not solve our problem—but at least it buys us time to do so. . . .

I'm no happier than anyone about getting involved in another squalid, secondary theatre in Asia. But we'll end up doing so sooner or later anyway because we won't be willing to accept another defeat. If so, the real question is not whether but how soon and how much! . . .

If we move in, we must exact in turn from Diem a whole series of iron-clad commitments.

WILLIAM BUNDY, "REFLECTIONS ON THE POSSIBLE OUTCOMES OF U.S. INTERVENTION IN SOUTH VIETNAM," DRAFT MEMO, NOVEMBER 7, 1961.

"Good" Scenarios

Scenario A: Diem takes heart and also takes the measures needed to improve efficiency, with only the 8000 man force and U.S. specialist help. Hanoi heeds our warning and lays low, so that control is reasserted in South Vietnam. (Laos is a big question mark here as in other Scenarios.)

Scenario B: The struggle continues to go against Diem, and his own efforts at improvement are feeble. Thus, the U.S. moves into the driver's seat and *eventually brings the situation* under control, using forces on the scale of *25,000 to 75,000*. Hanoi and Peiping do not intervene directly, and we do not attack Hanoi.

Scenario C: As the struggle becomes prolonged, the U.S. strikes at Hanoi (or Hanoi and Peiping [Beijing] intervene overtly). The U.S. wins the resulting conflict, i.e., obtains at least a restoration of the status quo, after inflicting such punishment on Hanoi and/or Peiping that further aggressive moves are forestalled for a long time to come.

"Bad" Scenarios

Scenario X: The U.S. decides not to put in the 8000 men, or later forces, and Diem is gradually overcome.

Scenario Y: The U.S. puts in the 8000 men, but when Diem fails to improve his performance pulls out and lets him be overcome.

Scenario Z: Moscow comes to the aid of Hanoi and Peiping, supplying all necessary equipment (including a limited supply of air-deliverable nuclear weapons to retaliate in kind against U.S. use) so that the outcome is a stalemate in which great destruction is wreaked on the whole area.

Of these, only A is truly a good outcome from all long-term standpoints—it stiffens us generally vis-à-vis the Bloc, holds the area (save perhaps Laos), does not discomfit us unduly in the neutral world, excellent for domestic U.S. will and drive. Only trouble is—it's unlikely! *However*, it is still so much better than any other that it is worth accepting some added degree of difficulty in achieving B and C to give A every chance to happen.

The choice between B and C is a hard one. . . . [O]ur case of aggression against Hanoi will not convince neutrals of its accuracy and justice, or major allies of its wisdom and practicality. On the other hand, B is a road that has almost no end in sight. The U.S. is poorly cast as a permanent protecting power, but the local capabilities would be so low at the end of such a struggle that we would almost have to assume that role. There is a very considerable chance that under continuing U.S. protection, South Vietnam and the area as a whole would become a wasting asset and an eyesore that would greatly hamper all our relations worldwide. On the whole, the short-term onus attached to C may be preferable. However, as we play the hand toward C (especially if we use Moscow as the channel to Hanoi) we may well raise the chances of Moscow acting to bring on Z.

On the "bad" side, X and Z are clearly nightmares. Though X means loss of the area for a long time to come, it is probably better in the long run than Z. The chances of the Soviets acting to bring about Z do not appear great in the short run, but we must certainly try to keep those chances low (e.g., by making our dealings with Moscow private).

Y is also a nightmare. It loses the area. Moreover, vis-à-vis the Bloc it would be worse than X, since they would take it as an almost final proof that we would not stand up. It might have some compensating gains in the neutral world, at least in the short run. But on the whole it seems the worst possible outcome.

The basic strategic issues are:

A. How long to give A a chance?

B. Whether B is preferable to the weighted odds of C vs. Z?

Source: From William Conrad Gibbons, *The U.S. Government and the Vietnam War: Executive and Legislative Roles and Relationships* Part II: 1961–64 (Princeton, N.J.: Princeton University Press, 1986), pp. 81–84.

Document 13
NIXON DOCTRINE

In 1969 President Richard Nixon began pulling the five hundred thousand American troops out of Vietnam, reversing the course that the two previous administrations had set. With the American troops coming home, the U.S. role in Asia was at last curtailed, and Nixon used the occasion to announce a new American policy of international relations that became known as the Nixon Doctrine, which in its nature was consonant with the new policy of détente that Nixon and his National Security Adviser, Henry Kissinger, were pursuing to lower tensions with the Communist bloc. The United States would no longer automatically protect Asian nations threatened by Communism (or anything else) unless they were specifically in a treaty relationship with Washington *or* they were threatened by a power with nuclear weapons. The implication was that if North Vietnam had begun its infiltration of South Vietnam in 1969, the United States would not have intervened, because this would have been considered an "internal security" matter. Neither, for that matter, would the United States have joined the Korean conflict, because there was no treaty commitment to that nation—although because North Korea was aided in its attack by a nuclear power (though not one using atomic weapons), this may have called for U.S. action.

The doctrine seemed tailored to address the cry "No More Vietnams!" More ambiguous was how it would govern the U.S. response to the kinds of threats that the Nixon Doctrine outlined: nuclear ones. If the criterion for response were a threat from a nuclear-armed power using its nuclear arsenal, what about a threat to U.S. security involving either a nuclear power not using atomic weapons (such as in Korea) or a non-nuclear power using conventional weapons but threatening U.S. vital interests (such as Iraq in the Persian Gulf in 1990–1991, when the United States quickly responded)? The doctrine was announced at a press conference in Guam, on July 25, 1969, just after Nixon had witnessed the splashdown of the Apollo 11 mission, the first to reach the moon.

Q: Mr. President, sir, on the question of U.S. military relationships in Asia, if I may ask a hypothetical question: If a leader of one of the countries with which we have had close military relationships, either through SEATO or in Vietnam, should say, "Well, you are pulling out of Vietnam with your troops, we can read in the newspapers. How can we know that you will remain to play a significant role as you say you wish to do in security arrangements in Asia?" What kind of an approach can you take to that question?

THE PRESIDENT: I have already indicated that the answer to that question is not an easy one—not easy because we will be greatly tempted when that question is put to us to indicate that if any nation desires the assistance of the United States militarily in order to meet an internal or external threat, we will provide it.

However, I believe that the time has come when the United States, in our relations with all of our Asian friends, be quite emphatic on two points: One, that we will keep our treaty commitments, our treaty commitments, for example, with Thailand under SEATO; but, two, that as far as the problems of internal security are concerned, as far as the problems of military defense, except for the threat of a major power involving nuclear weapons, that the U.S. is going to encourage and has a right to expect that this problem will be increasingly handled by, and the responsibility for it taken by, the Asian nations themselves.

I believe, incidentally, from my preliminary conversations with several Asian leaders over the past few months that they are going to be willing to undertake this responsibility. It will not be easy. But if the United States just continues down the road of responding to requests for assistance, of assuming the primary responsibility of defending these countries when they have internal problems or external problems, they are never going to take care of themselves.

I should add to that, too, that when we talk about collective security for Asia, I realize that at this time that looks like a weak reed. It actually is. But looking down the road—I am speaking now of 5 years from now, 10 years from now—I think collective security, insofar as it deals with internal threats to any one of the countries, or insofar as it deals with a threat other than that posed by a nuclear power, I believe that this is an objective which free Asian nations, independent Asian nations, can seek and which the United States should support.

Source: From *Public Papers of the Presidents, Richard Nixon, 1969* (Washington: Government Printing Office, 1971), pp. 548–49.

Document 14
EAST GERMANY AND THE POLISH SOLIDARITY MOVEMENT

In August 1980 the expanding Polish workers' movement Solidarity, led by Gdansk shipyard worker Lech Walesa and his Inter-factory Strike Committee, signed a treaty with the government of the People's Republic of Poland and its leader, Stanislaw Kania, First Secretary of the Polish United Workers' Party (PZPR). Despite its name, the latter organization served the ruling Communists and not the workers. Kania had signed the accords with Solidarity believing that he had no choice, as Solidarity's strength was growing rapidly and he wanted to avoid chaos.

Neighboring fraternal socialist states, however, looked on in alarm, including the German Democratic Republic (DDR), as well as the Soviet Union. The Gdansk accords outraged and panicked the Politburo of the East German Socialist Unity Party (SED) Central Committee (CC), whose members believed that "no one other than the Party itself, with the aid of scientific socialism, can express and realize the class interests of the Party."[9] Erich Honecker, General Secretary of the SED CC, here expresses his fear to Leonid Brezhnev, General Secretary of the CC of the Communist Party of the Soviet Union, that the Polish crisis would get out of control and "be the death" of socialism in Poland, as well as infect other socialist nations.

So great was Honecker's fear that in the fall of 1980 he ordered his own border with Poland sealed off, and his troops on combat alert in case they might be needed to intervene. Just as occurred in 1968 during the "Prague Spring" in Czechoslovakia, he wanted the Warsaw Pact nations to join together against the wavering satellite—here attesting that the Czechoslovak and Bulgarian "comrades" are in agreement with him—and he also hoped for a stronger role from Moscow in leading the effort. The Soviets had had little luck thus far in getting Kania to act decisively to stop the workers' movement, although in 1981 they would work through General Wojciech Jaruzelski to bring about martial law in Poland and to outlaw Solidarity. The movement revived, however, thanks to foreign support from both the United States and the Polish-born Pope John Paul II, and it eventually helped overthrow the old regime in Poland in 1989.

November 26, 1980.

Esteemed Comrade Leonid Ilyich!

In the Politburo of the SED CC we have discussed the current situation in the People's Republic of Poland, and have unanimously concluded that there is an urgent necessity to convene a meeting of the General and First Secretaries of the Communist Parties of our community of states. We believe that the situation developing in the People's Republic of Poland should be discussed with Comrade S. Kania in order to work out collective measures to assist the Polish friends in overcoming the crisis, which, as you know, has been intensifying day after day.

Unfortunately, one can already say that the Polish comrades' stopover in Moscow, and the timely counsel that you gave, had no decisive influence on the situation in Poland, which we had all been hoping for.

According to information we have received through various channels, counterrevolutionary forces in the People's Republic of Poland are on the constant offensive, and any delay in acting against them would mean death—the death of socialist Poland. Yesterday our collective efforts may perhaps have been premature; today they are essential; and tomorrow they would already be too late.

It would obviously be appropriate if we meet together in Moscow for a day right after the plenum of the PZPR CC, the decision of which, in our view, will not be able to change the course of events in Poland in any fundamental way.

So far as I know, Comrades Husak [of Czechoslovakia] and Zhivkov [of Bulgaria] also have been expressing their desire for us to convene on an urgent basis to discuss this question. It would be best to do so next week.

We believe that offering collective advice and possible assistance from the fraternal countries to Comrade Kania would only be to his benefit.

We ask you, esteemed Leonid Ilyich, to understand our extraordinary fears about the situation in Poland. We know that you also share these fears.

With Communist greetings,
E. Honecker

Source: From "The Warsaw Pact and the Polish Crisis of 1980–81: Honecker's Call for Military Intervention," Mark Kramer, author and translator, Cold War International History Project *Bulletin* 5 (Spring 1995), 124.

Document 15
"FOCUS OF EVIL IN THE MODERN WORLD"

In 1983, when President Ronald Reagan gave this speech, U.S.-Soviet relations were at a nadir. The repressive old Communist Leonid Brezhnev had recently died and his successor, Yuri Andropov, showed little sign of slackening off in the Cold War. Despite Western images of him as a whiskey imbibing, jazz-listening man of culture, Andropov was a former head of the KGB who had made his name in the crushing of the Hungarian revolution in 1956. The Soviets were consolidating their hold in Afghanistan and their advisers and proxies remained in Angola, Ethiopia, South Yemen, Vietnam, Cuba, and Grenada. Meanwhile, Reagan faced widespread pressure to initiate a nuclear freeze in the arms race, even as he had doubled the defense budget from 1979 to 1983, a buildup that supporters credited with helping to push the economically challenged Soviet Union over the edge, while critics charged that it mainly exacerbated the U.S. budget deficit while heightening tensions with Russia. Reagan was vilified for equating the Soviet Union with evil in this speech—no president had expressed these sentiments so blatantly before, not even Harry Truman, who faced the Soviets at the height of the Cold War. Many observers believed that he was making relations worse by such rhetoric, and reverting back to the days of "better dead than Red," as one of his following quotes indicates.

The speech has become something of a legend. At the time, critics charged that it demonstrated the president's stubborn opposition to better relations with the Soviet Union. Yet Reagan showed much flexibility in his dealings with a later (indeed, the last) Soviet leader, Mikhail S. Gorbachev, negotiating drastic reductions in arms, and indeed, it appeared that his earlier arms buildup had facilitated "peace through strength." Reagan's ultimate sentence in the following excerpt was surprisingly prescient, given the subsequent Soviet departure from eastern Europe and the demise of the Soviet Union itself in 1991.

Whatever sad episodes exist in our past, any objective observer must hold a positive view of American history, a history that has been the story of hopes fulfilled and dreams made into reality. Especially in this century, America has kept alight the torch of freedom, but not just for ourselves but for millions of others around the world. . . . During my first press conference as President, in answer to a direct question, I pointed out that, as good Marxist-Leninists, the Soviet leaders have openly and publicly declared that the only morality they recognize is that which will further their cause, which is world revolution. I think I should point out I was only quoting Lenin, their guiding spirit, who said in 1920 that they repudiate all morality that proceeds from supernatural ideas—that's their name for religion—or ideas that are outside class conceptions. Morality is entirely subordinate to the interests of class war. . . .

This doesn't mean we should isolate ourselves and refuse to seek an understanding with them. I intend to do everything I can to persuade them of our peaceful intent, to remind them that it was the West that refused to use its nuclear monopoly in the forties and fifties for territorial gain and which now proposes a 50 percent cut in strategic ballistic missiles and the elimination of an entire class of land-based intermediate range nuclear missiles.

At the same time, however, they must be made to understand we will never compromise our principles and standards. . . . [W]e can assure none of these things America stands for through the so-called nuclear freeze solutions proposed by some. . . . A freeze now would be a very dangerous fraud, for that is merely the illusion of peace. The reality is that we must find peace through strength. . . . A freeze would reward the Soviet Union for its enormous and unparalleled military buildup. It would prevent the essential and long overdue modernization of United States and allied defenses and would leave our aging forces increasingly vulnerable. . . .

A number of years ago, I heard a young father . . . addressing a tremendous gathering in California. It was during the time of the cold war, and communism and our own way of life were very much on people's minds. . . . I heard him saying, "I love my little girls more than anything. . . . I would rather see my little girls die now, still believing in God, than have them grow up under communism and one day die no longer believing in God." There were thousands of people in that audience. They came to their feet with shouts of joy. . . .

Yes, let us pray for the salvation of all those who live in that totalitarian darkness—pray they will discover the joy of knowing God. But until they do, let us be aware that while they preach the supremacy of the state, declare its omnipotence over individual man, and predict its eventual domination of all peoples on the Earth, they are the focus of evil in the modern world. . . .

So I urge you to speak out against those who would place the United States in a position of military and moral inferiority. . . . So in your discussions of the nuclear freeze proposals, I urge you to beware the temptation of pride—the temptation of blithely declaring yourselves above it all and label both sides equally at fault, to ignore the facts of history and the aggressive impulses of an evil empire, to simply call the arms race a giant misunderstanding and thereby remove yourself from the struggle between right and wrong and good and evil. . . .

Whittaker Chambers, the man whose own religious conversion made him a witness to one of the terrible traumas of our time, the Hiss-Chambers case, wrote that the crisis of the Western World exists to the degree in which it collaborates in communism's attempt to make man stand alone without God. . . . The Western World can answer this challenge, he wrote, "but only provided that its faith in God and the freedom He enjoins is as great as communism's faith in Man."

I believe we shall rise to the challenge. I believe that communism is another sad, bizarre chapter in human history whose last pages even now are being written.

Source: Ronald Reagan, "Remarks at the Annual Convention of the National Association of Evangelicals in Orlando, Florida," March 8, 1983, in *Public Papers of the Presidents, Ronald Reagan, 1983* (Washington: Government Printing Office, 1984) I: 363–64.

Document 16
GORBACHEV ASCENDANT

Mikhail S. Gorbachev succeeded Konstantin Chernenko in 1985 as General Secretary of the Communist Party of the Soviet Union and later, president of the Soviet Union. A lawyer by profession, Gorbachev was an intelligent, urbane man and by far the most charming leader that the Soviet Union had produced. Much younger than his immediate predecessors upon taking office, he wanted to revive Soviet Communism, which he saw as desiccated and deteriorating in the aftermath of the death of three of its leaders in as many years. He sought to institute a series of reforms to save the system. Unfortunately for him, these reforms represented too little, too late.

Rather than revive Communism, after a brief honeymoon among Soviet citizens, Gorbachev's policies of *glasnost* (openness) and *perestroika* (economic reconstruction), as well as a vigorous antialcohol campaign, succeeded in alienating nearly everyone. Reformers, though thrilled as all Soviet citizens were with the new opportunities to express themselves, objected to Gorbachev's half-hearted attempts to end central planning and his insistence that the Communist party retain its central role in the government. Thus, although Soviet citizens and other Europeans learned about the disastrous Chernobyl nuclear disaster in 1986 much sooner and more thoroughly than they had with previous catastrophes, the mechanisms that allowed a Chernobyl to be in place, such as rigid central planning at the expense of human safeguards, remained. Hard-liners objected to Gorbachev's effort to shed the empire—he would renounce the interventionist Brezhnev Doctrine in eastern Europe, as well as pull back from Afghanistan—and they staged a coup against him in August 1991.

The coup was foiled, but Gorbachev's Soviet Union nevertheless went out of existence just four months later. This was, perhaps, the surest sign of Gorbachev's success; he had contributed to democratizing the Soviet Union and allowed the first free elections, to the Congress of People's Deputies, in 1989, which eventually led to the breakup of the Soviet Union, albeit over Gorbachev's protests. After the Baltic nations and other republics had demanded their own freedom in the manner of the eastern European states, Russia too insisted on independence under its new leader, Boris Yeltsin. Gorbachev was already wildly unpopular, yet in 1996, he gamely ran for president of the Russian Federation against Yeltsin and several other candidates—receiving just under 1 percent of the vote. He remains far more highly esteemed in the West.

The following speech illuminates Gorbachev's ambitious peace initiatives toward the West, his goals for alleviating superpower tensions and the arms race, by which he also hoped to preserve his own state. It also shows his profound belief in the value of the Communist system and its staying power. He boldly states: "The Soviet state has proved repeatedly that it is able to meet any challenge." And with good reason—it had for seven decades. Yet just five years later his state collapsed.

We have one policy which expresses the interests of the Soviet people and takes account of the interests of all other peoples.

The 27th CPSU Congress produced a comprehensive analysis of all the controversies and interrelationships in today's world. What is needed to resolve its problems is an entirely new way of thinking, an innovative approach, and an awareness of the fact that the arms race and the development of military technology have reached a critical point. . . . [W]e understand that we exist side by side in world politics with an opposing system in terms of class and that from the point of view of safeguarding peace we are confronted by such a serious reality as the United States. At the same time, the leadership of that country still cannot drop past habits and, to all appearances, does not want to reckon with the reality of the Soviet Union.

This fact, however, does not stop us from seeking a way out of confrontation. . . . This is why we set out immediately after Geneva [Conference, November 1985] to translate the accords achieved there and the Joint Statement into practical actions:

—We extended our unilateral moratorium on nuclear explosions twice and offered immediately to begin talks on ending nuclear tests altogether; . . .

—Another major initiative was our Statement of January 15, which contains a concrete and clear plan for the elimination of weapons of mass destruction and for reductions in other weapons to limits that are adequate for defensive purposes;

—We took into account the anxiety of Europeans about medium-range missiles and tactical nuclear weapons and came up with a compromise option for the European zone;

—We suggested the mutual withdrawal of the Soviet and U.S. navies from the Mediterranean; . . .

In Geneva both sides agreed that just as in the nuclear arms race, there could be no winners in a nuclear war. But when we put forward a simple and clear, stage-by-stage plan for the reduction and elimination of nuclear arsenals, we were told: "No!"

Or another example: over the years they have kept harping that the Russians cannot be trusted because they do not permit on-site inspections. We have agreed to such inspections. In response, President Reagan offers us to "verify" not a ban on nuclear explosions but a procedure for improving nuclear weapons. . . . We naturally, have not accepted. . . . We put the matter differently: let us discuss both our proposal on ending explosions and the American proposal on verification. The only thing that the U.S. Administration seems to have retained from Geneva is talk about a new meeting between the U.S. President and the General Secretary of the CPSU Central Committee. . . . I'm for holding such a meeting. . . . But . . . it should mark a **step forward**, that is, produce **practical** results in ending the arms race.

One more thing. Our meeting can take place if the atmosphere of Geneva is preserved, or it would be more correct today to say **revived**. Just look at what is taking place. Soon after Geneva, an anti-Soviet campaign, full of every type of fabrication and insults to our country, was launched with a vengeance in the United States.

Subsequently, more serious matters have arisen, namely, the demand that the Soviet Union reduce the number of its diplomats in New York by 40 percent. An American naval squadron off the shores of the Crimea—and they did not conceal the fact that the action was sanctioned by the top authorities. An attack was launched against Libya to show America's might and to demonstrate that it was at liberty to do whatever it wished. A high yield nuclear explosion was carried out in Nevada with an obviously provocative purpose just before our moratorium expired. . . .

Does Washington think that it is dealing with people who are easily frightened? Do they believe that today it is possible to behave like reckless gamblers? . . .

And what about Western Europe? . . . [T]hey stand for peace in words, but for missiles in deeds. No, neither Britain nor France has demonstrated a serious approach in this respect.

Consider the attitude to the "strategic defense initiative." The West European governments and big businesses are using all sorts of pretexts for getting increasingly involved in that disastrous plan, and they are thus becoming participants in a new, even more dangerous round of the arms race. . . .

The USA is putting its Star Wars programme into full gear. The President claims that this is a defensive and non-nuclear programme. But the general, who heads that project, describes in public how the space weapon will be able to hit the enemy on earth, while the U.S. Secretary of Defense says that it includes nuclear components.

Let me state frankly: If, contrary to common sense, the U.S. persists in pursuing this policy, we shall find a convincing response, and not necessarily in outer space. We well know the potentials of contemporary science, our own potentials. There is nothing that the USA can do and we cannot. . . . To us, a ban on space-strike weapons **does not pose the problem of fearing to lag behind, but that of responsibility**. . . .

[T]he arms race will not wear us out, we cannot be taken from outer space, and shall not be outdone in technology. Nothing good will come of these attempts. . . . We shall not be taken by surprise. The Soviet state has proved repeatedly that it is able to meet any challenge. . . .

Certainly, nobody expected that the implementation of our programme to advance towards a world without wars and weapons would proceed smoothly, like a "Zhiguli" car driving down a good asphalt road. We are in for a long and tough struggle. Not only détente, but even a warming-up in Soviet-American relations does not suit certain circles . . . the circles associated with the business of manufacturing arms, those who work for the military-industrial complex which sends its representatives to the upper echelons of power and takes them back after they have loyally served its aims there. . . .

Our true friends—the socialist countries—support us in this great effort. We have a special responsibility towards them, that is, our common responsibility for the destiny of socialism. . . .

A majority of the world community supports preserving peace, including the governments and peoples of the non-aligned countries, of the Third World and the working people of the capitalist countries.

We want to preserve the achievements of Paris and Geneva. We shall not let ourselves be provoked, nor shall we pour fuel on the bonfire of the cold war which is currently being kindled. One should not play politics in this nuclear age.

Source: "From the Speech at a Meeting with the Working People of the City of Togliatti," April 8, 1986, in Mikhail Gorbachev, *The Moratorium: Selected Speeches and Statements by the General Secretary of the CPSU [Communist Party of the Soviet Union] Central Committee on the Problem of Ending Nuclear Tests* (January–September 1986) (Moscow: Novosti Press Agency Publishing House, 1986), pp. 91–98.

Document 17
END OF THE COLD WAR

In early 1992 President George Bush basked in the recent end of the Cold War in what would be his last State of the Union address. Though Reagan is the American president who correctly receives most credit for the U.S. contribution to ending the Cold War, the Berlin Wall fell and the Soviet Union collapsed during the Bush administration. These events were already set in motion by Gorbachev and the eastern European peoples, yet the Bush administration certainly facilitated the end of Cold War conflicts in Europe, Africa, Latin America, and the Middle East. The end of the Cold War is clearly evident in Bush's speech. He portrays the United States as the undisputed leader of the world, noting the recent victory in the Gulf War against Iraqi leader Saddam Hussein, and the end of the round-the-clock strategic bomber runs that for years had protected the United States. He declares that the world is satisfied and trusts the United States with its "prudent" power. Unfortunately for him, all this good news was not enough, for Bush was defeated in his bid for re-election in 1992.

The president, and millions of Americans, had great reason to celebrate the demise of the Soviet Union, to tout their successes and sacrifices. But Bush's assertion that America "won the cold war" is highly debatable. His flat statement that Communism had "died," moreover, is simply wrong. As of this writing, with the millennium in sight, Communists control the lives of millions with antiquated and oppressive notions of proper human behavior in the People's Republic of China, North Korea, and Cuba, although their days are likely numbered. Recently, old Communists have made new appearances,

> sometimes in the sheep's clothing of socialist parties, in the very eastern European countries that threw them out in the early 1990s.

I see the Speaker and the Vice President are laughing. They saw what I did in Japan [when Bush became violently ill at dinner], and they're just happy they're sitting behind me. [Laughter]

I mean to speak tonight of big things, of big changes and the promises they hold, and of some big problems and how, together, we can solve them and move our country forward as the undisputed leader of the age.

We gather tonight at a dramatic and deeply promising time in our history and in the history of man on Earth. For in the past 12 months, the world has known changes of almost Biblical proportions. And even now, months after the failed coup that doomed a failed system, I'm not sure we've absorbed the full impact, the full import of what happened. But communism died this year.

Even as President, with the most fascinating possible vantage point, there were times when I was so busy managing progress and helping to lead change that I didn't always show the joy that was in my heart. But the biggest thing that has happened in the world in my life, in our lives, is this: By the grace of God, America won the cold war.

I mean to speak this evening of the changes that can take place in our country, now that we can stop making the sacrifices we had to make when we had an avowed enemy that was a superpower. Now we can look homeward even more and move to set right what needs to be set right.

I will speak of those things. But let me tell you something I've been thinking these past few months. It's a kind of rollcall of honor. For the cold war didn't end; it was won. And I think of those who won it, in places like Korea and Vietnam. And some of them didn't come back. Back then they were heroes, but this year they were victors. . . .

This may seem frivolous, and I don't mean it so, but it's moving to me how the world saw them. The world saw not only their special valor but their special style: their rambunctious, optimistic bravery, their do-or-die unity unhampered by class or race or region. . . .

And there's another to be singled out, though it may seem inelegant, and I mean a mass of people called the American taxpayer. No one ever thinks to thank the people who pay a country's bill or an alliance's bill. But for half a century now, the American people have shouldered the burden and paid taxes that were higher than they would have been to support a defense that was bigger than it would have been if imperial communism had never existed. But it did; doesn't anymore. . . .

So now, for the first time in 35 years, our strategic bombers stand down. No longer are they on 'round-the-clock alert. Tomorrow our children will go to school and study history and how plants grow. And they won't have, as my children did, air raid drills in which they crawl under their desks and cover their heads in case of nuclear war. . . . There are still threats. But the long, drawn-out dread is over.

A year ago tonight, I spoke to you at a moment of high peril. American forces had just unleashed Operation Desert Storm. And after 40 days in desert skies and 4 days on the ground, the men and women of America's Armed Forces and our allies accomplished the goals that I declared and that you endorsed: We liberated Kuwait. Soon after, the Arab world and Israel sat down to talk seriously and comprehensively about peace, an historic first. And soon after that, at Christmas, the last American hostages came home. Our policies were vindicated.

Much good can come from the prudent use of power. And much good can come of this: A world once divided into two armed camps now recognizes one solid and preeminent power, the United States of America. And they regard this with no dread. For the world trusts us with power, and the world is right. They trust us to be fair and restrained. They trust us to be on the side of decency. . . .

Two years ago, I began planning cuts in military spending that reflected the changes of the new era. But now, this year, with imperial communism gone, that process can be accelerated. Tonight I can tell you of dramatic changes in our strategic nuclear force. These are actions we are taking on our own because they are the right thing to do. After completing 20 planes for which we have begun procurement, we will shut down further production for the B-2 bombers. We will cancel the small ICBM program. We will cease production of new warheads for our sea-based ballistic missiles.

This weekend I will meet at Camp David with Boris Yeltsin of the Russian Federation. I've informed President Yeltsin that if the Commonwealth, the former Soviet Union, will eliminate all land based multiple-warhead ballistic missiles, I will do the following. We will eliminate all Peacekeeper missiles. We will reduce the number of warheads on Minuteman missiles to one and reduce the number of warheads on our sea-based missiles by about one-third. And we will convert a substantial portion of our strategic bombers to primarily conventional use. . . .

For half a century, American Presidents have longed to make such decisions and say such words. But even in the midst of celebration, we must keep caution as a friend. For the world is still a dangerous place. Only the dead have seen the end of conflict. . . . I remind you this evening that I have asked for your support in funding a program to protect our country from limited nuclear missile attack. We must have this protection because too many people in too many countries have access to nuclear arms. And I urge you again to pass the Strategic Defense Initiative, SDI.

There are those who say that now we can turn away from the world, that we have no special role, no special place. But we are the United States of America, the leader of the West that has become the leader of the world. And as long as I am President, I will continue to lead in support of freedom everywhere.

Source: "Address before a Joint Session of the Congress on the State of the Union," George Bush, January 28, 1992, *Public Papers of the President, George Bush, I: 1992–93* (Washington: Government Printing Office, 1993), pp. 156–58.

NOTES

1. "X," "The sources of Soviet Conduct," *Foreign Affairs* 25 (July 1947): 575.

2. Frank Costigliola, " 'Unceasing Pressure for Penetration,' Gender, Pathology, and Emotion in George Kennan's Cold War," *Journal of American History* 83 (March 1997): 1309, 1312–13.

3. See Michael J. Hogan, *The Marshall Plan: America, Britain, and the Reconstruction of Western Europe, 1947–1952* (New York: Cambridge University Press, 1987), 293.

4. On Rand, also see Stephen J. Whitfield, *The Culture of the Cold War*, 2nd ed. (Baltimore: Johns Hopkins University Press, 1996), 129–31.

5. President's Directive, January 31, 1950, *FRUS* 1950, I: 236.

6. John Lewis Gaddis, *The United States and the End of the Cold War: Implications, Reconsiderations, Provocations* (New York: Oxford University Press, 1992), 55.

7. Quoted in Michael Schaller, *Douglas MacArthur: The Far Eastern General* (New York: Oxford University Press, 1989), 249.

8. Richard Gid Powers, *Secrecy and Power: The Life of J. Edgar Hoover* (New York: Free Press, 1987), 312.

9. "The SED Politburo and the Polish Crisis by the SED [East German Socialist Unity Party]-State Research Group," trans. Mark Kramer, in Cold War International History Project *Bulletin* 5 (Spring 1995), 121.

Glossary of Selected Terms

Brezhnev Doctrine: The concept, associated with CPSU General Secretary Leonid Ilyich Brezhnev (1964–1982), that socialist states should intervene to protect their fellow socialist states from counterrevolution. It was used most famously in Czechoslovakia during the Prague Spring of 1968 to crush the experiment there of "Socialism with a human face," when Soviet, Hungarian, and Polish forces all sent forces to restore the old regime. The doctrine died under Gorbachev's rule; he refused to intervene when the eastern European satellites left Soviet control beginning in 1989.

Carter Doctrine: An example of the heightened Cold War in the late Carter administration. In response to the Soviet invasion of Afghanistan and the revolution in Iran, Carter declared that "any attempt by any outside force to gain control of the Persian Gulf region will be regarded as an assault on the vital interests of the United States of America and such an assault will be repelled by any means necessary, including military force." This doctrine was designed to show to U.S. friends, like the Saudis, the American commitment to the region.

Central Intelligence Agency (CIA): Formed in 1947, along with the National Security Council and the Department of Defense, as part of the 1947 National Security Act, the CIA superseded the individual service branch intelligence agencies and is responsible for foreign intelligence gathering. It was modeled on the wartime Office of Strategic Services (OSS). The CIA was part of the large security state that developed after World War II, and during the Cold War was often used for secret operations, including the destabilizing and overthrow of foreign governments, as opposed to merely gathering intelligence.

China Lobby: Loose American group made up of anticommunists, including Republicans like Senator William Knowland (R-Calif.) and Rep. Walter Judd (R-Minn.) and journalist Henry Luce of *Time*, who blamed certain elements in the U.S. government for China's becoming Communist in 1949. Their targets included State Department China experts like John Stewart Service and the Institute for Pacific Relations (IPR), a left-leaning think tank on Chinese affairs which provided such advisers as Johns Hopkins University Professor Owen Lattimore to the government. (For an example of their views, see Isaac Don Levine's attack on Dean Acheson in Document 7).

Communism: In its purest sense, the economic theory of Karl Marx (1818–1883) that working people should own and control the means of production (as opposed to capitalism, where business owners are in charge). In practice, such egalitarian aims have been distorted by Communist governments in the Soviet Union, China, Vietnam, Cuba, and North Korea, which have been authoritarian, rigid, and oppressive, and have planned and run the means of production themselves, leaving out both working people and potential entrepreneurs. They have been bureaucratic and decidedly undemocratic, sharply curtailing civil liberties. With the exception of China, where the economy is actually much closer to a capitalist model, Communist systems have all been spectacular failures. (Communism is often called Marxism or Marxism-Leninism).

Containment: In 1947 State Department official George F. Kennan exhorted the United States to pursue a policy of "long-term, patient but firm and vigilant containment of Russian expansive tendencies."[1] His argument for containment, the most significant American Cold War doctrine, called for confining the spread of Communism to those areas in which it had already established itself. Under the aegis of containment, the U.S. military was able to preserve successfully the state of South Korea from takeover by the Communist North. Although Kennan protested that he had not meant for containment to be interpreted as a wholesale response to any hint of Communist expansion, some policymakers did see it that way, and containment inspired the disastrous U.S. intervention in South Vietnam. This effort finally undermined containment theory.

Decolonization: The process by which the former European colonial powers, including Great Britain, France, the Netherlands, and Italy, shed their holdings in Africa and Asia after World War II, owing to local independence movements, American pressure, and economic exigencies. In some cases, such as in India and Indonesia, native leaders took control relatively quickly. In others, Cold War imperatives preserved European control to ensure stability and prevent a Communist takeover. In Vietnam, for instance, the French stayed until 1954, propped up by Washington's support. Once independent, many former colonies became pawns in the Cold War as indigenous leaders, faced with economic and military needs that only the superpowers could satisfy, applied for aid. Egypt and Angola fell into the Soviet camp this way, and Ethiopia and the Congo into the American. During the 1970s, many of the former colonies joined the non-aligned bloc of nations in the UN, refusing to join the cause of either superpower.

Defensive Perimeter Speech: By mid-1949, Washington accepted the idea of an Asian "defensive perimeter," an island chain stretching from the Aleutians in the North to New Zealand in the South, and including Japan and the Philippines—but not the Asian mainland—as necessary to U.S. security. The Korean peninsula was left out. In a speech to the National Press Club on January 12, 1950, Secretary of State Acheson said: "The Asian peoples are on their own." Though Americans were "their friends . . . we can help only where we are wanted and only where the conditions of help are really sensible and possible." Thus, Asia's future "lies within the countries of Asia and within the power of the Asian people." This is exactly what Acheson had been saying regarding the "fall" of China in the China White Paper.[2] The "defensive perimeter" speech, however, was blamed by many for encouraging North Korea to invade South Korea in June 1950.

Détente: A French diplomatic term, referring to the lessening of tensions between powers. Although the Kennedy and Johnson administrations sporadically made efforts in this direction to improve relations with the Soviet Union, détente was pursued most systematically during the Nixon administration, especially by Nixon's National Security Adviser, Henry Kissinger. This initiative found a favorable reception with both Soviet leader Leonid Brezhnev and the Chairman of the Chinese Communist Party, Mao Zedong. It resulted in the SALT I treaty with Russia, as well as the diplomatic opening with the People's Republic of China in 1972. Yet, because many Americans mistakenly had believed that détente should introduce changes in the Soviet government itself rather than simply lower tensions, they became disenchanted. When American politicians judged that the policy was actually encouraging Soviet expansion, they soured on it and abandoned it by the late 1970s.

Domino Theory: American officials' belief, current in the 1950s and 1960s, that countries were like dominoes; once one "fell" to Communism, its neighbors would also fall. This theory underlay the American involvement in Vietnam, as authorities thought that the "fall" of South Vietnam would lead to Communist takeovers in neighboring countries like Thailand and Cambodia. This theory was often used in association with the "Munich" metaphor by a generation of politicians who had lived through World War II. As at Munich in 1938, when the European democracies did not stand up to Hitler but instead legitimized his conquests with appeasement, not standing up to Communism would encourage the same kind of dominolike expansion. (See Document 12.)

Flexible response: The Kennedy administration's defense policy, designed to be more nimble than the Eisenhower administration's "massive retaliation" nuclear-based response. The United States would increase ICBMs sevenfold, creating a 3:1 ratio over the Soviet Union; use Green Berets to conduct counterinsurgency against Communists in Vietnam; and step up civil defense. The policy included a political component as well, featuring covert operations designed to destabilize objectionable governments.

Free World: Euphemistic term (see NSC-68, Document 8) that U.S. officials used to describe the noncommunist world during the Cold War. Though certainly the Western democracies were "free," many of their allies in Latin America, Asia, and Africa were not. Indeed, Turkey and Greece, both authoritarian regimes, became part of the "free world" and received aid under the Truman Doctrine.

Iran-Contra Affair: The plan involved the selling of weapons to Iran, the foe of the Soviet-supported nation of Iraq, in order to free hostages in the Middle East, as well as to use the proceeds to assist the anticommunist Nicaraguan *Contras*. In the summer of 1985 the administration sold one hundred TOW missiles to Iran through Israel, with the aim of earning freedom for four hostages in Lebanon. Lt. Col. Oliver North of the National Security Council administered the aid to the *Contras*, and the CIA supervised flights of arms. The arrangement, which yielded only three hostages, continued until October 1986, when the Sandinistas shot a plane out of the sky carrying weapons to the *Contras*.

After Attorney General Edwin Meese was assigned to look into the operation, Oliver North, National Security Adviser Admiral John Poindexter, and North's secretary Fawn Hall shredded five thousand pages of documents, as well as secretly removed them (Hall stuffed extra sheets in her undergarments and boots when the shredder broke). However, material remained on the NSC's computer that included evidence of "the diversion of between $10 million and $20 million to the contras."[3] Reagan fired North and Poindexter, who were later convicted by a special prosecutor, but their convictions were overturned on appeal. Reagan himself was not implicated.[4]

Liberal-capitalist ideology: The political and economic system of the United States and the western European countries, as well as Japan, during the Cold War, characterized by a democratic system of government, a capitalist or mixed capitalist-socialist economy, and civil liberties, including a free press, freedom of speech, and personal freedoms to choose where and with whom to live, work, and recreate.

Mutually Assured Destruction (MAD): The U.S. strategic doctrine adopted after the United States and the U.S.S.R. approached parity in nuclear weapons in the late 1960s, designed to deter a first strike by the Soviet Union by assuring that its civilian population would be at equal risk in such a strike. Indeed, each nation could be destroyed many times over. Unfortunately, this doctrine meant that both sides' populations were held hostage to the forbearance of the other, something that Reagan pointed at in his proposal for the Strategic Defense Initiative in the 1980s, designed to prevent a nuclear attack.

NATO (North Atlantic Treaty Organization): Formed in April 1949 and originally comprised of Canada, Denmark, Iceland, Italy, Norway, Portugal, and the United States plus the Brussels Pact signatories (Britain, France, Belgium, Luxembourg, and the Netherlands). Greece and Turkey joined in 1952. It was a defense organization set up against the Soviet Union. After Germany joined in 1955, the Soviet Union established its own Warsaw Pact, which went out of business in November 1990. With the end of the Cold War, NATO has been responsible for peacekeeping in Serbia, among other missions. Its newest members include three former Soviet satellites, Hungary, Poland, and the Czech Republic.

Nixon Doctrine: In the summer of 1969, as he began pulling American troops out of Vietnam, President Richard Nixon announced a new American policy, which amplified his administration's move toward détente with the Communist bloc. The United States would no longer automatically protect Asian nations threatened by Communism (or anything else) unless they were specifically in a treaty relationship with Washington or they were threatened by a power with nuclear weapons.The doctrine was designed to reassure a war-weary nation that the U.S. would handle a crisis like Vietnam differently in the future, but it was nevertheless ambiguous, because it left unanswered how Washington would respond if a nuclear power using conventional weapons were to attack another Asian nation, for example.

Pentagon: The home of the U.S. Defense Department (DOD), and often used as a synonym for that department. It is named for the enormous five-sided building in which the department is located in Virginia just outside Washington, D.C., which was built during World War II. Tens of thousands of employees, both civilian and military, work in this building.

Reagan Doctrine: President Ronald Reagan announced the Reagan Doctrine in his 1985 State of the Union Address, demonstrating that the Cold War was still in high gear the year Mikhail Gorbachev came to office. This statement affirmed the U.S. government's assistance to "those who are risking their lives—on every continent from Afghanistan to Nicaragua—to defy Soviet-supported aggression and secure rights which have been ours from birth."[5] These "freedom fighters" included the Afghan mujahideen, the Angolan rebel forces of Jonas Savimbi, and the Nicaraguan *Contras*. All received officially authorized humanitarian or military aid or both from the United States, but even as Reagan spoke, his administration was secretly funneling money from Iranian arms sales to further assist the Nicaraguan *Contras* against the wishes of Congress, a deception that led to the Iran-Contra affair (*see* **Iran-Contra Affair**).

SEATO (Southeast Asia Treaty Organization): Set up by Secretary of State Dulles in 1954 after the fall of Dien Bien Phu, SEATO members included Pakistan, the Philippines, Thailand, Australia, New Zealand, France, Britain, and the United States. Indochina, including Vietnam, Laos, and Cambodia, was not permitted to join by the Geneva Accords. SEATO was much looser than NATO, lacking that organization's integrated command system, for example.

Truman Doctrine: In 1947 the British were no longer able to assist their former clients in the Mediterranean, Greece and Turkey, countries that were then threatened by a Communist insurrection and Soviet territorial demands, respectively. In the first application of the containment doctrine, Washington stepped into the breach and provided nearly half a billion dollars and a significant number of advisers to these two nations. Beside being a product of containment, the Truman Doctrine was also an example of the U.S. policy of European economic reconstruction made famous later that year through the Marshall Plan. American officials believed that such aid was necessary to fight Communism. Washington found authoritarian states like Greece and Turkey preferable to totalitarian regimes, which Truman and others saw as a threat to U.S. national security. Greece and Turkey thus became part of the Western orbit and eventually joined NATO.

United Nations: Organized at the Yalta Conference, and officially launched at San Francisco in the spring of 1945, the UN was based on the liberal principles of the Atlantic Charter (chiefly, the right of peoples to choose their own governments, which was signed by the anti-Nazi coalition in 1941). Its goal was to prevent the kind of isolation and economic nationalism, as well as the military disputes, that had led to World War II. The successor to the failed League of Nations, the UN was located in New York City and eventually grew to include most of the nations of the world. It was governed by a Security Council of five members—the United States, the U.S.S.R., Britain, France, and China. All other members belong to the larger General Assembly. During the Cold War, the UN sent forces into Korea, as well as settled disputes, provided relief, and carried out peacekeeping functions in the Middle East, Africa, and Latin America. At first influenced most by the United States and its allies, after decolonization in the 1960s the organization became dominated by the so-called nonaligned nations, who were often critical of the United States, which remains one of the UN's chief funders, if a sometimes delinquent one.

NOTES

1. "X," "The Sources of Soviet Conduct," *Foreign Affairs* 25 (July 1947): 575–76.
2. *Bulletin*, Department of State, January 23, 1950.
3. Michael Schaller, *Reckoning with Reagan: America and its President in the 1980s* (New York: Oxford University Press, 1992), 164.
4. Schaller, *Reckoning with Reagan*, 166.
5. Quoted in *Public Papers of the Presidents, Ronald Reagan 1985* (Washington, Government Printing Office, 1988) I: 135.

Annotated Bibliography

Acheson, Dean. Speech to the National Press Club, January 12, 1950. In U.S. Department of State, *Bulletin* (January 23, 1950): 111–19. Acheson's famous speech in which he outlines an American "defensive perimeter" in Asia that did not include the Korean peninsula.

Allin, Dana H. *Cold War Illusions: America, Europe, and Soviet Power, 1969–1989*. New York: St. Martin's Press, 1994. Argues that the U.S. exaggerated the Soviet threat, and underrated Western Europe's ability to hold up its end in the Cold War.

Alperovitz, Gar. *The Decision to Use the Atomic Bomb and the Architecture of an American Myth*. New York: Random House, 1995. Alperovitz is the leading exponent of the view that the U.S. decision to use the bomb was based on Cold War considerations, to intimidate the Russians and maintain a leading role in the Far East.

Ambrose, Stephen E. *The President*. Vol. 2 of *Eisenhower*. New York: Simon & Schuster, 1984. Packed overview of Eisenhower's presidency, very strong on foreign policy.

Ash, Timothy Garton. *The Magic Lantern: The Revolution of '89 Witnessed in Warsaw, Budapest, Berlin and Prague*. New York: Random House, 1990. An eyewitness account of the end of the Soviet empire in eastern Europe.

Bassett, Lawrence J., and Stephen E. Pelz. "The Failed Search for Victory: Vietnam and the Politics of War." In Thomas G. Paterson, ed., *Kennedy's Quest for Victory: American Foreign Policy, 1961–1963*. New York: Random House, 1995. Argues that Kennedy made a strong commitment to a noncommunist South Vietnam during his administration, and that he left a legacy of military involvement for Johnson rather than an exit strategy.

Bernstein, Barton. "Understanding the Atomic Bomb and the Japanese Surrender: Missed Opportunities, Little-Known Near Disasters, and Modern Memory." *Diplomatic History* 19 (Spring 1995): 227–273. Though suggesting the bomb was unnecessary, this article also questions myths regarding the American attack, elucidating the assumptions of U.S. officials in 1945 as well as the Japanese position at the time of the U.S. bombings.

Beschloss, Michael. *May Day: Eisenhower, Khrushchev, and the U-2 Affair*. New York: Harper and Row, 1986. Very readable study of the two men and their responses to the shoot-down of U-2 pilot Francis Gary Powers.

Bill, James A. *The Eagle and the Lion: The Tragedy of Iranian-American Relations*. New Haven: Yale University Press, 1988. Suggests that U.S. support of the shah's dictatorship made the Iranian Revolution in 1978 strongly anti-American.

Blum, John Morton, ed. *The Price of Vision: The Diary of Henry A. Wallace, 1942–1946*. Boston: Houghton Mifflin, 1973. Memoirs of the Secretary of Commerce including his famous disagreement with Truman administration policy toward Russia after World War II.

Boyer, Paul. *By the Bomb's Early Light: American Thought and Culture at the Dawn of the Atomic Age*, rev. ed. Chapel Hill: University of North Carolina, 1994. A fascinating look at the bomb's influence on popular culture during the early Cold War.

Cogan, Charles C. *Forced to Choose: France, the Atlantic Alliance, and NATO*. Westport, Conn.: Greenwood, 1997. Explores the French ambivalence towards NATO.

Cohn, Roy. *McCarthy*. New York: New American Library, 1968. Sympathetic portrait of the Wisconsin senator by his former assistant.

Costigliola, Frank. " 'Unceasing Pressure for Penetration': Gender, Pathology, and Emotion in George Kennan's Cold War." *Journal of American History* 83 (March 1997): 1309–39. Suggests that Kennan's imagery of the Soviet Union in the Long Telegram reflects gendered and psychological assumptions of that country and its foreign policy.

Cumings, Bruce. *The Origins of the Korean War*. Vol. 1: *Liberation and the Emergence of Separate Regimes, 1945-1947*. Princeton: Princeton University Press, 1981. Vol 2: *The Roaring of the Cataract, 1947–1950*. Princeton: Princeton University Press, 1990. Major study that argues for the domestic origins of the Korean War, and downplays the role of the Soviet Union or China in encouraging the North Korean invasion.

Dudley, William, ed. *The Cold War: Opposing Viewpoints*. San Diego: Greenhaven Press, 1992. A collection of primary sources highlighting key Cold War issues, such as containment and détente.

Dumbrell, John. *The Carter Presidency: A Re-evaluation*, 2nd ed. Manchester and New York: Manchester University Press, 1995. Sympathetic reappraisal of the Carter administration and its policies.

Eisenberg, Carolyn Woods. *Drawing the Line: The American Decision to Divide Germany, 1944–1949*. New York: Cambridge University Press, 1996. Critical analysis of American role in postwar Germany, which suggests that the division of Germany was not inevitable and attributes it to the interests of U.S. business in western Europe.

Feis, Herbert. *From Trust to Terror: The Onset of the Cold War, 1945–1950*. New York: Norton, 1970. An orthodox treatment of the origins of the Cold War, attributing its genesis to the Soviets.

Fukuyama, Francis. "The End of History?" *National Interest* (Summer 1989): 3–18. Argues that the demise of Communism demonstrates the ultimate triumph of Western values as forming the basis of governments.

Fursenko, Aleksandr, and Timothy Naftali. *"One Hell of a Gamble": Khrushchev, Castro & Kennedy, 1958–1964*. New York: W. W. Norton, 1997. Most complete account yet of the Cuban missile crisis, using newly available sources to show Kennedy's interest in détente with the Soviet Union, the close links between Castro and Khrushchev, and Moscow's willingness to use the missiles on Cuba.

Gaddis, John Lewis. *Strategies of Containment: A Critical Appraisal of Postwar American National Security Policy*. New York: Oxford University Press, 1982. Evaluates full scale and limited containment strategies against Communism, arguing that each had their advantages and disadvantages in deterring aggression.

———. *The United States and the End of the Cold War: Implications, Reconsiderations, Provocations*. New York: Oxford University Press, 1992. A collection of essays on the end of the Cold War, touching on themes including the role of nuclear weapons, espionage, and Ronald Reagan.

———. *We Now Know: Rethinking Cold War History*. New York: Oxford University Press, 1997. An overview of the Cold War to 1961, synthesizing the newest books on the subject, which finds Stalin chiefly to blame for the conflict.

Garthoff, Raymond. *Détente and Confrontation: American-Soviet Relations from Nixon to Reagan*, 2nd ed. Washington: Brookings Institution, 1994. Magisterial defense of détente blaming its decline on each side's differing expectations and arguing that the policy was an improvement over confrontation, even if it was only another phase of the Cold War. Clashes came during times of "flawed interaction," such as when the United States presumed that Russia was violating the spirit of détente.

———. *The Great Transition: American-Soviet Relations and the End of the Cold War*. Washington: Brookings Institution, 1994. Argues that détente began the transition to the end of the Cold War, and after Gorbachev revived this approach, Reagan responded boldly, although Bush's reaction was more cautious.

Gates, Robert M. *From the Shadows: The Ultimate Insider's Story of Five Presidents and How They Won the Cold War*. New York: Simon and Schuster, 1996. CIA veteran's account of his agency's role in the Cold War and its successful conclusion from the Nixon through the Bush administrations.

Gleijeses, Piero. *Shattered Hope: The Guatemalan Revolution and the United States, 1944–1954*. Princeton: Princeton University Press, 1991. Argues for the importance of domestic influences in understanding the impact of U.S. policies and intervention in Guatemala, and presents an indictment of that intervention.

Grose, Peter. *Gentleman Spy: A Life of Allen Dulles*. Boston: Houghton Mifflin, 1994. Well-researched, balanced biography of the founder of the modern CIA.

Hahn, Peter L. *The United States, Great Britain & Egypt, 1945–1956: Strategy and Diplomacy in the Early Cold War*. Chapel Hill: University of North Carolina Press, 1991. Suggests that U.S. hopes to assuage Egyptian nationalism were constrained by superpower conflict as well as Anglo-American relations.

Hamby, Alonzo L. *Man of the People: A Life of Harry S Truman*. New York: Oxford University Press, 1995. Interesting and multilayered analysis of the president.

Harbutt, Fraser. *The Iron Curtain: Churchill, America, and the Origins of the Cold War*. New York: Oxford University Press, 1986. Argues that Churchill had an influence in hardening Truman and other American officials' anti-Soviet attitudes in 1946.

Herring, George. *America's Longest War*. New York: McGraw Hill, 1995. A readable and useful overview that focuses chiefly on the U.S. role in the war and argues that American involvement was based on a flawed application of the containment theory.

Hershberg, James G. *James B. Conant: Harvard to Hiroshima and the Making of the Nuclear Age*. New York: Knopf, 1993. An outstanding biography of a leading Cold War academic consultant.

Hixson, Walter L. *George F. Kennan: Cold War Iconoclast*. New York: Columbia University Press, 1990. An interesting diplomatic biography of the author of containment doctrine, emphasizing his disagreement with policymakers' implementation of it.

Hogan, Michael J. *The Marshall Plan: America, Britain, and the Reconstruction of Western Europe, 1947–1952*. New York: Cambridge University Press, 1987. The best analysis of the plan, its origins, and its participants available.

———, ed. *Hiroshima in History and Memory*. New York: Cambridge University Press, 1996. An anthology of essays on the decision to use the bomb and its legacy in Japan and the United States.

Holloway, David. *Stalin and the Bomb: The Soviet Union and Atomic Energy, 1939–1956*. New Haven: Yale University Press, 1994. Excellent study of the crash Soviet bomb program that began after Hiroshima.

Hoopes, Townsend. *The Devil and John Foster Dulles*. Boston: Little Brown, 1973. Critical portrayal emphasizing the importance of the Secretary's crusading anticommunist agenda in framing Eisenhower Administration diplomacy.

Immerman, Richard H. *The CIA in Guatemala: The Foreign Policy of Intervention*. Austin: University of Texas Press, 1982. Contends that the intervention was based on Cold War fears rather than economic motivations.

Isaacson, Walter. *Kissinger: A Biography*. New York: Simon & Schuster, 1992. Excellent biography of Nixon's National Security Advisor and Secretary of State.

Isaacson, Walter, and Evan Thomas. *The Wise Men: Six Friends and the World They Made: Acheson, Bohlen, Kennan, Harriman, Lovett, McCloy*. New York: Simon and Schuster, 1986. Excellent, highly readable biography of these influential architects of U.S. Cold War policy.

Ivie, Robert L. "Diffusing Cold War Demagoguery: Murrow versus McCarthy on 'See It Now.' " In Martin J. Medhurst, Robert L. Ivie, Philip Wander, and Robert L. Scott, *Cold War Rhetoric: Strategy, Metaphor, and Ideology*. Westport, Conn.: Greenwood Press, 1990. An article that describes and analyzes the CBS journalist's process of effectively delegitimizing Joseph McCarthy through interviews with the senator on national television in 1954.

Johnson, Loch K. *America's Secret Power: The CIA in a Democratic Society*. New York: Oxford University Press, 1989. An overview of the CIA, demonstrating the difficult challenge it has faced, and not always met, in serving the requirements of national security while not curtailing civil liberties.

Kagan, Robert. *A Twilight Struggle: American Power and Nicaragua, 1977–1990*. New York: Free Press, 1995. Well-researched study of U.S. relationship with Sandinistas and Contras in the late Cold War.

Kaufman, Burton. *The Korean War: Challenges in Crisis, Credibility, and Command*. New York: McGraw-Hill, 1986. A diplomatic history of the war and the decisions related to it.

Kennan, George F. *Memoirs, 1925–1950*. Boston: Little Brown, 1967. Recollections of a leading Cold War policymaker who came to disagree with the way his containment thesis was implemented and called for negotiations with the Russians.

———. "The Sources of Soviet Conduct" (by "X"). *Foreign Affairs* 25 (July 1947), 566–82. George F. Kennan's influential and pseudonymously-published article in which he made his case for containment.

Khrushchev, Nikita S. *Khrushchev Remembers: The Last Testament*. Edited and translated by Strobe Talbott. Boston: Little Brown, 1974. Fascinating recollections from the former Soviet leader on his life in power.

Kissinger, Henry A. *Diplomacy*. New York: Simon and Schuster, 1994. A beautifully written, well-researched, and compelling survey by the former National Security Adviser and Secretary of State.

Klehr, Harvey, John Earl Haynes, and Fridrikh Firsov. *The Secret World of American Communism*. New Haven: Yale University Press, 1995. Eye-opening exposé of American Communist underground in 1930s and 1940s and its influence, using Soviet archives.

Klehr, Harvey, and Ronald Radosh. *The Amerasia Spy Case: Prelude to McCarthyism*. Chapel Hill: University of North Carolina Press, 1996. Lucid examination of the FBI's 1945 espionage case against the journal *Amerasia*, which shows how the Truman administration's downplaying of the case contributed to McCarthyist reaction and heightened anticommunist fervor in the early 1950s.

Lamphere, Robert J., and Tom Schachtman. *The FBI-KGB War: A Special Agent's Story*. 2nd ed. Macon, Ga.: Mercer University Press, 1995. A former FBI agent describes the agency's role in celebrated Cold War incidents like the Hiss and Rosenberg cases, with a post–Cold War afterword.

LeFebvre, Jeffery A. *Arms for the Horn: U.S. Security Policy in Ethiopia and Somalia, 1953–1991*. Pittsburgh: University of Pittsburgh Press, 1991. Analyzes the role that U.S. military aid to the Horn played in keeping Cold War allies in the region and countering the Soviets.

Leffler, Melvyn P. *A Preponderance of Power: National Security, the Truman Administration, and the Cold War*. Stanford: Stanford University Press, 1992. A seminal book that suggests that early Cold War fears about Soviet expansionism brought a "prudent" U.S. economic and military response, though policymakers exaggerated the importance of Soviet influence in the Third World and expended valuable resources in the process, thus hampering American freedoms—the very values they hoped to protect.

Lewy, Guenter. *America in Vietnam*. New York: Oxford University Press, 1978. Comprehensive, scholarly, and generally sympathetic portrait of America's Vietnam effort.

Lippmann, Walter. *The Cold War: A Study in U.S. Foreign Policy*. New York: Harper and Brothers, 1947. Contemporary critique of containment theory, written in response to Kennan's article, "The Sources of Soviet Conduct," in *Foreign Affairs* (July 1947). Lippmann argued that containment handed initiative over to the Russians, and he called for the removal of *both* American and Russian troops from Europe.

Lundestad, Geir. *The American "Empire" and Other Studies of U.S. Foreign Policy in a Comparative Perspective*. New York and Oslo: Oxford University Press and Norwegian University Press, 1990. Traces the rise and decline of the American "Empire" and shows how West Europeans and Japanese leaders sought U.S. economic and military assistance throughout the duration of the Cold War.

Maier, Charles S. *Dissolution: The Crisis of Communism and the End of East Germany*. Princeton: Princeton University Press, 1996. Uses newly available archives to explore the demise of the German Democratic Republic, long considered the Soviet bloc's economic powerhouse, which in fact rested on shaky foundations.

Marks, Frederick W. III. *Power and Peace: The Diplomacy of John Foster Dulles*. Westport, Conn.: Praeger, 1993. An engaging and strong defense of Eisenhower's controversial secretary of state.

Mastny, Vojtech. *Russia's Road to the Cold War: Diplomacy, Warfare, and the Politics of Communism*. New York: Columbia University Press, 1979. Traces the roots of Soviet influence in eastern Europe beginning during World War II.

McCormick, Thomas P. *America's Half-Century: United States Foreign Policy in the Cold War*. Baltimore: Johns Hopkins University Press, 1989. Suggests that the United States used economic clout to compel weaker nations to adapt to free market mechanisms, and military power to maintain the global system to its benefit.

McMahon, Robert J. *Colonialism and the Cold War: The United States and the Struggle for Indonesian Independence, 1945–49*. Ithaca and London: Cornell University Press, 1981. Suggests that U.S. economic pressure on the Netherlands owing to Cold War concerns helped to expedite Indonesian independence.

McNamara, Robert S. *In Retrospect: The Tragedy and Lessons of Vietnam*. New York: Random House, 1995. Best-selling, confessional memoir of the Secretary of Defense during the Kennedy and Johnson administrations, who recalls his doubts about the war while in that position.

Miscamble, Wilson D., C.S.C. *George F. Kennan and the Making of American Foreign Policy, 1947–1950*. Princeton: Princeton University Press, 1992. Sympathetic portrait of the father of containment.

Moïse, Edwin. *Tonkin Gulf and the Escalation of the Vietnam War*. Chapel Hill: University of North Carolina Press, 1996. Based on newly available evidence, this work argues that there was no North Vietnamese attack in the Gulf in 1964.

Nixon, Richard M. *Six Crises*. Garden City, N.Y.: Doubleday, 1962. The former vice-president and congressman reflects in a somewhat self-aggrandizing manner on his life in Washington, including the Hiss case, his disastrous Venezuela visit, and his 1959 trip to Moscow.

Paterson, Thomas G. *Contesting Castro: The United States and the Triumph of the Cuban Revolution*. New York: Oxford University Press, 1994. Suggests that the United States stuck too long by Batista, unwittingly facilitating the rise of Castro as the only alternative for fed-up Cubans.

Paterson, Thomas G., J. Garry Clifford, and Kenneth J. Hagan. *American Foreign Relations: A History since 1895*, 4th ed. Lexington, Mass.: D.C. Heath, 1995. A lively, useful, information-packed survey.

Philbrick, Herbert. *I Led Three Lives: Citizen, "Communist," Counterspy*. New York: McGraw-Hill, 1952. Breathless exposé by former FBI agent who acted as a Communist for the agency.

Powers, Richard Gid. *Not without Honor: The History of American Anticommunism*. New York: Free Press, 1995. Excellent overview of the American anticommunist movement, more nuanced than most, that highlights the different varieties of anticommunism.

———. *Secrecy and Power: The Life of J. Edgar Hoover*. New York: Free Press, 1987. Well-written, compelling overview of the life of the FBI chief.

Radosh, Ronald and Joyce Milton. *The Rosenberg File: A Search for the Truth*. New York: Holt, Rinehart, and Winston, 1983; 2nd ed., New Haven: Yale University Press, 1997. Classic study of the Rosenberg case which argues for their culpability. The second edition uses newly available documents.

Reeves, Richard. *President Kennedy: Profile of Power*. New York: Simon and Schuster, 1993. Close inspection of political life in the Kennedy White House, which argues that the president's driving ambition contributed to his successes.

Rotter, Andrew J. *The Path to Vietnam: Origins of the American Commitment to Southeast Asia*. Ithaca: Cornell University Press, 1987. Important study that shows how roots of the U.S. role in Vietnam were tied to the reconstruction of Japan as well as of western Europe, which was dependent upon the health of colonies like Malaya and Vietnam to supplement the Marshall Plan.

Schaller, Michael. *Reckoning with Reagan: America and its President in the 1980s*. New York: Oxford University Press, 1992. A critical analysis of the Reagan administration's policies.

Schlesinger, Arthur M., Jr. *A Thousand Days: John F. Kennedy in the White House*. Boston: Houghton Mifflin Company, 1965. A sympathetic, highly positive portrait of the Kennedy Administration by one of its members.

Schrecker, Ellen W. *No Ivory Tower: McCarthyism and the Universities*. New York: Oxford University Press, 1986. Discusses the relationship between academia and the anticommunist pressures of the 1950s.

Sherry, Michael S. *In the Shadow of War: The United States since the 1930s*. New Haven: Yale University Press, 1995. Comprehensive overview that argues that war and militarization have shaped many facets of American life from culture to politics.

Shultz, George P. *Turmoil and Triumph: My Years as Secretary of State*. New York: Scribner's, 1993. Balanced portrait that acknowledges acrimonious policy differences among the Reagan staff and is sometimes skeptical of the president's abilities, yet emphasizes the signal importance of the Reagan policy of "peace through strength" as a turning point in the Cold War.

Small, Melvin. *Johnson, Nixon, and the Doves*. New Brunswick, N.J.: Rutgers University Press, 1989. Interesting study that emphasizes the role of public opinion and protest on the two presidents during the Vietnam War.

Sodaro, Michael J. *Moscow, Germany and the West from Khrushchev to Gorbachev*. Ithaca: Cornell University Press, 1990. A discussion of Soviet relations with the two Germanies, with a particularly strong analysis of Gorbachev's approach.

Stokes, Gale. *The Walls Came Tumbling Down: The Collapse of Communism in Eastern Europe*. New York: Oxford University Press, 1993. Analyzes the fall of Communism in light of events in eastern Europe, with a special focus on domestic dissenters.

Stueck, William. *The Korean War: An International History*. Princeton: Princeton University Press, 1995. The best available examination of the war in an international context.

Tanenhaus, Sam. *Whittaker Chambers: A Biography*. New York: Random House, 1997. Fascinating, highly readable biography of the complex accuser of Alger Hiss.

Terrill, Ross. *Mao: A Biography*. New York: Harper and Row, 1980. Comprehensive, lively account of the Chinese leader's life and policies.

Weinstein, Allen. *Perjury: The Hiss-Chambers Case*. New York: Knopf, 1978; updated ed. New York: Random House, 1997. The best and most thorough survey to date on the espionage case, which suggests that Alger Hiss was indeed a spy.

Whitfield, Stephen J. *The Culture of the Cold War*, 2nd ed. Baltimore: Johns Hopkins University Press, 1996. An illuminating and entertaining survey of the Cold War's cultural manifestations in the United States.

Worland, Rick. "From the New Frontier to the Final Frontier: *Star Trek* from Kennedy to Gorbachev." *Film and History* 24 (1994): 19–35. A fascinating article that puts the television show into a historical and cultural context.

Zubok, Vladislav and Constantine Pleshakov. *Inside the Kremlin's Cold War: From Stalin to Khrushchev*. Cambridge: Harvard University Press, 1996.

Uses newly available archival materials to look at the personalities in the Soviet leadership and their motivations and views toward the Cold War.

———. "The Soviet Union." In David Reynolds, ed., *The Origins of the Cold War in Europe*. New Haven: Yale University Press, 1994. Argues that Soviet postwar foreign policy was shaped more by Stalin's arrogance and unwavering allegiance both to world revolution and Russian imperial ambitions than it was by Western threats to the Soviet Union.

VIDEOS

The American Pageant. 1996. Films for the Humanities and Sciences. CD-ROM. Images, recordings, video clips, primary sources, commentary, maps, and self-tests on U.S. history, including several segments on the Cold War.

The Berlin Wall. 1990. Films for the Humanities and Sciences. Discusses the history of the wall, from its erection in 1961 to its dismemberment in 1989.

Gorbachev and the Fall of the Soviet Union. 1996. Films for the Humanities and Sciences. Explores Gorbachev's life, his policies, and the collapse of his government.

Harry S. Truman. Produced by David Wolper and Jack Haley. History Television Network Productions, 1994. Discusses Truman's foreign policy leadership but not the debates surrounding it.

Inside the FBI. Produced by WETA and Channel 4, Great Britain. 1995. Uses interviews with agents and rare footage to complement a survey of current scholarship to produce a strong documentary.

J. Robert Oppenheimer: Father of the Atomic Bomb. Produced by Richard O'Regan. Claymont Productions in association with A&E Network, 1995. Introductory biography of the atomic scientist.

Kissinger and Nixon. Produced by Richard Borchiver. Turner Network Television, 1995. Based on Walter Isaacson's biography, an effective documentary that focuses on U.S. diplomacy and internecine political battles during the end of the Vietnam War.

The Marshall Plan: Against the Odds. Produced by the Educational Film Center and Christenson Associates. PBS, 1997. Overview of the Marshall Plan, its effects and legacies, including interviews with European beneficiaries.

Messengers from Moscow. Produced by PBS/BBC, 1995. 4 vols. Discusses the Soviet approach to the Cold War, based on interviews with former Soviet officials, focusing on events in Europe, Asia, the Third World, and the Soviet Union itself.

Post-Soviet Russia: Promises Deferred. 1997. Films for the Humanities and Sciences. Clashes over free enterprise reforms and nostalgia for communism are explored in this study of the economic changes instituted in Gorky, Russia.

Spy in the Sky. Produced by Linda Garmon. WGBH-Boston, 1996. Well-done exploration of the U-2 reconnaissance program and the shoot-down of Francis Gary Powers in 1960.

Vietnam: A Television History. Produced by PBS, 1983. 13 vols. An overview of the Vietnam conflict from the end of World War II until the fall of Saigon, told from the American perspective.

War and Peace in the Nuclear Age: A History of the Cold War. PBS, 1988. 13 vols. Survey of the Cold War discussing nuclear strategy, deterrence, proliferation, the Cuban Missile Crisis, the arms race, and the Strategic Defense Initiative.

Western Tradition. Produced by PBS, 1989. Vol. 49: *The Cold War*. Examines the U.S. role in financing European reconstruction, and subsequent economic developments in Europe.

WEB SITES

Chronology of U.S. History Documents, University of Oklahoma Law Center:
www/law.uoknor.edu/ushist.html

Cold War International History Project:
www.seas.gwu.edu/nsarchive/cwihp

Georgetown University Special Collections on Diplomacy, International Affairs, and Intelligence:
www/gulib.lausun.georgetown.edu/dept/speccoll/diplo.htm

Hanover College Collection of Speeches, Secondary Sources, Resources on Presidents:
www.history.hanover.edu/20th.carter.htm
www.history.hanover.edu/20th.eisenhow.htm
www.history.hanover.edu/20th.kennedy.htm
www.history.hanover.edu/20th.nixon.htm
www.history.hanover.edu/20th.reagan.htm

Mt. Holyoke College documents on the Cuban Missile Crisis:
www/mtholyoke.edu/acad/mtrel/cuba.htm

National Security Agency's Venona Project:
www.nsa.gov:8080/docs/venona/venona.html

Index

About the Author

KATHERINE A. S. SIBLEY is Assistant Professor of History at St. Joseph's University in Philadelphia. She is the author of *Loans and Legitimacy: The Evolution of Soviet-American Relations, 1919–1933* (1996), and her work on the Soviet-American relationship has also appeared in *Diplomatic History* and *Peace and Change*. Currently she is working on a study of interwar Soviet espionage against American industrial plants. She has received grants from the Hoover and Roosevelt presidential libraries, the Kennan Institute for Advanced Russian Studies, and the Society for Historians of American Foreign Relations.